By Alex F. Osborn

How To Think Up

Your Creative Power

Wake Up Your Mind

Applied Imagination

APPLIED IMAGINATION

Third Revised Edition

APPLIED IMAGINATION

PRINCIPLES AND PROCEDURES OF CREATIVE PROBLEM-SOLVING

THIRD REVISED EDITION

by Alex F. Osborn, L.H.D.

CHARLES SCRIBNER'S SONS

NEW YORK

1 3 5 7 9 11 13 15 17 19 K/P 20 18 16 14 12 10 8 6 4

PRINTED IN THE UNITED STATES OF AMERICA

Library of Congress Catalog Card Number 79-63255

ISBN 0-684-16256-3

Dedicated to
DR. T. RAYMOND MCCONNELL
of whom I was proud to be a colleague
when he was Chancellor and I was
Vice Chairman of the Council
of The University of Buffalo

Foreword

When I attended one of the earlier Creative Problem-Solving Institutes in Buffalo some years ago, I remember hearing a keynote speaker tell us: "Everything in the world remains to be done or done over. The greatest picture hasn't been painted. The ideal labor contract is yet unwritten. A windproof match, an airtight bottle cap, a lifetime lead pencil have not yet been conceived. The best way to train salesmen, an easy way to keep slim, a better way to pin diapers—all of these problems are unsolved. Not one product has ever been manufactured, distributed, advertised or sold as efficiently as it should be or someday must be. . . ."

No matter who you are or what you do, chances are you are in the market for ideas and welcome the chance to find ways to produce them. Of course, you cannot make yourself more creative than potentially you are, but psychologists tell us that exposure to certain principles and techniques and, above all, developing certain attitudes can help you approach your creative potential. This book, which appeared first in 1953 and has since become something of a classic, can helpfully point the way.

Until *Applied Imagination* first appeared, there had been surprisingly little written on the subject of creativity or creative problem-solving. Since this book appeared, however, there has been an enormous groundswell of interest in the subject, considerable research conducted at universities across the country, many books and articles published, and not only courses in creativity introduced on many campuses but, importantly, instruction in creative problem-solving techniques introduced into existing courses in many fields as well.

As the corpus of knowledge of the subject has increased through research and experience, the subject of creativity has been refined, codified, given a jargon all its own, and made more complex—a far cry from what it was in the 1940s and '50s when Alex Osborn wrote his half-dozen books on the subject, of which *Applied Imagination* is the best known. Many of the persons quoted in this book are no longer around or no longer in positions they held when this book first appeared, but what they had to say is still valid and may serve as useful springboards in our efforts to approach our creative potential. One could go through this "classic" layman's text on the subject and bring up-to-date all of the references and quotations, but such a tremendous undertaking would do little or nothing to enhance the truth of what was said in the first place.

Alex F. Osborn, for all the seeming self-assurance of his writing, was essentially an unprepossessing, modest, and wonderfully kind person, the rare kind of person who could be more concerned with the good he could do in encouraging others than in taking credit for ideas that were initially his own. His long career in advertising and, later, education was devoted either to being creative himself or to the development of creativity in others.

He was convinced that most of us fail to be as creative as potentially we could be, because we tend to "drive with the brakes on." He felt that all too often we allow ourselves to be creative and self-critical at the same time. Said he, "It is a little like trying to get hot and cold water out of the same faucet at the same time: the ideas may not be hot enough, the evaluation of them not cold or objective enough. The results will be tepid!" He felt it important to try to "stretch" people beyond their self-imposed limits in an oscillating process—first thinking up ideas and only later evaluating them. One might say he advocated alternating the current a bit in problem-processing.

Alex F. Osborn, the "O" in BBDO (Batten, Barton, Durstine & Osborn, Inc.), one of the world's largest advertising agencies, had a long and distinguished career that frequently placed him in situations that were difficult and demanding. But on the job and away from it he practiced what he preached in creativity. He practiced it in what he wrote or caused others to write, in his business, in civic, educational, and church activities, in leisure hours as a self-taught painter, and—in his last years—as founder and chairman of the Creative Education Foundation, an organization dedicated to teaching and research in creativity in all areas of life. As a matter of fact, he assigned all royalties from this book to support of the Foundation.

The Foundation has been responsible for a number of institutes and workshops held at different times of the year across the country. At State University College in Buffalo, N. Y., where the Foundation has its national headquarters, a master's degree in creative studies is now offered and the Foundation maintains probably the most extensive library of books, microfilms, articles, and papers on creativity and problem-solving in the world.

In *Applied Imagination* the author speaks of the importance of imagination in all areas of life—to individuals on and off the job, in business and the professions, at home and abroad, in government at the local, state, national, and even international level. He speaks of what is known about imaginative talent and how it can be broken down by such categories as age, sex, and educational background, and he speaks of factors, like worry, that can work against creativity. There are many common factors that can hold us back and cramp our creativity, like old habits, self-discouragement, premature criticism of results, timidity, and there are factors, like contagious enthusiasm, which can stimulate innovation. The book speaks of factors in our environment that can work for and against our creativity and ways in which creativity can be developed through games and puzzles, hobbies, reading, writing, and problem-solving exercises.

The author shows how to detect problems, how to define them properly and break them down into component parts or "bite-size" units that are more readily handled. He points out various techniques for processing problems and for evaluating proposed solutions. He shows how problem-processing can be done individually and in groups and how you can put to work such a simple device as the check-list in coming up with ideas.

William James wrote, "We forget that every good that is worth possessing must be paid for in strokes of daily effort. We postpone and postpone, until those smiling possibilities are dead."

Want to learn more about history or poetry or outer space or music? Want to master a foreign language or learn some special skill? It is astonishing how we can sneak up on such goals faster than we think possible if only we will make a regular stab at it, perhaps for just a few minutes each day. This came home to me in a Minnesota barbershop where a friend of mine was flabbergasted to hear an American barber speak fluent Spanish. "No, I have never been to Spain or South America," said the barber. "I have just taught myself Spanish here in the barber shop, studying between haircuts."

Here's hoping you will not race through this book but take "daily bites" at what it has to teach you, a bit at a time, realizing that it will not just be the principles and techniques that are important but attitudes. Instead of asking *can* a thing be done, Alex Osborn suggests we are going to want to make it a habit to ask instead *how* or *in what ways*. Perhaps we would do well to emulate the vaudevillian who was asked, "Do you play the violin?" and replied naively, "I don't know. I've never tried!"

A friend of mine once said, "We must be open-minded enough to realize that a thing may be true, even if we haven't heard of it before and may be true, even if we definitely disagree with it. We must seek for truth and not just for confirmation of our pre-conceived ideas."

Through exposure to certain principles and techniques and, above all, through development of new attitudes, it is possible, Alex Osborn maintains, to approach your creative potential. It is like driving a car with a governor on it that permits you only to drive 40 miles an hour. Remove the governor, and you go 60. This does not mean that the engine is more powerful. It just means that the governor which held you back has been taken away, and you are now getting the power that was in that engine all along. Exposure to certain techniques but, above all, cultivation of our curiosity and constructive discontent can help us remove governors and approach our true potential.

I had the great privilege of knowing Dr. Osborn for more than twenty-five years and serving as President of the Creative Education Foundation while he was its chairman. In my work as a writer, composer, lay preacher, and educator, I have experienced firsthand how rewarding it can be to put to work the ideas Alex Osborn offers in this book. May your own experience prove equally rewarding! Your own creativity may surprise you and enable you to talk like a woman I knew who had to take up cooking late in her life. "I rather dreaded it," she said, "until I found out how much the fire does!"

Lee Hastings Bristol, Jr., Mus.D.
President Emeritus
Westminster Choir College

Table of Contents

CHAPTER V

CHAPTER VI

CHAPTER VII

CHAPTER VIII

CHAPTER IX

CHAPTER X

CHAPTER XI

CHAPTER XII

CHAPTER XIII

CHAPTER XIV

APPLIED IMAGINATION

Third Revised Edition

Chapter I

The all-importance of imagination

FROM A functional standpoint our mental capacities might be over-simplified as follows:

1. Absorptive—the ability to observe, and to apply attention.
2. Retentive—the ability to memorize and to recall.
3. Reasoning—the ability to analyze and to judge.
4. Creative—the ability to visualize, to foresee, and to generate ideas.

Electronic brains can now perform those first three functions to some degree, but it still seems certain that no machine will ever be capable of the generation of ideas. Although Dr. Albert Einstein's statement that "imagination is more important than knowledge" might be challenged, it is almost axiomatic that knowledge can be more powerful when creatively applied.

The potential power of creative imagination is all but limitless. For example, Jules Verne hardly ever left the quiet of his home; and yet he found that his imagination could take him around the world, 20,000 leagues under the sea, and even to the moon. To those who scoffed at his ideas, Jules Verne retorted: "Whatever one man is capable of conceiving, other men will be able to achieve."

And now we have prototypes of Verne's imaginary submarine of 70 years ago—except that the modern ones are run by atomic power.

The fact that imagination is the pristine power of the human mind has long been recognized by the greatest thinkers. They have concurred in Shakespeare's conclusion that this divine spark is what makes man "the paragon of animals."

Civilization itself is the product of creative thinking. As to what ideas have meant in the forward march of mankind, John Masefield wrote: "Man's body is faulty, his mind untrustworthy, but his imagination has made him remarkable. In some centuries, his imagination has made life on this planet an intense practice of all the lovelier energies."

Doctor James Harvey Robinson went even further, saying: "Were it not for slow, painful, and constantly discouraged *creative effort,* man would be no more than a species of primate living on seeds, fruit, roots, and uncooked flesh."

No one will ever know to whom we should erect monuments for such indispensable discoveries as the use of fire. That and another creative triumph, the wheel, both came out of the Stone Age.

The main use of the wheel up until 1,000 A.D. was for war chariots. Then someone had the idea of using it as a backsaver in the form of a water wheel. By the time William the Conqueror took over England, over 5,000 mills in that tiny country were driven by water power.

"It was imagination," said Victor Wagner, "that enabled man to extend his thumb by inventing the vise—to strengthen his fist and arm by inventing the hammer. Step by step, man's imagination lured, led and often pushed him to the astonishing heights of power he now so apprehensively occupies."

A Yale professor has estimated that—thanks to the machines which have been created by man—the average person now has available to him a work power equal to the muscle power of 120 slaves.

That such progress can continue, Charles F. Kettering felt certain: "Every time you tear a leaf off a calendar you present a new place for new ideas and progress."

2. *Imagination made America*

It was only about 500 years ago that Europe began to rate the power of thinking, and especially creative thinking, on a par with the power of brute force. It was this new attitude that gave vitality to the Renaissance.

North America was the lucky beneficiary of the world's creative upsurge. As *The New Yorker* has said, "Ideas are what the United States are made of." Without doubt, our new heights in standard of living have been reached through creative thinking.

One new idea inherited by America from Europe was a way to use fire by means of an internal combustion engine. This gave birth to our automotive industry, without which America's standard of living would be far lower. For it alone gives gainful occupation to over 9,000,000 of us.

Agricultural ideas have made far richer the rich soil of our country. The creative genius poured into farm machinery by the McCormicks and the Deeres has enabled each farm hand to turn out far more food than formerly. When America was young, it took 19 farmers to feed one city dweller. Today 19 farmers produce enough food for themselves and for 66 other people.

Who in 1900 could have foreseen the changes in America that have since come about? From horse and buggy to car and plane and jet . . . from railroads and railway mail to transatlantic telephone and radio and television . . . from slow boat to the *Queen Mary.* (And now, more passengers fly the Atlantic than cross by boat.)

From gas lamps to indirect lighting . . . from sulphur-and-molasses to sulfathiazole . . . from hand-wound victrolas to hi-fi . . . from palm-leaf fans to air-conditioning . . . from coal stoves to electric ranges built into the wall . . . from cold cellars to home freezers . . . from ear trumpets to transistors.

And yet, it is only recently that the *value* of imagination has been fully recognized even in America. A few years ago, the Chrysler Corporation started to hail imagination as "the directing force" which "lights tomorrow's roads, explores today for clues to tomorrow, hunts better ways for you to live and travel." And the Aluminum Company has recently adopted a newly coined word, "imagineering," which means that "you let your imagination soar and then engineer it down to earth. You think about the things you used to make, and decide that if you don't find out some way to make them immeasurably better, you may never be asked by your customers to make them again."

Thus, competition has forced American business to recognize the importance of conscious creative effort. So much so, that, more and more, the heart and center of almost every successful manufacturing company is its creative research. Industrial research used to do but little more than take things apart in order to find out what caused what and why. The new research adds to such fact-finding a definite and conscious creative function aimed to discover *new* facts, arrive at *new* combinations, find *new* applications. Thanks to thinkers like Doctor James B. Conant, imagination's importance to science is now recognized as never before.

3. *Public problems need creativity*

But, alas, the newest and most pressing problems of our nation are not so much the improvement of *things* as the solution of *people*-problems. Overshadowing all such is our international impasse. We are applying plenty of research to this, but in the ineffective form of merely finding facts and making diagnoses. To arrive at new and good ideas which might solve the world's *people*-problems, there is *no conscious creative effort at all comparable to what scientific research is doing to better the products we use.*

"We'll explore and deplore, only that and nothing more," said a cynical senator concerning our national habit of going all out in fact-finding, and then petering out when it comes to applying creative thinking to the facts as found. In discussing this with David Lawrence, he remarked:

"In Washington in 1933, I had the opportunity of seeing thousands of letters received by congressmen, government officials, editors and columnists, all discussing the country's difficulties. The interesting fact was this. All the writers devoted some time to analyzing the causes of the situation and very intelligently, too, although all did not agree. However, once they had made such an analysis, they seemed to have expended their energy. The creative spark so badly needed was sadly lacking."

"The fundamental issue of our time," said Raymond Fosdick, "is whether we can develop understanding and wisdom reliable enough to serve as a chart in working out the problems of human relations." He recommended more research; and, undoubtedly, there should be more scientific study to clarify our public problems. But investigations cannot find solutions unless implemented with *ideas.* We would have failed in our atomic research if our scientists had not thought beyond the facts and beyond the known techniques. It was the *new* techniques they thought up, and the countless hypotheses they dreamed up, which solved the atom.

4. *Community problems*

In every community, there is a crying need for more creative thinking. Scores of municipal problems are begging for ideas—city-planning and traffic safety, for instance.

In New York, Robert Moses has shown what imagination can do. If, technically, he were the world's greatest engineer, he could not have done half as much for the New York metropolitan area as he has done through the creative power he has put into his planning.

William Zeckendorf has likewise endowed New York City with ideas. Some of his brainstorms may never work out, such as the city within itself in downtown Manhattan with a roof so large that it would serve as another La Guardia Field. He also thought up the new dream-town which has been created on the lower East Side to house the vast population of the United Nations Organization. John D. Rockefeller, Jr., thought well enough of this idea of Zeckendorf's to donate $26,000,000 with which to buy the land.

In traffic problems, ideas can save lives. My home town of Buffalo has been constantly rated by the National Safety Council as at, or near, the top of all large cities in prevention of traffic deaths. This record is mainly due to the creative thinking of the volunteer head of the local safety setup, a manufacturer named Wade Stevenson. One new idea was to dramatize the virtue of good driving. Instead of handing out summonses, the police handed out flowers. On one evening, Patrolmen William Collins and James Kelly ordered 25 women drivers to the curb, then complimented them on their careful driving and handed them fresh orchids.

To make democracy work as it should, it is vital to get out the vote. Pontiac, Michigan, adopted a new idea to that end. All the churches of that city rang their bells simultaneously once an hour while the polls were open on election day.

5. *America's domestic problems*

There is hardly a phase of national life which does not cry for improvement; and in nearly every case, the key is more and better creative thinking. Take the baffling problem of labor and capital, for instance. "The solution is not yet in sight," said U. S. Senator Irving Ives, "but if we would put half the effort into thinking up *ideas* for straightening out our labor snarl as we put into finding *facts,* we could save years in bringing order out of our industrial chaos."

If you were Secretary of Labor wouldn't you like to have a creative group of your own, with absolutely nothing else to do but think up ideas—new ideas for you to judge, to adopt, to modify or combine for your use?

Some enemies of America hope that her downfall will come through collapse of the nation's finances. The problem of taxation is therefore vital. Why is it that we have so long stumbled from one expedient to another instead of creating a long-term plan of sound taxation?

In our national problems, we need the best thinking of our most creative people. Some of them are occasionally invited by Washington to lend a hand, especially in wartime. During the first World War, Thomas Edison was called in, not to contribute his scientific knowledge, but to think up how to save the farmers. It was he who suggested the plan which, in substance, became the "ever-normal granary."

Why does Washington make so little use of our creative citizens in peacetime? One reason is that too much power of judgment is asked of them—judicial ability which is impossible without a deeper knowledge of the subject than can be quickly acquired. Why not ask such creative minds to perform a *creative* function only? Why not *divide* each problem so that one set of experienced experts will take care of the fact-finding and judicial judgment, while the creative consultants will concentrate solely on suggesting idea upon idea?

6. *International salesmanship*

No matter how many good ideas we may think up to solve our problems on the local and national levels, we may still be lost unless we are creatively sharp enough to cut our international knot. One great challenge is how to ingratiate America to the rest of the world.

American ingenuity did much to win our last fighting war; but, in the cold war since then, Russia's ideas have been hot enough to drive our country back on the European front, step by step. "Ideas will have to be fought with ideas," said Ernest Hauser. . . . "In our attempt to hold the line against Russia in Europe, we have not even begun to use ideological weapons."

If Drew Pearson had relied upon legislators and bureaucrats to bless his Friendship Train, that idea of his would probably have died a-borning. But he went ahead on his own and, almost singlehanded, showed how America can shower gifts in a way that can make foreign recipients recognize our generosity and appreciate our donations.

The Dunkirk idea was another hopeful example. "This latter-day miracle," wrote Meyer Berger, "originated in this smoke-blackened city on stormy Lake Erie. It spread with astonishing swiftness to cities all over the United States. Dunkirk, N. Y., took Dunkerque, France, to be a kind of sister city. Her little people established warm kinship with the little people of the North Sea Dunkerque. Americans in other states looked upon this sisterhood and found it somehow heart-filling and genuine. They moved toward similar adoptions."

The Dunkirk idea was a project which our Federal Government might well have done something about—not by way of taking it over, but by way of sponsorship. While at war, Washington rightly hopes to organize local volunteer bond-selling campaigns throughout the country. Just so, our government might well put its weight behind a movement like this, which, if multiplied nationally, could build more friendships in Europe than billions of dollars shoveled out of our treasury in cold-blooded routine.

The Friendship Train, the Miracle of Dunkirk—these are models of what we need, and there is hope that more and more will come. For example, why not have naturalized Americans write home to their families in Europe and tell them the truth about America? This idea *was* put into action by millions of our citizens to help keep Italy from bowing to Moscow in the 1948 election.

"The most effective inspirer of letters," according to Drew Pearson, "was Generoso Pope, the Italian-American newspaper publisher in New York, who organized letter-writing clubs and committees among Italian-Americans throughout the United States. He estimates that over 2,000,000 letters were written to Italy alone. . . . Equally effective can be letters written to the countries just inside the Iron Curtain. . . . Individual Americans can automatically enlist in the people's army for peace by getting busy in all sorts of ways to build up American friendship."

Why not seek suggestions from amateurs for our cold war just as we sought them for our last World War? The National Inventors' Council brought in 200,000 ideas between 1942 and 1945—many of them looked "crazy" at first—but in the net they helped speed our armed forces to victory.

Or why not set up a group of creative people in the State Department with just one function—to suggest new ways and more ways to win the friendship of the rest of the world? All week long this group could sit and pile up alternatives. A committee of trained statesmen could then pick out from that week's crop the few ideas which they deemed most promising. In some such way we need to put more creative power to work on our international problems. We need more boldness. We need *audacity* in persuasive ideation, *just as we need audacity in armed conflict.*

7. *International statesmanship*

Even *more creative* thinking is needed in our international *statesmanship* than in our international *salesmanship.* We will spend billions of dollars and mountains of imagination preparing for war. And yet to ward off war, what will we do? Will we let ourselves be the victims of events, or will we think up the moves which may "*make* circumstances"? If the armed forces need a General Staff to create our military strategies, don't we need a creative group to plan our peace strategies?

The need for more and better ideas is frequently stressed by our national leaders—even by our Secretary of State. In a message to all State Department employees, both here and overseas, Dean Rusk made these two points in these words:

1. "We want to stimulate ideas from the bottom to the top of the State Department."

2. "The infant mortality rate of ideas—an affliction of all bureaucracies—must be reduced."

It has been rightly said that ideas made America. But, now ideas may unmake America. Not our ideas, but the ideas of our enemies—particularly Russia and Cuba.

Castro's ideas did much to kill our prestige all over the world. His tractors-for-prisoners idea nauseated most of us. But, as an idea, it was brilliant. And it worked. It succeeded in making monkeys out of us. And it helped make Castro a god in the eyes of Cuba.

Even if an idea like that were moral, it would be unlikely ever to see the light of day the way we operate. A bureaucratic underling would hardly dare to stick his neck out with anything so wacky. If he did, his brain-child would be smothered to death in its infancy by the criticism of his colleagues or his superiors. If the idea ever did reach the top, it would probably take so long that, by then, it would be a dud.

If our government had been geared for idea-production, we might have been able to throw Castro's bomb right back. This could have been done with the right kind of counter-idea—like the one Richard Nixon suggested, the idea of accepting Castro's proposal with the proviso that Cubans be given the right to vote.

The round-by-round record of our bout with Russia is an indictment of our ingenuity. Khrushchev put his finger on our weakness when he publicly challenged the West to *initiate* some concrete ideas to blunt the threat of war.

We have to be even *more* productive of good ideas than our enemies. Our imaginations are handicapped by our desire to adhere to our moral code. Then, too, as long as our press remains free, we are virtually forced to stick to the truth. If an American leader should say that black is white, he would be laughed out of power. With Russia, however, the sky's the limit. The Soviet leaders are free to fabricate big lies at any time and quickly put them into orbit.

The least our government could do would be to conduct a pilot-type of experiment—a six-month's try-out of a panel of able ideators whose only duty would be to think up ideas —just as the only duty of many scientists is to think up missiles.

It would be best for such a board of strategy to be inaugurated without ballyhoo and to operate in secrecy. And, of course, it should be made up of men both highly creative and also well versed in international affairs. If only one worthwhile suggestion came out of a whole year's work by such a group, the cost would be a peanut compared to the cost of a single missile. And it is quite likely that good ideas could do more than missiles to save our nation's life.

* * *

This chapter has covered some of the applications of imagination to local, national and international problems. Later chapters will set forth the part that creativity can play in every vocation, every profession, and in almost every phase of personal living.

TOPICS

1. John Masefield said: "Man's body is faulty, his mind is untrustworthy, but his imagination has made him remarkable." To what extent do you believe this to be true? Discuss.

2. What are some of the inventions that built up the automotive industry? Discuss.
3. What community problems are in need of creative thinking? Discuss.
4. To what extent has America's per capita production of food increased, and why?
5. Which of the problems now personally pressing you is most in need of a creative solution?

EXERCISES

1. What solutions of downtown parking problems can you suggest?
2. What ideas can you think up to encourage motorists to drive safely?
3. If you had a son who was Communistically inclined, what would you do to straighten him out?
4. What means would you suggest to get more citizens to go to the polls?
5. Name all possible uses for a common brick. (This exercise was suggested by Dr. J. P. Guilford.)

REFERENCES

BURLINGAME, ROGER, *Engines of Democracy; Inventions and Society in Mature America.* New York. Charles Scribner's Sons, 1940.

FORBES, R. J., *Man the Maker.* New York. Henry Schuman, 1950.

GUILFORD, J. P., "Creativity," *American Psychologist.* September 1950, pp. 444–454.

MUMFORD, LEWIS, *Technics and Civilization.* New York. Harcourt, Brace and Company, 1938.

RICKARD, THOMAS A., *Man and Metals.* New York. McGraw-Hill Book Company, Inc., 1932.

ROBINSON, JAMES HARVEY, *Mind in the Making.* New York. Harper & Brothers, 1939.

RODGERS, CLEVELAND, *Robert Moses.* New York. Henry Holt and Company, 1952.

ROGIN, LEO, *The Introduction of Farm Machinery in Its Relation to the Productivity of Labor in the Agriculture of the United States during the 19th Century*. Berkeley. University of California Press, 1931.

WEAVER, HENRY GRADY, *Mainspring*. Detroit. Talbot Books, 1947.

Chapter II

Universality of imaginative talent

"WHO, *me?* Why I couldn't think up an idea if I tried." Only a moron could truthfully say that; for there is overwhelming proof that imagination is as universal as memory.

Scientific tests for aptitudes have revealed the relative universality of creative potential. The Human Engineering Laboratories analyzed the talents of large groups of rank-and-file *mechanics* and found that two-thirds of these rated *above* average in creative capacity. An analysis of almost all the psychological tests ever made points to the conclusion that creative talent is normally distributed—that *all* of us possess this talent to a lesser or greater degree—and that our creative efficacy varies more in ratio to our output of mental energy than in ratio to our inborn talent.

Scientific findings are borne out by the countless cases in which ordinary people have shown extraordinary creative power. Stuart Chase has gone so far as to say that most of the best ideas are originated by amateurs. The war furnished overwhelming proof that the rank and file can shine creatively when stirred by a patriotic urge. Literally millions of ideas were brought forward by people who never thought of themselves as at all creative.

"During the war," said President John Collyer of B. F. Goodrich, "suggestions came in from our employees at the rate of 3,000 per year. And we found that about one-third of these were good enough to deserve cash awards." The Ordnance Department saved over $50,000,000 in 1943 alone, as a result of ideas thought up by rank-and-file employees.

The fact that war spurred many, many people to think up so many good ideas helps prove that nearly all of us are gifted with creative talent; and it helps prove the part that effort plays in activating this talent.

Even when it comes to art, creativity is no rarity. "Everybody is original. Everybody can design—if not supremely, at least beautifully." So said Henry Wilson, teacher of art teachers.

2. *The age factor in creativity*

"Experience takes away more than it adds," wrote Plato. "Young people are nearer ideas than old people." With due respect to Plato, how could he say that while listening to the 60-year-old Socrates as he presented one new idea after another?

The career of Alexander the Great might seem to reinforce Plato's contention. But a study of Alexander's life shows that before he conquered Persia at the age of 25, he had been highly creative in many ways other than military. After 25, his creativity was paralyzed by vanity. From then on, his only new idea was beardlessness—to shave his face so that he might again look as young as when winning the world. How could such creative talent dim down and die out so soon? The answer is that his *effort* died first, and, as a result, his creativity dwindled.

Plato's opinion might also seem to be confirmed by the life of Robert Louis Stevenson. But he was still writing brilliantly when he died at the age of 44. Had he been of normal health instead of consumptive, and had he lived his three-score-and-ten, Stevenson would undoubtedly, have written as well, or better, after 60 as before 40—as did Goethe, Longfellow, Voltaire, and many other immortals in the creative field.

In some cases, abnormal talent does flame early in life and then burns out. Hence the term "infant prodigies." But it could not have been such precocity that prompted Plato's remark. Nor could such be the basis of a similar opinion voiced by Oliver Wendell Holmes when he said: "If you haven't cut your name on the door of fame by the time you reach 40, you might as well put up your jackknife."

Holmes' own life belied that statement. Until he was 48, he was an unknown physician and professor. His literary fame started with his *Autocrat of the Breakfast Table,* which he wrote when nearing 50. His most creative period was between then and when he wrote his biography of Ralph Waldo Emerson at the age of 75.

The career of Holmes' own son likewise refutes the theory that creative power necessarily wanes with youth. Chief Justice Holmes wrote his first great book, *The Common Law,* when he was 72. During the panic of 1933, when Holmes was over 90, the President of the United States leaned upon him for suggestions on how to pull the nation through its crisis.

"Writers die young," they say. But this, too, is untrue. Milton lost his sight when 44, wrote *Paradise Lost* when 57, and wrote *Paradise Regained* when 62. David Belasco still wrote successful plays when he was over 70. Mark Twain, at 71, turned out two books—*Eve's Diary* and *The $30,000 Bequest*.

Julia Ward Howe wrote *The Battle Hymn of the Republic* when she was 43. But Alexander Woollcott once told me the best writing she ever did was *At Sunset,* which she penned at 91. The first time George Bernard Shaw won a Nobel Prize was when he was nearing 70.

Thomas Jefferson retired to his homestead in Virginia when he was 66. Visitors at Monticello are amazed at the many innovations he thought up in his 70's and 80's. Benjamin Franklin was likewise both a statesman and an inventor. He was also a creative writer. One of his masterpieces was his appeal to Congress for the abolition of slavery. He wrote that in 1790, when he was 84.

Among creative scientists, Doctor George Washington Carver, at 80, was still turning out new ideas—so many that *The New York Times* hailed him as "the man who has done more than any other man for agriculture in the South." An earlier scientist, Alexander Graham Bell, perfected his telephone when 58, and when past 70 solved the problem of stabilizing the balance in airplanes.

Psychologist George Lawton maintains that our mental power can keep on growing until 60. From then on, according to Lawton, mental ability ebbs so slowly that, at 80, it can still be almost as good as at 30. And specifically, when it comes to creative talent, Lawton holds that although older people are apt to lose other faculties such as memory, "creative imagination is ageless."

Scholarly evidence that creativity can defy the calendar has been advanced by Professor Harvey C. Lehman of Ohio University. One of his studies covered notables who in their day had thought up ideas of importance to the world. Of the 1,000 or more creative achievements listed by Professor Lehman, the median age at which such creativity occurred was 74.

A patent counsel of the General Electric Company plotted

the records of the number of patents taken out by prolific inventors and found that, in some cases, their inventions became fewer as the men became older. But, here again the explanation is probably that of relative driving-power. It seems humanly inevitable that some people will slacken effort after they have won success. Feeling secure in well-paid positions and in expectation of comfortable pensions, such men are less likely to apply as much creative effort as they did while on the way up. Thus, in comparison to the past, America's progress in the realm of personal security may tend to deprive the nation of creative contributions formerly made by older people.

Even if our native *talent* should not grow, our creative *ability* can keep growing year after year in pace with the *effort* we put into it. "Imagination grows by exercise," said W. Somerset Maugham, "and contrary to common belief, is more powerful in the mature than in the young."

3. *The sex factor in creativity*

The female may be inferior to the male in musculation, but not in imagination. In fact, the Johnson O'Connor Foundation found from 702 tests of women that their creative aptitude averaged as much as 25 per cent higher than that of men.

As further indication that the idea-fluency of females may be superior to that of males, Edwin J. MacEwan of Paterson, New Jersey, recently reported his experience as the instructor of a class in creative thinking comprised of 32 high school seniors. According to his finding, the *girls* showed a 40 per cent superiority over the boys in fluency of ideas.

Further corroboration is found in the record of the firm I formerly headed. Over the years we have held more than

1,000 "brainstorm" sessions—conferences which are strictly confined to the thinking up of ideas on specific problems, with criticism deferred until later. The women members of such groups have consistently averaged more ideas than their male colleagues.

Most housewives work their imaginations far more than most husbands do. The man's job is usually routine, while the woman is on her own almost every hour of the day. Few women realize how much creative power they have to use. When a wife is successful in handling her husband, how else does she do it but by continually thinking up the right idea to keep him contented? And what ingenuity a woman must use in shopping, in thinking up meals, in prettying up the garden, in rearranging the furniture, in getting her youngsters to do this and not to do that!

When wartime workers were thinking up so many ideas, women won the limelight. Bernice Palmer was featured in *Life* for having thought up eight devices to speed up production of engine parts. "One of her most useful inspirations," said *Life,* "came when she remembered the way her mother had made doughnuts."

No woman would deny that she "racks her brains" for Christmas gifts. This means that she *does* have imagination, and *works* it when driven by duty or affection. During the whole year, few men do more creative work than she does at Christmas—in thinking up new and different presents for her husband, her children, Aunt Julia, Cousin Tillie, and all the others on her Christmas list. In most cases she also has to think up all those gifts which are tagged: "Merry Christmas from *Daddy.*"

You can't be a good mother without using imagination. When baby won't eat, you don't give up at the first howl of protest. You think up a way to get her to eat. Sheer instinct pushes parents into the habit of thinking up whatever will benefit their offspring.

Miss Florence Gray is a math teacher and an in-law of mine. She was chosen to write a tribute to her principal on his golden anniversary. "I can't do it," she said to me in despair. "I never have any ideas." I told her that psychological tests showed school teachers as a class to have a high degree of creative imagination—that as a successful school teacher she undoubtedly had plenty of talent—and that all she had to do was to try hard enough.

Later she told me that her tribute "To Our Beloved Principal" had made a hit. I asked her how she had gone about it. "After I saw you that night," she said, "I tried to think up ideas before I retired. I jotted some down and then went to bed. During the night I kept jumping up and jotting down more ideas. In the morning, to my amazement, I had plenty of good ideas to work on. My tribute almost wrote itself the next day." Miss Gray no longer underestimates her creative power.

The number of female stars in the field of creativity is growing apace. Many husbands have known firsthand how highly creative a woman can be—especially the husbands in the long and brilliant list of creative partnerships made up of married couples.

Admittedly, however, the record of noteworthy creativity is higher among males than females, as Professor Harvey C. Lehman of Ohio University has shown in another of his studies. But it is only during the last few minutes of history that women have had a chance to spread their creative wings. As Doctor Paul Popenoe pointed out in his analysis of the psychological differences between sexes, "These differences are acquired rather than inborn, and are visibly diminishing as woman passes to a wider life."

Scientific research on the question of the relative creativity of the sexes has been inconclusive. Dr. E. Paul Torrance of the University of Minnesota conducted an exploratory study on "Sex-Role Identification and Creative Thinking." The results showed no significant relationships between the total creativity scores and either of the masculinity-femininity scores, for either males or females.

Likewise, Dr. G. A. Milton of Stanford University conducted an investigation into "The Effects of Sex-Role Identification upon Problem-Solving Skill." One implication indicated by Dr. Milton was to the effect that "masculine" men will solve problems more readily than "feminine" men; and, similarly, the more masculine women will be better problem-solvers than women who have greater identification with the feminine role.

4. *The educational factor in creativity*

"To be extremely intelligent is not the same as to be gifted in creative work," wrote Doctor L. L. Thurstone. "Students with high intelligence are not necessarily the ones who produce the most original ideas. The Quiz Kids are often referred to as geniuses. They would undoubtedly score high in memory functions. . . . But it is doubtful whether they are also fluent in producing ideas."

According to scientific tests for creative aptitude, there is little or no difference between college or non-college people of like ages. Doctor William H. Easton, a man of many degrees, remarked: "Education is not a vital factor. Many highly trained persons are sterile creatively, while others accomplish outstanding results in spite of an almost total lack of formal instruction."

History records that many great ideas have come from those devoid of specialized training in the problem involved. The telegraph was worked out by Morse, a professional painter of portraits. The steamboat was thought up by Fulton, likewise an artist. A school teacher, Eli Whitney, devised the cotton gin.

Early in the war, a new shell-fragment detector was thought up by an unscientific employee of New York City's transit system. From Pearl Harbor on, that device saved many a life. There were many such cases where untrained people have creatively outthought the highly trained.

5. *The factor of effort in creativity*

When it comes to creative efficacy, neither the extent of our knowledge nor the potency of our talent is as vital as our driving power. To illustrate, let us suppose that you were sitting here with me on the 16th floor of this building, and I were to say to you: "Here's a pad and pencil. Please write down, within one minute, just what you would do if you knew that this building would immediately tumble to the ground as the result of an earthquake." Your answer might be, "I'm sorry, but I wouldn't have an idea."

On the other hand, suppose I were to stage that same scene so as to seem *real* to you—by having a good enough actor rush into my office and shout: "*This building is going to fall down within two minutes!*" If you believed him, you undoubtedly would think up one or more ideas instantaneously.

There are some geniuses whose lamps *seem* to need no

rubbing. Alexander Woollcott and I were college mates. His native brilliance dazzled and perplexed me. I had to rub hard to get any rays at all from my little lamp, while his seemed so big that all he needed to do was brush his sleeve against it. And yet, the more I saw of him throughout his later life, the more I realized that his secret was not so much his creative *talent* as his mental *energy.*

From a strictly physical standpoint, we have far more gray matter than we could ever use, even if we worked our minds to capacity. It is literally true that most of our brain centers (such as those which enable us to speak and to read) are in duplicate. The stand-by twin remains idle until its opposite number is injured or diseased. The spare can then be trained to take over. Louis Pasteur had a stroke which destroyed half his brain; yet he made some of his greatest discoveries after that.

Comparatively speaking, the mechanical complexity of the human brain is of the order of 100 billion, while that of the most advanced digital computer is of the order of 100 thousand. Thus, considering the brain only as a mechanical entity, it has a million times more potential than any electronic counterpart.

Ants are known for their organizational ability. And yet, an ant's entire system comprises only 250 nerve cells, whereas the human brain comprises some 10 billion such cells. The fact is that nearly all of us have far more mental capacity than we ever use.

The influence of heredity on creative ability is still open to question. Environment is a baffling factor. For example, Professor Ellsworth Huntington of Yale studied the inventiveness of descendants of Pilgrims. He compared the number of their patents with the number granted to sons of later immigrants. His findings showed that the presence of colonial blood insured a higher degree of creativity. But, as Arnold Toynbee has indicated, Yankee ingenuity was due more to *effort* than to inborn talent. The early New Englanders had to fight the Indians, the cold, the forests, and the rocks in the soil; and that environment built up the habit of effort which stepped up their creativity.

As Brooks Atkinson has said, it is the "driving force" of creativity which is so "remarkably unequal"—not the degree of native *talent.*

TOPICS

1. What evidences are there that creative talent is a widely distributed gift?
2. What evidence is there that creative ability need not wane with age? Discuss.
3. Do men actually excel women in creative aptitude? If this is a fallacious belief, what are the reasons? Discuss.
4. Are students with the highest IQ's necessarily the ones who can produce the most original ideas? Discuss why or why not.
5. Do you believe Yankee ingenuity to be an inherited or an acquired characteristic? State reasons for your belief.

EXERCISES

1. If you were teaching this course, what problem would you suggest for solution by the class at this point?
2. If the student in front of you fell off his seat in a faint, what would you do? And then what?
3. Make a note of every opportunity you have had to use your creative imagination since awakening this morning.
4. Write down at least three cases where ingenuity on your part—or on the part of one of your family or friends—either improved or actually saved a situation.

5. List every possible use that might be made of a brush, of the size and kind usually used for painting a house.

REFERENCES

AUSTIN, MARY, *Everyman's Genius.* Indianapolis. Bobbs-Merrill Company, 1925.

BROADLEY, CHARLES V. and MARGARET E., *Know Your Real Abilities.* New York. Whittlesey House, 1948.

BROMILEY, DENNIS B., "Some Experimental Tests of the Effect of Age on Creative Intellectual Output." *Journal of Gerontology,* January 1956, pp. 74–82.

LEHMAN, H. C., "Man's Most Creative Years: Quality versus Quantity of Output." *Scientific Monthly.* November 1944, pp. 384–393.

LEHMAN, H. C., "Optimum Ages for Eminent Leadership." *Scientific Monthly.* February 1942, pp. 162–175.

McCLOY, WILLIAM, "Creative Imagination in Children and Adults." *Psychological Monographs, 231.* 1939.

MARKEY, F. V., *Imaginative Behavior of Pre-School Children,* Child Development Monograph *18.* Teachers College, Columbia University, 1935.

MEARNS, HUGHES, *The Creative Adult.* New York. Doubleday and Company, 1940.

MILTON, G. A., "The Effects of Sex-Role Identification upon Problem-Solving Skill." *Journal of Abnormal and Social Psychology.* September 1957, pp. 208–212.

MOGENSON, A. H., "Every Worker Has Ideas." *Factory Management.* April 1935, pp. 147–148.

ROCKWELL, J. G., "Genius and the I.Q." *Psychological Review.* September 1927, pp. 377–384.

ROSSMAN, J., "A Study of the Childhood, Education, and Age of 710 Inventors." *Journal of the Patent Office Society.* May 1935, pp. 411–421.

TORRANCE, E. P., "Sex-Role Identification and Creative Thinking." Minneapolis. Bureau of Educational Research, University of Minnesota, 1959.

Chapter III

Creative and non-creative forms of imagination

THIS TEXT seeks mainly to cover the *creative* type of imagination, especially in its application to problem-solving. Nevertheless, for the purpose of fuller comprehension, this chapter will outline other forms of imagination.

The fact is that far too much is still to be discovered about the workings of the human mind. Although scalpels are cutting through much of our ignorance about our physical gray matter, the world is still in the dark as to what sparks our thinking functions, and still vague about how our minds work.

On the other hand, electronic brains built out of metal and plastics can now do almost everything human minds can do. To some extent they can even perform feats of judgment. But, according to Doctor Howard H. Aiken, head of Harvard's Computation Laboratory, these mechanized minds can *never* achieve that highest type of human thinking—creative imagination.

2. *"Non-controllable" workings of imagination*

As a term, imagination covers a field so wide and so hazy that a leading educator has called it "an area which psychologists fear to tread." For imagination takes many forms—some of them wild, some of them futile, some of them somewhat creative, some of them truly creative. These forms, in turn, fall into two broad classes. One consists essentially of the kinds which *run themselves* and sometimes run away with us. The other class is made up of the kinds we can run—which we can *drive,* if and when we will.

The less controllable group includes unhealthy forms such as hallucinations, delusions of grandeur, persecution complexes, and similar maladies. Delirium is a less chronic phase of the same form. Nightmares are akin to delirium.

Inferiority complexes are still another form. Until recently, such ills were seemingly beyond control. But psychiatry has found ways of correction; and Doctor Harry Fosdick and Doctor Henry Link have helped by buttressing psychiatric therapy with religion.

Still another form of twisted imagination is the martyr complex, sometimes called the "wounded-hero" complex. This consists of imagining hurts to one's feelings and exaggerating such hurts to the point of morbid self-pity. Hypochondria is a similar form; but it makes the victim "enjoy" his imaginary ills.

A basic cause of such complexes, according to Doctor Josephine A. Jackson, is the "desire to run away from difficulty—to *misuse* one's imagination as a way to flee from reality." This concurs with Freud's theory that "every neurosis has the result—and therefore probably the purpose—of forcing the patient out of real life, of alienating him from actuality."

Dreams are a more common form of uncontrollable imagination. These phenomena have long been looked upon as one of the most mystic phases of the human mind. In the fifth century before Christ, Heraclitus observed: "The waking have one and the same world; the sleeping turn aside, each into a world of his own."

The *speed* of our dreams is most mystifying. As a little

boy, I had the flu and after my temperature had gone down, my folks bundled me up and sat me at the dinner table. I tried to eat my broth, but felt too weak. I heard my father start to tell something about a trolley car, and, the next thing I knew, I was lying on the floor. I had fallen off my chair in a faint. My father had jumped up, had emptied a glass of water into his napkin, and had swabbed my face. Only a few seconds elapsed between fainting and waking, but in that moment I had dreamed so much—as I could later recall in detail—that it would take *hours* to live what I had dreamed. There was more action in that dream than in the average drama. What magic our imaginations must possess when, in two seconds, we can dream the equivalent of 2,000 words!

Daydreaming is the most common use of non-creative imagination. Sometimes called reverie, this is for some of us the usual form of our so-called thinking. It takes less than no effort. We merely let our imaginations join hands with our memories and run here and there and everywhere—without design and without direction, except as set by our prejudices, our desires, or our fears.

Doctor Josephine Jackson warns that daydreaming may become unhealthy when, "instead of turning a telescope on the world of reality—as positive imagination does—this negative variety refuses even to look with the naked eye." Victor Wagner has called daydreams "the rat-holes of escape from the stubborn realities of the workaday world." But with children, daydreaming is natural and is less harmful than with grownups. The young gain innocent pleasure from merely imagining their desires to be gratified. But when this habit carries on into later life, such reverie is almost sure to grow into vicious phantasy.

Worry is a non-creative form of imagination, all too normal and too often accepted as uncontrollable. Doctor Harry Fosdick has labeled it "anxious fear." Since this is a trait of human beings from which animals seem relatively immune, Doctor Fosdick regards this characteristic as "a tribute to one of man's supreme endowments—imagination." He likens worry to running reels of morbid movies through our minds. "But," he says, "we can *change* those reels. We can substitute for destructive and fearful imaginings, positive and constructive pictures of life, its meaning and its possibilities. Thus we can prove at last that 'as man thinketh so is he.' "

When based on imaginary troubles, worry is a fussy phase of fear. Real fear is a deeper emotion. When founded on facts or probabilities, fear is a form of anticipative imagination which can bring out the best in us, mentally and physically. It can stir us to prepare for the worst while hoping for the best.

And then there are the so-called blues. Sometimes these depressions are due to untoward events or other external causes. Often they come out of one's own chemistry, as during the aftermath of influenza. But no matter what the source, it is often true that our despondency persists because our imagination is running away with us, instead of being ridden by us with a strong enough rein.

3. *Functions that tend toward the creative*

"Just imagine!" When you hear people say that, they are probably referring to forms of imagination which are *almost* creative, quite controllable, and generally enjoyable—such as *visual imagery*. This is the power to see things in the "mind's eye." Through this talent, any of us can create a mental picture of almost anything whenever we wish.

That photographic type of imagination can take several

forms. The one in which memory plays but little part might be termed *speculative imagery*. You may never have visited Victoria Falls, but you could lie down, look at the ceiling, and make yourself "see" the great cataract.

Another phase of imagery might be called *reproductive imagination*. Speculative imagination may work in any tense, but reproductive imagination works only in the past. It enables us deliberately to bring pictures *back* into our minds.

Although reproductive and speculative imageries tend to flash on and off at their own whim, we nevertheless can direct these photographic powers almost at will. This is likewise true of the third phase of visual imagery called *structural visualization*. Scientific tests give great weight to this talent. Johnson O'Connor described it as "an inherent sense for three-dimensional forms, an instinctive ability to construct in the mind's eye from a flat blueprint a clear picture of a solid object." This skill is important to physicists and other scientists, and, says Mr. O'Connor, "aviators probably use it in bringing a plane to the ground—certainly in blind flying."

All three visual forms of imagination—whether fairly photographic or almost mathematically exact—are highly controllable, as we all know from the way we can operate our own mental cameras at will.

A more nearly creative form of imagination serves as a *bridge* by which we can put ourselves into another's place. We all use this *vicarious* imagination most of the time. Sympathy is one of its facets. Without vicarious imagination we could not "feel for others."

That same form is often used to pretend we are someone else, as in a child's play-acting. Little Teddy makes believe he is a railroad engineer. Barby loves to dress up in her mother's dinner dress. All through life this passive form enables us pleasurably to change places—a fact which largely explains why over 100 million movie tickets are bought each week in America. For, as Walt Disney has said, people go to theaters mainly to lose themselves in the lives of those whom they see and hear. The same brand of imagination accounts for the fact that every week 45 million American women listen to at least one soap opera.

Vicarious imagination also tends to determine what the public chooses to read. One day the newspapers blared out an announcement by President Truman that the national deficit would be $7,000,000,000 less than expected. Hidden on the same page of one newspaper was a little story about three local boys putting a dog's broken leg into splints. The average woman could put herself into the boys' place more easily than into Truman's shoes. A survey showed that only eight per cent of the women readers remembered the President's announcement, whereas 44 per cent recalled the dog story.

The Golden Rule embodies the noblest use of vicarious imagination. To "do unto others," we have to imagine how *they* would like to be treated, as well as know how *we* would like to be treated. A similar need for imagination marks every act of kindness, such as the selection of gifts. This not only calls for putting oneself into another's shoes, but also for thinking up long lists of alternatives. To a degree, this calls for *creativity,* since we seldom pick the right gift without imaginative effort.

If we tried harder to put ourselves into each other's shoes, there would be more concord and less conflict in human affairs. Dr. Paul Moody, President of Middlebury College, believed in literally changing places in order to facilitate a figurative changing of shoes. When he called a student into his office for disciplinary purposes, he would ask him or her to sit in the President's chair behind the desk. Dr. Moody would then sit in the student's chair. According to Dr. Moody, this physical exchange of positions made the student more likely to see the problem from the viewpoint of the college.

The key to tact is likewise to put yourself in the other's place; and tact has to do with what you do—or do not do—as well as what you say, or do not say. Environment and training make tact more or less instinctive. But this use of our vicarious imagination does call for a will to please, and should even call for effort. The greater our creative power, the more tactful we should be expected to be.

4. *Creative forms of imagination*

That brings us within a short step of creativity, but let's first look at another phase that might be called *anticipative imagination.* In its most passive use it is the foresight which stops little boys from touching live coals. If you said to a baseball pitcher, "Go out there and use your imagination," he would probably say, "Huh?" Although he may be bankrupt in inventive creativity, he may be rich in anticipative imagination. He has to think ahead for every pitch. With the catcher's help, he has to outguess the batter. All guessing calls for anticipative imagination. Most of us have an idea as to which way the cat will jump. The enjoyment of this form of imagination is the spice of gambling.

The highest form of anticipative imagination is *creative expectancy.* "When we look forward to something we want to come true, and strongly believe that it will come true, we can often make ourselves *make* it come true." That is the nub of creative expectancy, as stated by Doctor Albert Butzer. It is a faculty that characterizes the champion, whether he be a Babe Ruth, a Henry Ward Beecher, or an Abraham Lincoln.

As to truly *creative imagination*, its functions are mainly twofold. One is to *hunt*, the other to *change* what is found.

In its hunting function, our talent can serve us as a searchlight with which we can find that which is not really new, but is new to us. When we thus explore, it is well to throw our beam into dark corners. In this way men like Newton lighted up unknown but existent truths such as the law of gravity. This is *discovery* rather than invention. But, for invention or discovery, we should always swing our searchlight here, there and everywhere. The more alternatives we uncover, the more likely we are to find what we seek—and this is often found in the obvious.

When beaten by personal problems, we are apt to wail, "Oh why, oh why didn't I think of *that?*" We rue the failure of creative imagination to light our way; whereas we should face the fact of *our* failure to think up enough alternatives.

The *hunting* function should not be too sharply set apart from the changing function. But let's look at this changing function by itself for a moment. Just as imagination can be used for light, so it can also be used for heat. As a cooker, imagination can bring together those things or thoughts which are not new of themselves but can be cooked up into that which *is* new. In this way, we can do more than discover—we can invent—we can produce ideas that never before existed.

On leaving home one morning I passed through the kitchen. My wife and daughter were busy with pencil and pad, pondering the problem of that day's meals. They were swinging their mental searchlights over all types of meat, fish and groceries. In their hunt, they discovered the materials they wanted. Later, they cut them, mixed them, cooked them, and added this and that seasoning. Flour became popovers. Chicken, bean sprouts and noodles became chow mein. Thus their imaginations used both hunting power and mixing power. Their final technique was *combination* —often called the essence of creative imagination.

As applied to ideation, the oft-used term of *synthesis* is inadequate. Even the act of bringing things together into new combinations may take more than synthesis alone. Often it calls for breaking a problem into separate parts and then regrouping them. Analyzing, hunting, combining and otherwise changing—these are all parts of creative research. Scientific experimentation calls into play all of these activities and more.

Unlike other forms of imagination, the truly creative is seldom automatic. Even when it seems to work without our bidding, it is usually because we have been trying to make it work. Therefore, creativity is more than mere imagination. It is imagination inseparably coupled with both intent and effort.

Physiologist R. W. Gerard described creative imagination as the "action of the mind which produces a new idea or insight." The key word in that statement is *action*. And when Joseph Jastrow termed creative effort "the imagination that looks forward, foresees, supplies, completes, plans, invents, solves, advances, originates," it is significant that there is not a single passive verb in his whole list.

Although we can understand much of how imagination works, and how to work it better—the mysticism of the creative spark cannot help but impress anyone who contemplates. One question is: "What sparks the spark?" Mortal man may never know the answer. It is a deeper secret than life itself; and we have not yet learned what makes the heart beat. Henry Morton Robinson described its activating force as "a kind of electrical timing apparatus called the 'pacemaker.'" But—what activates the activator?

Creative imagination is just as mystic or more so. According to Richard Roberts, it is understandable only as another evidence of divinity. "There is at work in the world," said he, "an influence which may be described as creative, wherever it operates. It is capable of reinforcing life and enhancing natural faculty. For this there is impressive evidence."

TOPICS

1. Of the essential capacities of the mind, which do you think the most important? Why?
2. Is imagination vital to the Golden Rule? Why or why not?
3. What is creative expectancy? To what extent can we deliberately make this work in our favor?
4. Name at least five types of non-controllable imagination.
5. Distinguish between speculative, reproductive, structural and vicarious imagination and give examples of each.

EXERCISES

1. You are left alone with a complete stranger. List six introductory topics of conversation which would be interesting yet not controversial.
2. Suggest a single word of your own coinage to describe each of the following: a supper made up of left-overs . . . butts and ashes left in a receiver after a long evening . . . crumbs in the bed

. . . a crowd rushing out on a football field before game's end
. . . a party of 10 men and one girl.

3. Write a classified ad offering for sale a vest-pocket exercising kit, an untraceable poison, a bed-making machine. (This exercise suggested by *The London Spectator.*)
4. Name practical uses for each of the following combinations of objects: volley ball and steel spring . . . 13 empty pop bottles and 72 ounces of water . . . a stick, a hinge, and a board one-half inch thick and three feet square.
5. What uses could be made of a silk hat other than as a head covering?

REFERENCES

ABT and BELLAK, *Projective Psychology.* New York. A. A. Knopf, 1950.

ANASTASI, ANNE, and FOLEY, JOHN P., JR., "A Survey of the Literature on Artistic Behavior in the Abnormal." *Psychological Monographs,* 237, 1940.

ANDREWS, MICHAEL F., ed., *Creativity and Psychological Health.* Syracuse. Syracuse University Press, 1961.

BARTLETT, F. C., "Types of Imagination," *Journal of Philosophical Studies.* January 1928, pp. 78–85.

CASON, HULSEY, "The Nightmare Dream." *Psychological Monographs.* 1935, p. 209.

COWLING, DONALD, and DAVIDSON, CARTER, *Colleges for Freedom.* New York. Harper & Brothers, 1947.

DEXTER, EMILY S., "What Is Imagination?" *Journal of General Psychology.* January 1943, pp. 133–138.

DOWNEY, J. E., *Creative Imagination, Studies in the Psychology of Literature.* New York. Harcourt, Brace and Company, 1929.

FERNALD, M. R., "Diagnosis of Mental Imagery." *Psychological Monographs.* 1912, p. 58.

GERARD, R. W., "The Biological Basis of Imagination." *Scientific Monthly.* 1946, pp. 477–499.

GORDON, K., "Imagination; a Psychological Study." *Journal of General Psychology.* January 1935, pp. 194–207.

HARGREAVES, H. L., "The Faculty of Imagination." *British Journal of Psychology Monograph, Supplement 10.* 1927.

INDUSTRIAL RESEARCH INSTITUTE, *The Nature of Creative Thinking.* New York. New York University Press, 1952.

KUBIE, LAWRENCE S., *Neurotic Distortion of the Creative Process.* Lawrence, Kansas. University of Kansas Press, 1958.

MEIER, N. C., "Reconstruction Imagination." *Psychological Monographs.* 1939, p. 231.

PATRICK, CATHERINE, *What is Creative Thinking?* New York. Philosophical Library, 1955.

PEAR, T. H. and OTHERS, "The Relevance of Visual Imagery to the Process of Thinking." *British Journal of Psychology.* July 1927, pp. 1–29.

ROE, ANNE, "A Study of Imagery in Research Scientists." *Journal of Personality.* June 1951, pp. 459–470.

SQUIRES, P. C., "The Evolution of the Creative Imagination." *Scientific Monthly.* May 1931, pp. 447–453.

STETSON, R. H., "Types of Imagination." *Psychological Review.* July 1896, pp. 398–411.

Chapter IV

Factors that tend to cramp creativity

DOCTOR L. L. THURSTONE commented on the devastating effect of negative reaction toward a strange problem or a new idea. He pointed out that almost any proposed idea can be shown to be wrong, immediately and logically. He went on to say: "Sometimes the proof is so convincing that one is tempted to discard further thought about the new proposal. Even when this negative attitude is associated with high intelligence, the result is not likely to be creative."

Our thinking mind is mainly two-fold: (1) *a judicial mind* which analyzes, compares and chooses; (2) *a creative mind* which visualizes, foresees, and generates ideas. Judgment can help keep imagination on the track, and imagination can help enlighten judgment.

Judicial effort and creative effort are alike in that both call for analysis and synthesis. The judicial mind breaks facts down, weighs them, compares them, rejects some, keeps others—and then puts together the resultant elements to form a conclusion. The creative mind does much the same, except that the end product is an idea instead of a verdict. Then, too, whereas judgment tends to confine itself to facts in hand, imagination has to reach out for the unknown—almost to the point of making two and two equal something more than four.

In the average person, judgment grows automatically with

years, while creativity dwindles unless consciously kept up. Circumstances force us to use our judicial mind every waking hour. From rising to retiring—from childhood to the end—we exercise our judgment. And by exercise it grows, or should grow, better and stronger.

Then, too, education strengthens our judgment. Over 90 per cent of our schooling tends to train our judicial faculties. Still another influence tends to do the same—it's stylish to be an unerring judge. "He's a wonderful man—he never makes any mistakes." You hear that 10 times as often as you hear, "He has imagination *and* he makes it *work.*"

The research conducted by Dr. E. Paul Torrance of the University of Minnesota has confirmed the fact that imagination tends to contract as knowledge and judgment expand. These scientific investigations are set forth in his book, *Guiding Creative Talent.*

This same phenomenon was detected by Ribot, a psychological investigator of some 50 years ago. His findings indicated the conflict that exists between judgment and imagination, and the resultant decline in creativity during the early years of most individuals. According to Ribot, imaginative power initially grows faster than reason, but then tends to wane while reason rises in ascendancy.

The fact that moods won't mix largely explains why the judicial and the creative tend to clash. Unless properly coordinated, each may mar the working of the other. The right mood for judicial thinking is largely negative. "What's wrong with this?" . . . "What's the out about that?" . . . "No, that won't work." Such reflexes are right and proper when trying to judge.

In contrast, our creative thinking calls for a positive attitude. We have to be hopeful. We need enthusiasm. We have to encourage ourselves to the point of self-confidence. We have to beware of perfectionism lest it be abortive. Edison's first lamp was a crude affair. He could have hung onto his imperfect model while he tried and tried to make it better. Or he could have junked the whole idea. He didn't do either. His first electric lamps were better than candles, kerosene lamps, or gaslights—so he introduced them. Then he went to work on improvements.

Doctor Suits of General Electric has declared that the positive attitude is "a characteristic of creative people."

Even those who seem most anticreative are endowed with imagination. But theirs is of the negative type, while the truly creative tend to be positively inclined. Negative people are likely to listen to an idea with only one thought in mind: "What holes can I poke in that?" Often this type of destructive imagination is so amazingly fluent that it can speedily snatch objection after objection right out of the blue.

Judgment and imagination can help each other if kept apart when they should be kept apart. In creative effort we have to be a Jekyll-and-Hyde. From time to time, we must turn off our judicial mind and light up our creative mind. And we must wait long enough before turning up our judicial light again. Otherwise, premature judgment may douse our creative flames, and even wash away ideas already generated.

Especially in approaching a creative problem, we should give imagination priority over judgment and let it roam around our objective. We might even make a conscious effort to think up the wildest ideas that could possibly apply. For at this point, we are just warming up our think-up apparatus —limbering up our imagining muscles. Instead of laughing at such preliminary flashes—fantastic as they might seem—we should put them down on paper. One of them might turn out to be as sensible as a door key.

One highly creative friend of mine makes it a rule to exclude outside judgment until he has thought up all possible ideas. To those who prematurely try to pick flaws he says: "I don't want your judgment—not yet. Just now I want more and better ideas. What have you to suggest?" Even in the larger scope of world progress, judgment, in the form of common convictions, can block scientific advance. For, as stated by Doctor James B. Conant, "a well-established concept may prove a barrier to the acceptance of a new one."

A point to be kept in mind is that in most creative efforts there is no need for any decision as to relative merits of our ideas *until* we come to the question of which one, if any, is to be used. At this time we should be as cold in our criticism as we have been warm in our enthusiasm during the creative process. And when it comes to judging, if we can *test,* rather than opine, so much the better. Personal judgment can't help but be tinged with environmental prejudices. Seldom can it be as objective as it should be.

It used to be that when picking a title for a movie, directors, executives, and everybody else would wrangle all over the lot. But most titles are now selected by scientific testing. The best among all those suggested are exposed to theater goers by investigators. They record the many Tom-Dick-and-Harry reactions, which are then scientifically boiled down to a final judgment—a judgment far keener than that of any man. As Talleyrand remarked: "There is only one person who knows more than anybody, and that is everybody."

2. *Previous habits hinder problem-solving*

One reason why many of us tend to function less creatively as we mature is that we become victimized by habit. As a result of education and experience, we develop inhibitions which tend to rigidize our thinking. And these inhibitions habitually militate against our attacking new problems with an imaginative approach.

Frank Hix of General Electric has called this block "functional fixation." Experimental psychologists have given it various names such as "problem-solving rigidity," "mechanization," "set," and "*Einstellung.*"

The cramping effect of this block has been brought out in two research projects at Stanford University, conducted by Dr. Robert E. Adamson and Dr. Donald W. Taylor. Reports of these studies have been published in the *Journal of Experimental Psychology*, one under the title of "Functional Fixedness as Related to Problem-Solving," the other under the title of "Functional Fixedness as Related to Elapsed Time and to Set."

From the point of view of most experimental psychologists, our ideation processes tend to be dependent upon our life history. All that we have seen and done—and particularly those actions and thoughts which have been most frequently successful—become a part of our mental attitude. Such habit is useful in the solution of problems which we have previously encountered. When similar problems come up again, we have at hand solutions which have proved workable in the past.

However, when we face a new problem, we tend to limit our thinking to the solutions we have used for similar problems. When none of these work—and we are faced with the need of thinking up new solutions—we then are forced to combine parts of different habitual acts into new actions—to synthesize, in a novel way, some of the parts of previous actions. This process was described by the late Professor Clark Hull of Yale University. Part of his thesis was that intelligent behavior in problem-solving involves "the assembly of habit segments never previously associated with each other."

We can help ourselves to that end by bearing in mind the principles and procedures set forth in this book. For, in a way, we have to *de*-condition ourselves—to root out the habit of restricting our ideation within the limits of past experience, and thus to let our imagination run *loose* in seeking clues to the solutions of new problems.

An outside influence to that same end is encouragement by others. This was brought out in an experiment by Emory L. Cowen at the University of Rochester. One-half the tested students were subjected to critical stress; the others were treated with praise. In a series of Luchins' water-jar tests, the "praise" group showed 37 per cent fewer rigid responses than the "stress" group. This reduction in rigid behavior was attributed to the anxiety-diminishing effects of the experimenter's reassurance.

A cogent offset to inhibitive habit is a technique popularly known as "brainstorming." Brainstorm sessions are exclusively creative conferences. All participants are led to ideate in a consciously uninhibited atmosphere. The very spirit of the group encourages that which a director of research has called "wild stabs." Thus the chains of habit are broken, and ideas flow freely without being dammed by previous experience.

The underlying principle of that kind of "free-wheeling" (so-called by Dr. J. R. Killian, Jr., President of M.I.T.) is the separation of ideative thinking from critical thinking—with judgment deferred until a maximum number of tentative solutions are thought up. This principle will be fully explored in later chapters.

According to Fritz Kahn, author of *Design of the Universe,* free-wheeling tends to be more difficult for the highly educated than for the relatively uneducated. He cites Faraday's epoch-making idea and then quotes this comment by the late Albert Einstein: "This discovery was an audacious mental creation which we owe chiefly to the fact that Faraday never went to school, and therefore preserved the rare gift of thinking freely."

3. *Self-discouragement as a deterrent*

My long experience as a creative coach has impressed me with the way so many of us undermine our creativity by self-discouragement. Our creative efforts will always breed discouragement by *others* as long as nearly everyone likes to throw cold water. But *self*-discouragement—what a stifler of creativity this so often is, and how uncalled for! We should remember that even the Pasteurs fumbled and stumbled, and that most of the world's truly great ideas were laughed at when first suggested.

Self-confidence used to be an American trait. So much so that our English cousins regarded our ancestors as swashbuckling and boastful. Even up to the first World War, Americans looked up to the D'Artagnan type. Mysteriously, the style changed and modesty became the mark of the model American. Self-effacement has been glorified to the point that many young Americans are almost ashamed to advance ideas. As a result, many brainchildren of great promise are strangled by their own parents before anyone ever hears of them.

Another tendency that militates against creativity is a yen to "conform." This carries the curse of conventionalism; and "convention is a great discourager of originality." The fear of "looking foolish" goes with wanting not to seem different. This complex has stood in the way of many whom I have tried to coach. At the risk of sermonizing, I have reasoned with them:

"Which is worse—to look foolish to others, or to look foolish to yourself? Some may think that some of your ideas are half-baked; but what could be sillier than for you to let that stop you from trying to make the most of your mind?" And I have tried to point out to them that truly intelligent people admire creative effort, realizing as they do that almost all the good in the world came from ideas that many condemned as "foolish."

The fear of looking foolish is an all-too-common emotional block. Few of us are conscious of this anticreative trait. Not so Dr. James Bryant Conant. While President of Harvard University, he kept on his office wall a drawing of a turtle, with this motto: "Behold the turtle. He makes progress only when his neck is out."

Unfortunately, and sometimes erroneously, we have looked upon some of the world's most creative figures as unenviable egotists. "A regular cock-a-hoop show-off" is what Musselman's grandmother called the man who created the coaster brake. Paul de Kruif noted the "scornful cockiness" of Pasteur. And of Leeuwenhoek who gave us the microscope, de Kruif wrote: "His arrogance was limitless. In his day, Leeuwenhoek was regarded by all who knew him as the man with the swollen head."

The flamboyance of George Bernard Shaw may have been due largely to a pose designed to attract the limelight. As a boy he was pathetically self-deprecating. "I suffered such agonies of shyness," wrote he, "that I sometimes walked up and down the Embankment for 20 minutes or more before venturing to knock at the door. . . . Few men have suffered more than I did in my youth from simple cowardice." To conquer his timidity, he learned to speak in public; in his early attempts he deliberately made himself seem like a man of cocky confidence, even though his knees were shaking all the time.

As a matter of fact, the great majority of the notably creative have been modest to the point of humility. I have known more than a few men high up in creative research, and I have yet to meet one whom the world doesn't regard as a greater man than he regards himself. In almost every case, when asked the secret of their success, they have claimed that their imaginative talent is far below the genius level—and that whatever they have achieved has come mainly from just trying and trying, in the face of repeated failure.

4. *Timidity tends to abort ideas*

When due to our expecting too much of ourselves, diffidence may reflect conceit rather than modesty. One night, a group of us went into a huddle to think up a new radio show. All of us oldsters came through with ideas; but the youngsters just listened. I knew one of them to be gifted with far more creative talent than I, so I asked him: "Why didn't you do some pitching?" He explained to *his* satisfaction, but not to mine: "I was afraid you might not think my ideas as good as you'd expect of me." He held back, not because he felt he was creatively sterile, but because he prided himself too much. What a shame! The chances are that at least one of his ideas would have been better than most of ours.

On the other hand, I have found that timidity usually stems from genuine doubts of one's ability to be creative. Such "doubts are traitors," quoth Shakespeare, "and make us lose the good we oft might win by fearing to attempt." Surely there can be no reasonable doubt that we do have imaginative talent, or that we can use it better if we will.

But even when we do think up, we are too often held back by hesitation to give out. Years ago, a private secretary in a big company faced a dim future. His personality was meek, and his duties were routine. And yet, over the years, I saw that man step ahead of scores of others and become one of the top three in his great corporation. Here's his own explanation of his success: "During the first 10 years I got nowhere because, even though I did think up ideas, I was afraid to suggest them to anybody. Then one day I made up my mind that the worst that could happen would be that somebody might laugh at me. After a few of my suggestions had been adopted, I became bold—so bold that I never hesitated to pass along any idea that I was able to think up."

When we keep on creating, even trivially, we tend to form a habit. Getting started soon becomes less of a problem. The more we try, the more we instinctively do, as Victor Wagner urged when he said: "Ask questions, dig for facts, gather experience, watch the breaks. And at every stage of the game, peer beyond the end of your nose, learn that two and two can make 22 and zero as well as four—and above all get your heaven-sent gift of imagination to work. Once that trick becomes a habit, as it always does, you will realize that imagination, like faith, can and often does move mountains."

Timidity tends also to halt us after we get started on a creative project. Even Edison had to fight off this gremlin in his early days; but in later life, according to a man who worked with him, "his experimental failures appeared to be merely parts of his day's work, and served as signals for the starting of other experiments."

Many a creative scientist has had to whistle in the dark to keep himself going. Ronald Ross ran up against a stone wall in India while in hot pursuit of a way to overcome malaria; but, instead of being stopped, Ross kept on until he ran across a promising clue. He made the most of this by wiring back to London from Calcutta that the mystery of malaria was almost within his grasp and that, within a few weeks, he would solve it to the glory of old England. This turned out to be overoptimistic as to time, but not as to final achievement.

In the early days of the ethyl-gas research, the young scientists went to Boss Kettering with this protest: "We would like to do something in the world and we don't want to be kept on this problem forever, because we don't see any hope of ever working it out."

Kettering was about to leave for New York. "Let me have a couple of days to think this over," he replied, "and when I come back I'll see if I can't work out something for you." On the way back to Dayton, he picked up a newspaper which announced: "University Professor Discovers Universal Solvent." The next morning he showed this item to the boys and said, "Here's one we'd better try before we quit."

So they went ahead again, and that led, finally, to the successful use of tetraethyl lead. "The point of this story," said Kettering, "is that there will always be dark days, but if your conviction of the value of the problem is such that you go right ahead in spite of the difficulties, the chances are that you will achieve success in the end."

5. *Encouragement cultivates ideation*

Even though Thomas Carlyle was right in saying, "a certain amount of opposition is a great help to a man," creativity is so delicate a flower that praise tends to make it bloom, while discouragement often nips it in the bud. Any of us will put out more and better ideas if our efforts are appreciated. Unfriendliness can make us stop trying. Wisecracks can be poison—as was brought out by Balzac's epigram, "Paris is a city where great ideas perish, done to death by witticism." *Every* idea should elicit receptivity, if not praise. Even if no good, it should at least call for encouragement to keep *trying.*

A boss is at his best when both a suggester of ideas and a creative coach. During the years when E. M. Statler was building up his staff from a one-hotel team to a national organization, he did not pride himself so much on his own ideas as on his ability to coax ideas out of others. Here's what he once told me:

"When I was a bellboy at the McClure House in Wheeling, I got one of the best ideas I ever thought up. I had to run up and down stairs toting pitchers of water. I knew it could be cleaner, and I also knew that a lot of guests wanted ice water but hesitated to call a bellboy. That's what led me to the idea of piping ice water to each guest room. Now that I am running my own hotels, I never fail to realize that some bellboy of mine could dish up just as good an idea as that.

That's why I let everybody know that we *want* their ideas. And when anybody suggests anything, I make sure that he is praised for his effort—and ultimately rewarded if the idea is any good. In that way I coax them to keep trying."

E. M. Statler had come up from the bottom and was the owner. It is much harder to induce such an attitude in supervisory employees. Whenever a management can lead superintendents and foremen to act as creative coaches, a happier and harder-hitting organization is sure to result. "Ideas are generated best in an organization by friendliness," said Ernest Benger of Du Pont. "No stimulus to creative effort is so effective as a good pat on the back. We should do anything possible to encourage people to get more and better ideas."

Corporations have found that the more encouragement they can put into their suggestion systems, the better they will work. The B. F. Goodrich Company has gone so far in this that even a foolish notion still elicits encouragement, as in the case of this idea which landed in the suggestion box: "I suggest that shude put Gloss windows in Dores in Mens and Women tolit for safty When two men mit nither one can see eich other and often makes cowlision." The head of the Suggestions Department tactfully pointed out that some privacy would be lost if glass doors were put on toilet compartments. His letter ended with, "However, any time you have further ideas, we want to hear from you."

In another instance, a worker who could hardly read or write seemed to have some kind of an idea. An engineer was assigned to interview him and, after two hours of patient probing, he got what the man had on his mind. The idea turned out to be so valuable that any engineer would have been proud to have thought it up.

General Mills has made praise a company policy. Vice President Samuel Gale originated a citation for outstanding creative work. On a special form with "Good Deed of the Day" printed on top, he issued a bulletin to the executive staff in praise of whatever had come to his attention as worthy of an orchid. Most big companies fear that naming names in this way may stir up envy, but Mr. Gale's "Good Deed of the Day" specifically addressed itself to the individual to be congratulated; and the system worked.

6. *Intimates can encourage best*

The discouragement that hurts creativity the most is that which comes from those we love. Within a family, praise is at its greatest premium. Parents should stop, look, and listen before ever uttering the slightest discouragement of a child's creative efforts. Praise helps a child creatively when given face to face, but is even more powerful when spoken to others and overheard by the child.

Most of us are highly imaginative in childhood, and yet many of us grow up to be non-creative. One reason for this may be that as a nation we have not made enough of the *importance* of ideas. Another reason is that most parents are guilty either of active discouragement, or, at least, of lack of active encouragement of their children.

A friend who has prospered from his creative efforts told me he got his start when, as a little boy, he showed his father a gadget he had thought up so that he wouldn't have to stand on a stool in order to turn off the gas light. All he had done was to saw a notch in the top of a stick. With this, he could reach up to the gas fixture, slip the notch over the valve, and turn off the gas without climbing. His father told him his idea was "terrific"; and that night at the dinner table, with guests present, he told the story over again with emphatic praise of his little boy's ingenuity. That encouragement made the lad realize that he *could* think up ideas and that it was fun to try. This faith paved his way to success.

According to the late Justice O. W. Holmes, his father made meals a training ground for creative effort by offering a prize for the wittiest remark his children could think up at the table.

Doctor Roma Gans has stressed the need to build self-confidence in the young; and she further points out that there's a difference between a child's willingness to try *three* things—getting two successes and one flop—and trying only *one* thing that can be perfectly done. In her opinion, a perfectionist point of view can't help but cramp creative effort.

Brothers and sisters tend to be somewhat sadistic toward each other, and to look for a laugh in anything the other has done or has tried to do. It may be too much to hope that a brother will *encourage* his brother in creative sallies, but how much less harm he would do if he resisted the temptation to *discourage.*

Uncles, aunts, and grandparents are more inclined to enhearten rather than to dishearten. An uncle I know found that his nephew, aged five, had gone to a fire with a pad and crayons and had drawn pictures of the flames, the windows, and the ladders. Strongly believing that there can be no such thing as too much praise in fanning the creative flames of the young, the uncle later wrote to the lad the first typewritten letter he had ever received, and in this he said: "Your pictures of the fire were so good that I showed them to the people in my office. They all felt the same as I did about how real you made the fire look. I am glad that you like to draw and hope you will keep on drawing. Perhaps someday you will be a great artist, and we'll all be proud of you. For your birthday I am getting you some new crayons. Next Christmas I am going to ask Santa to send you a box of paints."

One way to gird our wills against discouragement is to realize that most of the greatest ideas were at first greeted with sneers. When John Kay invented the flying shuttle, it was considered such a threat to labor that weavers mobbed him and destroyed his mold. When Charles Newbold worked out the idea of a cast-iron plow, the farmers rejected it on the grounds that iron polluted the soil and encouraged weeds. In 1844, Doctor Horace Wells was the first to use gas on patients while pulling teeth. The medical profession scorned this new idea as a humbug. When Samuel P. Langley built his first heavier-than-air machine—flown by steam—the newspapers dubbed it "Langley's folly" and scoffed at the whole idea of self-propelled planes.

Let's remember that we can throttle our own creative talent by self-discouragement. Let's also remember that we can likewise throttle the creative talent in others. For all of us, a good rule is always to encourage ideas—to encourage speaking up as well as thinking up. Nothing else makes sense because the essence of creativity is to keep on trying and trying, harder and harder—and that's almost too much to expect of human nature if, on top of all other blocks to creative effort, we also have to surmount the curse of discouragement.

A combination of a creative climate and the constant use of creative procedures can do much to help a business grow. For example, 10 years ago W. J. Lutwack started a company on a "shoestring." Today that business is the leader in its field. Here is Mr. Lutwack's explanation:

"The creative climate we have fostered has been the key to our success. Our executives and staff regularly get together to think up ways and means to solve production problems, to create new items, to explore and develop new markets and new uses. Mutual encouragement is the absolute rule. A negative attitude is never permitted until after we have thought up plenty of ideas from which to choose."

TOPICS

1. Distinguish between judicial thinking and creative thinking. Discuss.
2. What should be one's attitude toward a new idea? Discuss.
3. How should judgment be controlled in its application to creative thinking?
4. Hollywood producers often adopt a different title when they make a movie out of a book. Why do they do this? How do they decide?
5. Why is discouragement so great a threat to creative efficacy? Discuss.

EXERCISES

1. List five ideas which might be used further to lessen intolerance toward Negroes in this country.
2. If you were to teach a course in algebra, what would you do to make it more interesting and more important to your students?
3. Write down the title of the last moving picture you saw. Now suggest five other titles you think might well have been chosen.
4. E. M. Statler won fame for his innovations in hotel service. What additional ideas can you think up along this line?
5. In what ways could the physical characteristics of the usual textbook be improved?

REFERENCES

ADAMSON, ROBERT E., "Functional Fixedness as Related to Problem-Solving: A Repetition of Three Experiments." *Journal of Experimental Psychology*. Vol. 44, 1952, pp. 288–291.

ADAMSON, ROBERT E. and TAYLOR, DONALD W., "Functional Fixedness as Related to Elapsed Time and to Set." *Journal of Experimental Psychology*. February 1954, pp. 122–126.

BERGLER, EDMUND, "Unconscious Mechanisms in Writer's Block." *Psychoanalytical Review*. April 1955, pp. 160–167.

FOUNDATION FOR RESEARCH ON HUMAN BEHAVIOR, *Creativity and Conformity*. Ann Arbor. 1958.

GETZELS, J. W. and JACKSON, P. W., *Creativity and Intelligence*. New York. John Wiley and Sons, 1962.

HART, HORNELL and OTHERS, "Preliminary Conclusions from a Study of Inventors." *Proceedings of the American Sociological Society*. 1927, pp. 21, 191–194.

HASBROOK, E., "The Conditions of Creative Work." *Progressive Education*. December 1931, pp. 648–655.

INDUSTRIAL RELATIONS NEWS, *Company Climate and Creativity*. New York. 1958.

JOELSON, EDITH A., "Creative Thinking." *Journal of the American Society of Training Directors*. September 1957, pp. 7–13.

LIGON, ERNEST, *A Greater Generation*. New York. The Macmillian Company, 1948.

LIPPITT, R., "An Experimental Study of the Effect of Democratic and Authoritarian Group Atmospheres." *University of Iowa Studies in Child Welfare*. 1940, pp. 16, 145–195.

MCEACHRON, K. B., JR., "Developing Creative Ability in an Educational System." *Journal of Engineering Education*. 1947–1948, pp. 55, 122–128.

MEARNS, HUGHES, *Creative Youth*. New York. Doubleday and Company, 1930.

MEARNS, HUGHES, "Demon of Inhibition." *Junior-Senior High School Clearing House*. February 1930, pp. 346–350.

MEARNS, HUGHES, "Providing for Creative Self-Expression." *New York State Education.* December 1936, pp. 201–203.

NEF, JOHN U., *War and Human Progress.* Cambridge. Harvard University Press, 1950.

OVERSTREET, HARRY ALLEN, *The Mature Mind.* New York. W. W. Norton and Company, 1949.

STEVENSON, A. R., JR., and RYAN, J. E., "Encouraging Creative Ability." *Mechanical Engineering.* September 1940, pp. 673–674.

THURSTONE, L. L., "Creative Talent." *Psychometric Laboratory, University of Chicago,* No. 61. December 1950.

TORRANCE, E. P., *Guiding Creative Talent.* Englewood Cliffs, N. J., Prentice-Hall, Inc., 1962.

VEATCH, JEANNETTE, "The Structure of Creativity." *Journal of Educational Sociology.* November 1953, pp. 102–107.

WIGGAM, ALBERT EDWARD, *The Marks of an Educated Man.* Indianapolis. Bobbs-Merrill Company, 1930.

Chapter V

Our new environment—
its effect on creativity

For those of us who are in non-creative pursuits, today's environment provides too little imaginative exercise. It was otherwise a generation or so ago. Circumstances forced most of our forefathers to practice creativity at every turn, no matter what their calling. They could keep their ingenuity in training without reaching out for imaginative exercise.

The spirit of effort which led our forebears to make the most of their creative talent came partly from environment and partly from heredity. According to Edna Lonigan, it came mainly from "the English seafarers who ventured out from their sunless island in search of a livelihood, and learned how to manage new and strange employments, in which the penalty of failure was death."

Forebears like those from England were the first to enrich our national bloodstream with ingenuity. As time went on, almost every country added to our inheritance. The call of the new America fell on the deaf ears of the lazy and the unimaginative, whereas the same call was a clarion to those of greater gumption. From such sources, there came into our nation what Paul Hoffman has described as "the discontented, youthful, and pioneering spirit which forever quests for that which is better." The essence of this spirit was hard work. The result was a climate which cultivated creative imagination as never before anywhere in the world.

America's ingenuity was called "Yankee" for good reason. New Englanders creatively contributed by far the most to our early development. "The home of the New Englanders," said Arnold Toynbee, "was the hardest country of all." Their creative power was built up by the need to overcome their obstacles.

During our colonial period, all manufacture in our country was practically forbidden by the English Parliament. Therefore, New Englanders had virtually no experience to guide them when they started to industrialize, at the beginning of the 19th century. Almost every detail of making goods had to be thought up—almost as if no goods had ever been manufactured anywhere. One idea followed another; one enterprise after another was conceived and started.

The opening of our West served as another impetus to our creative effort. Again the brothers and sisters strong in imagination and gumption left their cosy homes and took the same westward direction as their European forefathers had taken. Like their forebears, they had to force their muscles and minds to the utmost or fail; they had to think up new ways to solve new problems. Their creative instincts were sharpened on the stones of adversity.

Meanwhile, many of our forebears had to become jacks-of-all-trades; and out of this fact came an ever greater inventiveness, as typified in the case of Thomas Davenport, the young blacksmith from Vermont. He changed the world through his invention of the electromagnet, out of which came the electric motor. He had no training in electricity or any other science. He started doing the work of a grown man when he was only 10 and, as apprentice to a blacksmith, served without pay until he was 21. He read a lot, but above all else, he did this and that and the other thing with his hands, guided by his imagination and his will. It was men like Davenport who brought about our industrial revolution in the form of mass production.

His work made Davenport more and more creative, whereas most of today's Americans tend to grow less and less creative as they mature. This fact is stressed in William Sheldon's book, *Psychology and the Promethean Will.* He points out that most youngsters are highly creative, but that their creativity ebbs from adolescence on. Sheldon calls this "the dying back of the brain." And he adds that this tragedy happens to so large a percentage of our people that it is generally accepted as unavoidable.

The disciplines of education and the pressures of living tend to enhance our critical faculties at the expense of our imaginative ability. This is another reason why we are almost certain to become less and less creative unless we deliberately do something to conserve and develop the imaginative talent with which we were born.

As to the ever-growing softness of the American environment, President Griswold of Yale has sounded a national alarm in these words: "Amidst the easy artificiality of our life . . . our creative powers have atrophied."

We lose what we don't use. This is an axiom which applies to brain as well as to brawn.

2. *Urbanization versus imagination*

"The country bore the country town and nourished it with her best blood," said Oswald Spengler. "Now the giant city sucks the country dry, insatiably and incessantly demanding and devouring fresh streams of men."

Whereas 50 years ago two-thirds of our people lived on farms and in rural villages, over two-thirds of us now crowd our metropolitan areas. And the day is in sight when up to 77 per cent of us will be city dwellers.

Urban life tends to sap imaginative strength in all except the few who work in the arts and in creative phases of business and science. Most of those in routine jobs practice ingenuity far less than those who work on farms. One proof that a non-urban background is more likely to foster creativity is found in the disproportionate preponderance of country-born leaders among those listed in *Who's Who.*

A committee of educators with a grant from the Carnegie Foundation recently conducted a five-year survey to determine the geographical origin and the economic backgrounds of those who had made good as creative scientists. In interpreting the committee's findings, *Newsweek* editorially commented: "The conclusion is that creative research is a grass-roots business. . . . It thrives where memories of frontier days still linger."

Most metropolitan dwellers have had no need to be craftsmen. "Around the corner" there have been specialists who could be called upon to fix the plumbing, paper the walls, paint the house, and all that. The very speed of the telephone and the motor-car have spread specialism and have thus contributed to a widespread slump in ingenuity. In the early days of the automobile, motorists simply had to "get out and get under"; but now, when stalled, we just phone the nearest garage for a tow. Even professional drivers no longer whet their resourcefulness on their motor troubles. A fouled spark plug is enough to stump most of today's taxi-drivers.

"Modern civilization," said Doctor Alexis Carrel, "seems to be incapable of producing people endowed with imagination. . . ." And, if Spengler is right, a most destructive phase of American civilization is our exodus from country to city—with the resultant debilitation of creative power through "urbanitis."

3. *Decline in creative incentive*

Compared with our ancestors, and compared with the rest of the world, nearly all Americans are relatively prosperous. Easy living not only numbs creativity, but tends to make us overcritical—supercilious toward those who "stick out their necks." This attitude tends to cramp the creative power of both the sneered-at and the sneerers.

Group spirit used to encourage those who tried hard. The "go-getter" was looked up to; the pace-setter was admired. This is far less so today; in fact, the opposite is too often true, as in the case of the welder who was fined by his union for working "too hard" in order to earn more money for his family.

Recent polls reveal that over half of all Americans no longer believe that hard work pays. This carries a real threat to creative power. For belief in the rewards of hard work did much to make our people ingenious; and the loss of that belief can do much to tear down their creative urge.

Our new "why-try?" philosophy carries with it a "don't-take-a-chance" complex. Almost every poll of high-school seniors as to what employment they prefer puts civil service at the top of the list. A similar mania for safer and easier berths was one of the causes of the decline of France, according to Henri Le Chatelier.

Taxes have done much to reduce creative incentive. When the Senate was debating the income tax in 1909, a member declared that if Uncle Sam could take one per cent of a citizen's income, he would take 10 per cent or even 50 per cent. To which Senator Borah responded angrily: "Such talk is nonsense. The American people would never stand for a tax of 50 per cent." And now the income tax rate on top incomes reaches as high as 94.5 per cent.

High taxation was mainly caused by war. In that way, as well as in others, the World Wars contributed to a decline in creative power, although they did serve as spurs to our creative scientists. America entirely depended upon Germany for scientific laboratory glassware until World War I forced American ingenuity to solve that problem. The same was true of dyestuffs.

War, however, has a crippling effect on artists and writers. "The qualitative decline of creative imagination in the fields of literature and the theatre during war," said Leslie Pearl, "is one of those phenomena so frequently observed and so widely discussed that it has become almost a truism."

In World War II, over 11,000,000 Americans spent an average of one and a half years in uniform. Most of them were seldom or never called upon to exercise their imaginations; theirs was but to do as told. Thus some 50 billion man-hours were spent between 1940 and 1945.

Except for the way war spurs creative thinking on the part of military leaders and inventors, the net effect of our global strife has been to make our national environment less and less creative.

4. *The creative trend in education*

Many educators believe that our changed environment should call for more training in creativity. Some even fear that much of our educational program has tended to stifle imagination—that whereas kindergartens cultivate this talent, the primary and secondary grades usually tend to smother imagination.

An outstanding leader in seeking solutions to this problem is Warren W. Coxe, New York State's Director of Educational Research. Most of his staff's energies are now devoted to surveying ways and means by which schools throughout that state can change their teaching programs to insure that they will do less to cramp imagination, and do more to encourage creativity.

Some authorities on higher education are likewise concerned with this problem, partly because scientific testing has revealed that, although college graduates should rate higher than non-college people in creative aptitude, they do not. According to Doctor J. P. Guilford, the most common complaint concerning college graduates as researchers is that "while they do assigned tasks with a show of mastery of the techniques they have learned, they are much too helpless when called upon to solve problems where new paths are demanded." A study by the Brookings Institute confirmed this paradox.

A well-filled mind is certainly essential to creativity, since facts are the wherewithal of ideas. But grave danger lurks in memory-stuffing. In his *The Aims of Education,* Alfred North Whitehead warned: "We must beware of what I call 'inert ideas'—ideas that are merely received into the mind without being utilized, or tested, or thrown into fresh combinations." And yet nearly every curriculum stresses the intake and retention of such data.

Another deterrent is what one educator calls the "academic attitude—the acquisition of a spirit of mellow tolerance and scholarly insight, to the sacrifice of the creative impulse."

The fact is that the generation of ideas often requires an almost irrational enthusiasm—at least until verification shows that we have misfired. According to Charles Kettering, even duds can be steppingstones by which to reach worthwhile ideas.

"*Passivity* is the most dangerous pitfall in contemporary education," was the conclusion of a group of college professors. To offset this deterrent, students need to acquire a true evaluation of the part that effort plays, especially in creativity. That's why one professor of English goes out of his way to explode the popular notion that writers are "born," and that what they write just writes itself. He cites the autobiographies of authors as evidence to the contrary. He agrees with Thomas Huxley that a fundamental purpose of education is to teach students that the most valuable trait they can acquire "is the ability to make yourself do the thing you have to do, when it ought to be done, whether you like it or not."

Pre-college schooling tends to be anticreative, as a rule, even in the teaching of art, according to Stanley Czurles, Director of Art Education at New York State College for Teachers. He has said: "A child is highly creative until he starts at school. Then, under traditional procedures, almost all our teaching tends to cramp his imagination. For instance, when in the traditional manner all pupils are given pieces of paper, all of the same color; are told just how to fold and mark them, all in the same way; are shown just how and where to cut, all in the same pattern; the result is that every child comes out with exactly the same design. There is no stimulation of the imagination, no incentive for creativeness. How much better it would be to have the pupil select the color, cut and fold so as to explore various possibilities, according to his individual initiative. In this way we would fan the creative spark, whereas, through standardization, we tend to stifle it."

Some progressive schools are exponents of creative exercise. And so are some trade schools. Commissioner Grace of Connecticut reported: "Recently, I visited one of our trade schools. Its laboratory was built from the junkyards, from the castoff materials of industry, and from whatever could be picked up here and there around the community. Boys designed the instruments and the appliances; the laboratory is their creation. We need more of this. The opportunity to create should be provided in every school and class." Dean John B. Wilbur of M.I.T. wrote this: "The educator has the special obligation of encouraging and helping his students to develop their mental faculties; in short—but not too accurately—the students should be taught how to think." He then went on to stress the need to develop "the informal mental processes" which he described as "judgment, wherein reflection on past related experience leads to the formulation of values through comparison and discrimination . . . imagination, wherein some process of the mind leads to the formulation of mental images or concepts."

TOPICS

1. To what extent do you agree with Thomas Huxley on the fundamental purpose of education?
2. Do you believe that hard work "pays off" either in school or on a job, the way it used to? Why or why not?
3. Would you say that discontent stimulates the creative spirit? Why or why not?
4. "Creative research is a grass-roots business." Do you agree? If so, why? If not, why?

5. If adversity was the driving power behind many of the world's most creative people, how were they able to maintain and increase their creativeness long after they became famous and prosperous? Discuss.

EXERCISES

1. Think of at least five ways, not now being used, to strengthen school spirit at the school you attend or attended.
2. Name five inventions which the world could use to advantage which have not yet been invented.
3. What improvements in a bus would you suggest for the comfort and convenience of passengers?
4. Write five imaginary headlines that you would most *like* to see in tomorrow morning's newspaper.
5. "Your mind is like a parachute; it's no use unless it's open." To a similar result, complete the following: "Life is like a Bible;—" "Love is like a flying saucer;—" "Love is like Grandma's spectacles;—" (This exercise suggested by *The London Spectator*.)

REFERENCES

BROWN, K. I., "To Create: to Cause to Come into Existence; Place of Creativity in the Liberal Arts." *Journal of General Education*. October 1948, pp. 34–40.

DONHAM, W. B., *Education for Responsible Living*. Cambridge. Harvard University Press, 1944.

ELLINGER, R. G. "Education for Creative Thinking." *Education*. February 1946, pp. 361–363.

GREENSLET, FERRIS, *The Lowells and Their Seven Worlds*. Boston. Houghton Mifflin Company, 1946.

MCCONNELL, T. R., "Learning by Thinking." *School and Society*. March 18, 1939, pp. 343–347.

MEARNS, HUGHES, "Creative Education in College Years." *Progressive Education*. May 1946, pp. 268–269.

MEARNS, HUGHES, "Creative Learning." *Challenges to Education, War and Post-War*. Philadelphia. Pennsylvania University School of Education, 1943, pp. 157–166.

PEARSON, DONALD L., *Creativeness for Engineers*. Donald L. Pearson, P. O. Box 413, State College, Pennsylvania, 1960.

ROGERS, D., "Teaching Children to Think Creatively." *Peabody Journal of Education*. March 1952, pp. 268–273.

SHELDON, WILLIAM H., *Psychology and the Promethean Will*. New York. Harper & Brothers, 1936.

SPENGLER, OSWALD, *The Decline of the West*. New York. Alfred A. Knopf, 1926.

STEWART, G. W., "Can Productive Thinking Be Taught?" *Journal of Higher Education*. November 1950, pp. 411–414.

STEWART, G. W., "Higher Education in Creativeness." *Journal of Higher Education*. January 1946, pp. 31–39.

THORNDIKE, ROBERT L., "How Children Learn the Principles and Techniques of Problem-Solving." *Yearbook National Society for the Study of Education*. Bloomington. Public School Publishing Company, Part 1, 1950, pp. 196–216.

WHITEHEAD, ALFRED NORTH, *The Aims of Education*. New York. The Macmillan Company, 1929.

WOOLRICH, W. R., "Creative Engineering Research: Its Stimulation and Development." *Journal of Engineering Education*, 53, 1945–1946, pp. 565–571.

ZIRBES, LAURA, *Spurs to Creative Teaching*. New York. G. P. Putnam's Sons, 1959.

Chapter VI

Ways by which creativity can be developed

"TALENT IS our affair," said Gustave Flaubert. We can let our creative gift shrivel through disuse, or we can build it up by taking on those activities which are most likely to cultivate imagination—and to provide it with exercise.

That this talent can be developed is beyond question. Psychologists long ago accepted the tenet that any primary ability can be trained—that even an average potential can be developed by exercise. By practicing mental arithmetic, adults can more than double their ability to calculate. As to the effect of exercise on memory, many people, through practice, have doubled their power of recall.

Even distinctly emotional traits can be changed for the better through exercise. The more we practice kindness, the kinder we become. By practicing good cheer we become cheerier ourselves. Even a sense of humor can be developed by training—at least the University of Florida so believes. Its experimental course in this subject proved so effective, that such teaching is now a permanent part of that university's curriculum.

Exercise is needed to develop minds as well as bodies. Walt Disney advises us to look on our imagination-apparatus as mental muscles. "The more a muscle works," said Doctor Carrel, "the more it develops. Activity strengthens it, instead of wearing it out. Like muscles and organs, intelligence and moral sense become atrophied for want of exercise."

When Shakespeare referred to "the rich advantage of good exercise," he indicated that practice varies in degrees of value. Best of all, of course, is actual *doing*—the actual combining of effort with imagination. Thus creative power can be retained or regained—and "it can actually be stimulated into growth," according to Professor H. A. Overstreet and nearly all other students of the mind.

2. *Experience provides fuel for ideation*

To develop creativeness, the mind needs not only to be exercised, but to be filled with material out of which ideas can best be formed. The richest fuel for ideation is experience.

Firsthand experience provides the very richest fuel, since it is more apt to stay with us and to bubble up when needed. Secondhand experience—such as superficial reading, listening, or spectating—provides far thinner fuel.

At the age of 12, Thomas Alva Edison was a candy butcher on Grand Trunk trains. He published a newspaper when still less than 14. Between times, he bought and sold vegetables, and, while still in his teens, he worked in a telegraph office. So much did he learn firsthand that, by the time he was 22, he had perfected the Universal Stock Ticker and had sold it to Western Union for $40,000. Such firsthand experience helps explain Edison's life-long record of creative triumphs.

Travel is one kind of experience that tends to feed imagination. The high spots linger long in our memories and strengthen our power of association—so much so, that years later, we may give birth to an idea that would not have come to us had we not gone somewhere and seen something.

The creative value of travel depends on the effort we put into it. When my partner, Bruce Barton, circled the globe many years ago, he kept a diary—not only of his experiences, but also of the ideas he thought up each day. This record has greatly enhanced the carry-over value of that trip. Many a time I have seen him pick up that diary and pluck from it some thought of his for use in the weekly editorials which he wrote for more than 50 newspapers throughout the country.

Percy Grainger, as he traveled from recital to recital, did a lot of his composing. He sang and hummed and whistled as he worked. Such creative activity would be mildly noteworthy if done in Pullmans. But Grainger always rode in day coaches, where concentration was well-nigh impossible, and where singing, humming and whistling elicited jibes from fellow passengers.

A woman, about to spend 10 hours in a day coach with her two young sons, dreaded the way they would bombard her with: "Mother, what will I do now?" So she told them at the start: "Here are two pads and pencils. Write down everything you can think up to do on a train ride. I will give you a dime for each good idea you list." As a result, she paid her 10-year-old $2.30 and her seven-year-old $1.20. I have seen the 35 ideas they thought up. Some of them are worth putting into pamphlets for distribution on trains.

A type of travel which forces imagination into play at every turn is the kind advocated by Episcopal Bishop Edward R. Welles. One summer, he and his wife took their four children on a camp-as-you-go trip to Alaska. In discussing that experience, Mrs. Welles remarked: "The more you depend upon yourself, the better able you are to think up ideas. That is one reason the Bishop and I chose to travel with our family the way we do—to out-of-the-way places and in a rough-it-as-we-go manner. We believe that this kind of travel has helped develop imaginative strength, not only in our children, but also in us parents."

Vagabonding has helped make many a man far more creative than he otherwise would have been. One outstanding example of this was Eugene O'Neill. He worked his way all over South America and across the Atlantic. Thus, by the time he was 24, he had stored up a mountain of rich ore, out of which his imagination could refine the gold with which his plays are laden.

Lowell Thomas is another who has built up his imagination by meanderings off the beaten paths. His most sensational trip was to forbidden Tibet with his son. The book which Lowell, Jr., wrote about that can't fail to stir the reader's imagination. Just think what those firsthand experiences must have done to strengthen the imaginative muscles of the Thomases!

Whether our travel be "out of this world," or into the suburbs, it does add to our experience; thus it adds to the knowledge out of which imagination can generate ideas. It also steps up our automatic power of association. Travel likewise tends to open our minds, and thus, too, makes for ideation.

Personal contacts can also do much to feed and to stimulate imagination. This is especially true of contacts with the very young.

Adults whose professions constantly expose them to children offer living proof that grown-ups can grow in imagination as a result of working with little ones. Teachers of kindergartners and of lower grades are creative to an exceptional degree. Aptitude testers report that 58 per cent of them rate extraordinarily high in imagination, compared with other occupational groups.

To get the most creative help from children, we must meet them more than halfway; we must mentally commune with them as does a newspaper woman I know. She helps to keep her imagination bright by joining her children in thinking up figures of speech. When they take a Sunday afternoon drive, they play a game in which they try to describe what they see —not in terms of literal description, but rather by association.

"Freddie, what does the valley make you think of?"

"Well, Mother, it reminds me of the quilt on Tommy's bed —the way the fields are laid out."

"It's like our colored blocks, side by side," pipes up seven-year-old Johnny.

A white-puffed cloudy day is a source of endless imagining—full of Indian chiefs, buffalo, birds and fish. A sunset becomes "a strawberry soda, turning finally to chocolate."

Doctor Rudolf Flesch drove home the point that the creative value of contacts with children largely depends on the attitude of the adult: "If you try to talk down to children, they will quickly find you out and shut you up. But if you can take the anchor off your adult imagination—what a wonderful realm you enter with them!

3. *Playing games—solving puzzles*

The average person spends much of his leisure on games. Some of these can help develop imagination; others cannot.

There are about 250 kinds of sedentary games. On analysis, only about 50 of these entail creative exercises.

Then, too, much depends on how we play. In chess, for instance, we can either be "book players," and make all moves from memory—or we can make each move a creative adventure, as does a scientist who is one of the best chess players I know. "Instead of playing chess by rote," he told me, "I continually try to think up new and dashing ways to gain my goals. This makes the game more fun and better mental exercise."

Some claim that checkers provide more creative exercise than chess. They agree with Edgar Allan Poe: "In chess, where the pieces have different and bizarre motions, what is complex is taken for what is profound. In checkers, any advantage gained by either party is gained by superior acumen."

Among parlor games, "Twenty Questions" gives no creative exercise to those who merely answer yes or no, although the *questioner* does have to run his mind around energetically in search of alternatives. A far better exercise is charades, as revised by Elsa Maxwell, and now called "The Game." This provides creative effort on the part of all participants. It not only challenges the ingenuity of those who enact, but also makes the viewers try hard to imagine the meaning of each gesture and facial expression.

Outdoor sports tend to bring our minds more or less into play, depending upon how we go at them. In baseball, for example, the catcher must use his imagination the most. He has to think up an endless list of alternatives before he squats. The over-all team strategy revolves around him. The creative training a catcher receives usually pays off in later life, as evidenced by the long list of catchers who have stood out as big-league managers.

In football, the quarterback must call upon his creative imagination every minute his team is on the offensive. His reasoning may be largely intuitive; but, even while walking back to his huddle, a good quarterback must apply hard creative thinking as to what play to call for next. This fact is recognized by sports writers. Often you see quarterbacks described the way Ray Ryan described Don Holland: "His play-calling was daring and imaginative."

Ollie Howard, who broadcasts about angling, claims that more creative imagination is used in fishing than in any other sport. "From the Stone Age, when survival itself depended on the imagination of primitive man, to this modern day of self-appointed Izaak Waltons, success in the pursuit of fish has depended on the ability of the angler to use his creative wits," says Mr. Howard.

Thomas Edison, according to his son Charles, definitely believed in puzzle-solving as a creative exercise. Nowadays we can combine creative practice with relaxation by solving crossword puzzles, like those in the Sunday edition of *The New York Times.* To unriddle them, we must work our minds backward and forward. But mainly, we must *work* our minds; and that, of itself, tones up our creative fibre.

A more strenuous exercise can be had in doing "Double Crostics," which an 80-year-old woman, Elizabeth Kingsley, originated. She rightly claimed: "Mere knowledge alone cannot solve my Double Crostics. I construct them so that they require creative thinking above all else."

An even more strenuous workout is to create and decipher codes. As a pastime, this dark science of secret communication is as old as Egypt. Civilians who make a hobby of cryptograms not only exercise their creativity to the limit, but also train themselves for service in our nation's defense. When all-out war comes, many of them are given crucial responsibilities almost overnight.

4. *Hobbies and fine arts*

There are about 400 known hobbies, most of which have to do with acquiring, rather than creating. The collecting hobbies tend to build knowledge and train judgment, rather than stimulate imagination. Since hobbies vary so widely in the degree of creative exercise they offer, we might better choose those which call for imaginative effort.

By and large, handicrafts provide creative exercise to a greater degree than collecting. There seems to be a reciprocal influence between brain activity and manual activity of the right kind. According to Alfred North Whitehead, "The disuse of handicraft is a contributory cause to the brain-lethargy of aristocracies."

Handicrafts do more for us creatively if and when we think up the designs as well as carry them out. This is true of basket-making, embossing, wood-carving, metalworking, modeling, and a score of other such crafts. Turning scrap into something useful or ornamental likewise challenges creativity. A recent book by Evelyn Glantz shows 401 worthwhile objects she has produced from odd pieces of wood, paper, cloth, bottles, boxes, and other pieces of junk. With the guidance of Peter Hunt's *Workbook*, anyone can "make something out of nothing," and in doing so can find a happy and profitable outlet for creative energy.

We can vigorously exercise imagination by trying to think up new hobbies. I saw one such in the glassmaking department of General Electric's research laboratory. During his lunch hour, a young scientist was at "work" making a ship model out of glass. What a stiff training for his imagination —to think up his designs and then, at every turn, to invent ways to make sails and spars and ropes out of molten silica!

A. Edward Newton recommended: "Get a pair of hobby-horses that can safely be ridden in opposite directions." Many of our creative giants of literature have kept stables of such steeds. Victor Hugo not only made furniture; he also invented furniture. He not only painted pictures, but delighted in turning a blob of ink, while still wet, into a fascinating design. One of these rapid-fire creations of his is a black spider in a web, with infinitesimal demons crawling up the strands.

The fine arts call for imagination—for "bringing something into existence," as Aristotle put it. This is true of music, sculpture, painting, and even aesthetic dancing. But the creative good we get out of an art depends on how we go at it. For example, when we passively listen to music we merely set a mood for imagination; but when we are trying to compose, we actively exercise our creativity—as does Eugene McQuade, a New York lawyer, who often spends his time on his commuting train trying to work up new scores.

Painting and drawing can't fail to put imagination through its paces. Every stroke of brush, pen, or pencil tends to turn on that automatic power of ours called association of ideas. Eugene Speicher likened painting to playing with electricity. "Touch one part of the canvas," he said, "and something immediately happens to some other part."

5. *Creativity thrives on reading*

As Francis Bacon declared, "Reading maketh a full man." It supplies bread for imagination to feed on, and bones for it to chew upon. But to get the most out of our reading, we must be selective; and a good test as to what to read might well be this simple question: "How good an exercise for my creative mind will this provide?"

Our imaginations are whetted by the right kind of fiction, such as that written by Dickens, Dumas, Conrad, and Kipling. Most of the lesser novels, however, provide but little more than pleasant escapes. The better mysteries, however, can give us good creative workouts—if we read them as if we were participants rather than spectators—and especially if we stop as soon as the clues are in hand, and try to think out "who done it."

Short stories are short mainly because they leave so much to imagination. To gain the most creative exercise from these, we might well try to outwit the author by reading the first half, then thinking up and writing down our own outline for the latter half. By emulating O. Henry's snap-the-whip endings, we can provide our imaginations with strenuous practice.

"The most rewarding form of reading is biography"—in the judgment of Harry Emerson Fosdick. Any life worth publishing can't fail to reveal an inspiring record of ideation. Doctor Albert G. Butzer believes in the Bible as a source of creative development for those who read it right. William Lyon Phelps likewise has recommended Bible-reading for mental training.

Among the periodicals, the *Reader's Digest* is recommended by Walt Disney in these words: "Your imagination may be creaky or timid or dwarfed or frozen at the points. The *Reader's Digest* can serve as a gymnasium for its training." Travel magazines like *National Geographic* and *Holiday* help fill the fuel tanks of our imagination. Women's magazines not only do that for their readers but often run articles which inspire creative effort. Periodicals like *Popular Science* provide a creative atmosphere, and serve as showcases for new ideas.

Too many of us let our minds serve solely as sponges while reading. Instead of such passivity, Elliott Dunlap Smith of Yale has urged active effort—enough energy to "*exercise* our power of creative thought." George Bernard Shaw went so far as to write his own outline of each book he was about to read before he even opened it.

In *How to Read a Book,* Mortimer Adler distinguishes between *information* and *enlightenment* as results of reading—a distinction that determines the extent to which reading can foster creative imagination. To gain enlightenment we must think as we read. Thus more ideas "come to us" from reading. Often they are sparked by passages wholly unrelated to the creative thought we generate.

Reading provides far better creative exercise when we make notes as we go. For one thing, this induces more energy on our part. In Albert Bigelow Paine's life of Mark Twain the biographer wrote: "On the table by him, and on his bed, and on the billiard-room shelves, he kept the books he read most. All, or nearly all, had annotations—spontaneously uttered marginal notes, title prefatories, or concluding comments. They were the books he had read again and again, and it was seldom that he had not had something to say with each fresh reading."

Professor Hughes Mearns, a pioneer in the teaching of creativity, summed up as follows: "The right sort of reading is rich in vitamins. Those who have been deprived of its energizing units may suffer later dangers in abbreviated lives. We must in honesty admit, however, that many are able to thrive upon its near substitute, a rich reading of experience; but that requires a much longer process."

6. *Writing as a creative exercise*

Writing can do much to train imagination. Scientific tests rate "facility in writing" as a basic index of creative aptitude. Arnold Bennett insisted that "the exercise of writing is an indispensable part of any genuine effort towards mental efficiency."

We need not be "born" writers in order to write. Every author was once an amateur. Matthew Arnold, a plodding school inspector, suddenly found himself hailed as a man of letters. Anthony Hope was a barrister named Hawkins. Joseph Conrad sailed before the mast for 16 years before he discovered he was a novelist. Conan Doyle, a physician, created Sherlock Holmes as a hobby. A. J. Cronin was likewise a family doctor, and so was Oliver Wendell Holmes. Charles Lamb clerked in India House, and started writing to overcome his boredom. Stephen Leacock taught at McGill University for many years before he found that his quill could tickle us. Longfellow was a language teacher. Anthony Trollope was a postal inspector. Herman Melville was an obscure customs official for 20 years.

Recent surveys tell us that nearly 2,500,000 Americans are trying to write for money. Most of them will hope for too much too soon, and will fall by the wayside—stopped by discouragement. But many others will make out well over the long run, according to A. S. Burack, editor of *The Writer*. He estimates: "For every person who hits the jackpot in writing and achieves big money and fame, there are at least 30 or 40 who make comfortable incomes or supplement their earnings by writing a few hours a day."

Some highly successful authors still stick to their regular jobs. Ed Streeter, who wrote *Dere Mabel* and *The Father of the Bride,* early became a banker, and stayed on as vice president of a New York trust company long after his writing had won wide acclaim.

If we use our imagination, rejections need not cause dejection. For one thing, we can put ourselves in the shoes of the greatest authors and realize how they kept going under a barrage of turndowns. W. Somerset Maugham began writing when he was 18; but 10 years elapsed before he could sell enough to make his keep.

Even if we never try to write professionally, there are many forms of amateur effort on which to sharpen our creative wits. Even letter-writing can provide helpful training if we go at it right.

One of my young friends practices by writing his own gag lines for magazine cartoons and sometimes tops the caption chosen by the editors. Another tears a picture from a magazine and writes a short story around it. A woman who is easily irritated by radio commercials occasionally rewrites one the way she would like to hear it.

An industrial engineer who had never written "anything" attended a course in creativity at the University of Buffalo. His instructor, Robert Anderson, asked him to write a story for children. I saw the manuscript which Boyd Payne turned out. It's a tale about a chicken—a Cinderella story entitled "Chickendrella." The scene is Coop Town. The main characters are Flossie Feathers and Brewster Rooster, who live on Cockscomb Avenue. It's a story that would delight any child. It helps prove that nearly all of us have it in us to write—even though we have never written, and have never thought we could.

We can also exercise imagination through word-play. For example, synonym-hunting can be an exciting game, as proved by a mixed group of all ages who spent an evening thinking up ways of saying "superficial." We hit upon 27 synonyms other than those listed in our thesaurus. One of the graphic words we thought up was "horseback." A "horse-back survey" certainly paints more of a picture than does a "cursory survey."

That kind of game also makes a good twosome. Two of my young associates set out jointly to think up synonyms for *acumen.* They knew that a professor and I had thought up 38; so they were bent on beating that mark. They won. In three hours (on a train) they listed 72 words, phrases and figures of speech meaning acumen—34 more than Professor Arnold Verduin and I had been able to dream up in the hour we had spent on the same project.

Another good exercise is to create figures of speech. These can be as simple as those which a group of us thought up: "As superficial as a Bikini bathing suit" . . . "As superficial as a cat's bath." Or, they can include an ironic twist, as when Dorothy Parker likened superficiality to "running the gamut from a to b." In his book, *Teaching to Think,* Julius Boraas strongly recommended as a creative exercise any such effort to think up figures of speech.

7. *Practice in creative problem-solving*

The most direct way to develop creativity is by *practicing* creativity—by actually thinking up solutions to specific problems.

Such exercise has been the essence of nearly all the 1,000 or more courses that have been conducted in creative problem-solving. As a rule, instructor lecturing has been subordinated to student participation in the form of active problem-solving.

As reported in the Foreword of this book, the resultfulness of such teaching has been scientifically evaluated by the research conducted by Dr. Arnold Meadow and Dr. Sidney Parnes at the University of Buffalo. Students who had taken semester courses in creative problem-solving were paired against comparable students who had had no such course. The findings clearly confirmed the fact that creative ability can be substantially improved by means of a 13-session course in creative problem-solving in which this book is used as the text.

The most significant test showed that those who had taken courses were able to average 94% better in production of good ideas than those without benefit of such a course.

These tests were based on quantity of good ideas produced within the same period of time. The researchers scored as "good" ideas only those which were potentially useful and relatively unique.

The technical reports of these findings have been published in the *Journal of Applied Psychology* and the *Journal of Educational Psychology*.

TOPICS

1. Of all the trips you have taken, which one did the most to stimulate your imagination? Analyze the reasons why, and why other trips did not.
2. Do you believe children should be encouraged or discouraged in their "pretending"? Discuss.
3. To what extent do you agree with Francis Bacon that "reading maketh a full man"?

4. Do you think you could write a book? Why, or why not?
5. True or false. "The more you practice kindness, the kinder you get"? Discuss.

EXERCISES

1. Put a blob of ink on a piece of paper and blot it quickly. Make a list of the objects the resultant smear resembles.
2. Cut out six cartoons from a magazine, omitting the original captions. Suggest an alternate legend for each.
3. In less than 100 words, write an outline of an original story for children.
4. List all the words, phrases and figures of speech (including slang) that you can think of which might be used instead of the word "absurd."
5. It is a rainy, cold day. Think up 10 ways a child of eight could amuse himself indoors by using imagination.

REFERENCES

ADLER, MORTIMER, *How to Read a Book*. New York. Simon and Schuster, 1940.

ALGER, JOSEPH, *Get in There and Paint*. New York. Thomas Y. Crowell Company, 1946.

ANDERSON, HAROLD H., ed., *Creativity and its Cultivation*. New York. Harper & Brothers, 1959.

BARTLETT, G. M., "Can Inventive Ability Be Developed in Engineering Students?" *Journal of Engineering Education*. 1933–1934, pp. 41, 276–288.

BOWER, MARVIN, *The Development of Executive Leadership*. Cambridge. Harvard University Press, 1949.

CHURCHILL, WINSTON S., "Painting as a Pastime" from *Amid These Storms*. New York. Charles Scribner's Sons, 1932.

CORNELL, P., "Where to Find Selling and Advertising Ideas." *Printers' Ink*. May 13, 1926, pp. 17–20.

GOLDSTEIN, J. J. and OTHERS, "Thinking Can Be Learned." *Educational Leadership*. January 1949, pp. 235–239.

GREGG, ALAN, "Travel and Its Meaning." *Scientific Monthly*. March 1950, pp. 151–156.

HUNT, PETER, *Peter Hunt's Workbook*. New York. Prentice-Hall, Inc., 1945.

LIGON, ERNEST, *Their Future Is Now*. New York. The Macmillan Company, 1939.

MASON, JOSEPH G., *How to Be a More Creative Executive*. New York. McGraw-Hill Book Company, 1960.

MEADOW, ARNOLD and PARNES, SIDNEY J., "Evaluation of Training in Creative Problem-Solving." *Journal of Applied Psychology*. June 1959, pp. 189–194.

MYERS, R. E. and TORRANCE, E. P., *Invitations to Thinking and Doing*. Minneapolis. Perceptive Publishing Company, 1961.

PARNES, SIDNEY J. and HARDING, HAROLD F., eds., "Can Creativity Be Increased?" from *A Source Book for Creative Thinking*. New York. Charles Scribner's Sons, 1962.

Chapter VII

The creative problem-solving process

THE CREATIVE problem-solving process ideally comprises these procedures: (1) *Fact*-finding. (2) *Idea*-finding. (3) *Solution*-finding.

Fact-finding calls for problem-definition and preparation. Problem-definition calls for picking out and pointing up the problem. Preparation calls for gathering and analyzing the pertinent data.

Idea-finding calls for idea-production and idea-development. Idea-production calls for thinking up tentative ideas as possible leads. Idea-development calls for selecting the most likely of the resultant ideas, adding others, and reprocessing all of these by such means as modification and combination.

Solution-finding calls for evaluation and adoption. Evaluation calls for verifying the tentative solutions, by tests and otherwise. Adoption calls for deciding on, and implementing, the final solution.

Regardless of sequence, every one of those steps calls for deliberate effort and creative imagination.

Let's start with problem-definition. The importance of this part of the creative problem-solving process was stressed by Albert Einstein in these words: "The formulation of a problem is far more often essential than its solution, which may be merely a matter of mathematical or experimental skill."

It is only occasionally that an important new idea is accidentally stumbled upon; and it usually turns out that the stumbler had been hard on its trail. Seldom is it a case of aimless luck, as in the story of the plumber who carelessly dropped a piece of steel pipe into a batch of molten glass and, on pulling it out, found that he had hit upon a way to make glass tubing.

We cannot consciously increase the crop of fortunate accidents, but we can produce more ideas by conscious creative effort; and in this process, it pays to focus our aim. We should first make our target as clear as possible.

Sometimes we must originate the problem itself. At other times the problems are thrust upon us by force of circumstances. In scientific and in business organizations, problems are often assigned to staff-members, with the targets well defined. Other assignments may carry helpful hints, as when the National Inventors' Council during the war put out lists of "Inventions Wanted."

2. *Thinking up new problems*

Sensitivity to problems is a valuable trait. The lack of it is illustrated in the story of a young man who had taken a course in creative problem-solving and had later told his instructor that he'd been fired from his job. When asked why, the ex-student said:

"I don't know. After taking your course, I was prepared all right. If they'd given me some problems to solve, I know I could have solved them. But they didn't give me problems. They just gave me one whale of a *mess!*"

One reason why Americans get better and better goods

for their money is that our manufacturers *reach out* for targets—consciously search for problems, the solution of which can spell opportunity. For example, recognition of shrinking as a shortcoming in men's shirts led to the multi-million-dollar idea of Sanforizing. Here's the story of how the target was picked and how the aim was set:

The problem grew out of the manufacturer's inability to give consumers as good a fit in shirts as in collars. The trouble was that collars had always been washed after being made, while if shirts were washed that way, they would lose some of their fine finish—would look as though they were not new, but had been through the laundry. So, on his own initiative, Sanford Cluett decided to find a way to shrink cloth without putting it in water.

At the cotton mills Mr. Cluett saw that, in the finishing process, the cloth was always *pulled* through the various processes of bleaching and mercerization. In fact, the cloth was sewed together into strips as long as 14 miles, and then pulled through the mill. This naturally distorted the fabric. He discovered that if this distortion were taken out, most of the shrinkage would be eliminated. So he built a machine which automatically restored the cloth to equilibrium—in other words, pushed the stretch back.

The Sanforized process was designed for cotton goods only. Its success led to other aims. One result is a similar process called "Sanforset" which stabilizes rayon. A still newer process eliminates felting in wool. This case typifies how we can reach out for targets by grasping problems, and how one target can create another.

Creative triumphs have come also from diving off the deep end in search of unseeable problems. Faraday went at it blind when, in 1831, he discovered how electricity could be produced. He had no target. He merely wondered what would happen if—between two poles of a horseshoe magnet—he were to mount a copper disc and make it *spin.* To his amazement, electric current was what the spinning disc produced.

Doctor Charles M. A. Stine did not know what he was after when he started the search which resulted in nylon. His associates have told me that his outstanding trait was curiosity. There would probably be no nylon had he not decided to start a blind hunt.

Dr. Stine inaugurated a program of fundamental research in the Du Pont Company without specific objective, but believing that out of new scientific knowledge important developments would spring. Among the men engaged in this research was Dr. Wallace H. Carothers, who wanted to make larger molecules than had ever been made before, whether or not they had any practical application. He broke the world's record for molecular size of synthetic substances by producing polyesters and polyamides. Dr. Julian Hill noted that one of these polymers in plastic condition could be pulled out into a fiber. Over a hundred chemists, physicists, and engineers participated in the research which ensued on these new compounds, eventually giving the world the synthetic fiber, nylon.

Now and then someone asks a question which leads to a precious answer, and yet his name is lost in oblivion. One example of this was reported by the Department of Agriculture. Baby pigs are often crushed by their mothers rolling over upon them. An unknown thinker-upper asked whether pig mortality in a farrowing house could not be remedied by simply tilting the floor. This led to a system which is now working well. Since mama pigs like to lie down with their backs uphill and the piglets like to travel downhill, the tilted floor tends to keep the baby from under the recumbent old lady. The Department of Agriculture has reported that these tilted floors have cut down this cause of pig mortality by as much as 25 per cent. The price of bacon would be higher had it not been for that unknown's going out of his way to create a target.

3. *Clarification and dissection*

We need not only to pick our problem but also to point it up. We should make the target clear. "Specify your problem consciously," urged Brand Blanshard of Yale. "Coin it at the beginning into a perfectly definite question."

As John Dewey has said, "A problem well stated is half solved." Clarification not only throws light on the target, but helps to put it in perspective. "It brings it into relation with other known facts so as to facilitate examination," as Matthew McClure put it.

By all means, let's *write out* the problem. To help force creative action, we might even write it to somebody else and commit ourselves to find *an* answer, if not *the* answer, by a certain date. And let's not stop with merely posing the problem. Also let's remember that before we can phrase a problem we must determine the real nature of the problem. Only then can we properly set our aim or aims.

Doctor Walter Reed is one of our immortals mainly because he took pains to set the *aim* in the war against yellow fever. The *problem* was thrust upon him. On arrival in Cuba as head of the yellow-fever commission, he went over the most recent death list and asked about each case. He found that the latest to die had not even been near any other victim.

"You mean to say this man had no contact whatsoever with the disease?" asked Major Reed.

"None," was the reply. "He was in the guardhouse for six days with six other men and he was the only one to catch it."

"Well, if you are right about this," said the Major, "then something must have crawled or jumped or flown through the guardhouse window, bitten that prisoner, and then gone back where it had come from. I am convinced the time has come to set aside our microscopes and learn how yellow fever spreads from man to man. The poison is probably carried by an insect, and that may be a mosquito."

After all the bleary-eyed efforts to track down the cause of yellow fever through the usual microscope techniques, Major Reed, in that one observation, had set the aim that led to solution. Through his finding the right focus—plus the heroism of the volunteers who served as human guinea pigs—a vaccine against yellow fever was eventually produced. And 40 years later, our soldiers were able to chase our enemy through infested jungles and swamps, and yet be immune to that once dread disease.

As Charles F. Kettering has explained, "The process of research is to pull the problem apart into its different elements, a great many of which you already know about. When you get it pulled apart, you can work on the things you don't know about."

Questions can be keys to that kind of dissection. For instance, if asked to dream up a new outside sign for your church, you might start by writing down headings like these: Purpose? Location? Design? Material? Illumination? Lettering? Erection? Under each of these you might spell out subquestions. For example as to purpose, should it be: 1. To remind parishioners of services? 2. To attract visitors? 3. To build good will? All told, you could thus list about 30 points which would clarify the objective, indicate data to be sought, and help you get further faster with your creative thinking.

In problem-definition we should begin with a wide focus and then use a narrow focus to define the sub-problems. As Professor John Arnold of Leland Stanford has said: "Knowing what you are looking for helps you to recognize it when you see it. But in the case of innovation, how do you know what you are looking for? You don't, unless you state your problem so broadly, so basically, so all-inclusively and generically, that you do not preclude even the remotest possibility—so that you do not pre-condition your mind to a narrow range of acceptable answers."

In line with Professor Arnold's teaching, Emerson's mousetrap problem was really a sub-problem. The initial problem could well have embraced a total need such as: "How to get rid of mice." Thus, the problem would at first include all possible means of mouse-extermination—such as poisoning, asphyxiation, electrocution, and even cats. This all-inclusive problem could then be broken down into its basic components. "How to make a better mousetrap" could become one of the sub-problems. And then, within this sub-problem, we could ask ourselves a series of specific questions. "How can I make it better-looking?" . . . "Cheaper?" . . . "Easier to use?" . . . "Safer for the housewife?" . . . "Lighter in weight?" If we happened to have a research staff, we might well assign one of these aims to each man or group.

Similarly, Albert V. Carlin of the U. S. Weather Bureau breaks down a general problem into its more manageable components. When confronted with the problem of how to improve the hurricane warning system, he chose these three sub-problems: (1) How to make certain that everyone in the hurricane belt received the warning. (2) How to make certain that everyone who received the warning understood it. (3) How to make certain that everyone who understood it knew what to do about it.

The Buffalo Pottery Company started with this problem: "How can we reduce manufacturing costs?" This problem was too broad. Manufacturing costs embrace nearly everything in a plant. So the next step was to break out the 31 items comprising "manufacturing costs." This list was then boiled down to the 17 factors most subject to cost reduction. The problem selected for initial creative attack was this: "What mechanical method can we think of to substitute for hand labor at points of manufacturing change?"

Although this was a specific problem, it concerned seven positions in the plant, and each position called for a specific solution. After this set of problems had been processed (for each of the seven positions), the 16 other opportunities for cost reduction were subjected to creative problem-solving, one at a time.

Here's an ultra-scientific example from General Electric of the method of composing a problem so as to be limitless in approach and yet specific in purpose. The General Engineering Laboratory received a request from an operating department to suggest a device by which a lamp could be turned on when you walked into a room, "so you would not have to fumble trying to find the lamp switch and knock the lamp down and fall over a chair and break your leg." The brainstormers took two weeks to define the problem. At the end of this time they made a proposal to the operating departments that for a certain figure and in a certain length of time, they would think up a device to meet the specifications. In the given period and within the budget, the brainstorm group came up with what has since been marketed under the trade name of "Touchtron." You simply touch the side of the lamp and the lamp turns on. You touch it again and the lamp turns off.

It was G. E. executive C. Frank Hix, Jr., who reported that case. He commented that "it is hard to go anywhere in General Electric today without finding this time-taking type of problem approach being used by our engineering staffs." The point is that it often pays to take plenty of time to point up a problem.

One psychological reason for taking time to contemplate a problem was brought out in the Rokeach experiments with 250 students at Michigan State College. These tests bore out the hypothesis that by taking more time for perception of a problem, a less rigid and more creative attack is more likely to ensue.

Walter Chrysler saved his small pay as a young railroad mechanic in order to buy a huge $5,000 Pierce-Arrow sedan —just to take it apart, put it together again, and see what he could see. He wanted to find a way to make a better motorcar and went at it, according to Ray Giles, by asking himself specific questions such as. "Why wouldn't brakes on all four wheels stop the car even better?" . . . "Why not keep the lubricating oil in better condition by having it run through a filter all the while?" . . . "Wouldn't tires of bigger diameter give a smoother ride?"

"No wonder when that young fellow later brought out his first Chrysler automobile it was the sensation of that year's auto show," concluded Ray Giles.

Personal problems are usually complex; and these, too, are more likely of solution if broken down into their simpler components. For example: If upset over her husband's morals, a wife would face the basic problem of "How can I make him a better man?" But that covers too much ground for creative attack. She might better start by making a list of influences which corrupt him, and another list of influences which might reform him. She could then single out her targets, such as: "How can I get him to attend church with me?"

Dr. Edgar E. Robinson, Professor Emeritus of History at Stanford University, has frequently remarked, "It is striking how many ideas we humans have for action to be taken by someone else." So perhaps that wife might better set her aims on what she might do to help, rather than try to reform him. For example, she might consider how she can help make his life happier; or how she can arrange for more opportunities for him to enjoy the fishing he so loves.

4. *One aim may lead to another*

Just as one idea leads to another, one aim often leads to another. This has been true of even the greatest scientists. As Paul de Kruif has said, "Microbe hunters usually find other things than they set out to look for."

In June of 1922, I went through the General Motors research laboratory at Dayton. My guide was the research director, Charles Kettering. We peeked into a little room where three men were at work around a little stationary engine which was exhausting through the hole in a window. "What are they doing?" I asked Mr. Kettering.

"Oh, I told them they ought to be able to change gasoline so it would give the motorist five times as many miles per gallon." They never found what they were after, but they did hit on the idea of lead, and that resulted in Ethyl gasoline. Their search had changed its aim and as a result, instead of increasing the mileage of gasoline, they had decreased its knocking.

The Corning Glass people aimed to make globes for railroad lanterns so strong that they would not crack even when bombarded by icy sleet. They hit that mark all right, and railroads became safer as a result. But in doing that, they perfected a new kind of glass that could be used in millions of homes. Thus the aim to make better lanterns led to the aim to make glassware that could withstand the heat of ovens. The women of America have since bought nearly 500 million pieces of Pyrex ware in which to bake, serve and store. That innovation then led to Flameware for top-of-stove use.

Research directors recognize that aims often change. Doctor Howard Fritz told me how one of his scientists had started on a pursuit which led to a by-product of his work, which then became his life's work. The by-product became the product known as Koroseal. This is not an unexpected turn of affairs in organized creativity, according to Doctor Fritz. As Doctor L. L. Thurstone has pointed out, problem-solving often calls for "reformulating the problem itself and then solving the new problem."

Not only a specific aim, but even a basic aim may change. Very few people know that Henry Ford planned to go, not into the automobile business, but into the locomotive business. His first creative exploit as a young man on his father's farm was to build a steam engine. His life's aim was to make railroad equipment. It was not until he was nearly 40 that he set his aim on passenger cars.

It pays to assay our aims. The U. S. Patent Office is crowded with "good" ideas that are no good for anything.

Countless people have spent countless hours and pounds of creative energy on projects of no useful purpose.

Personally, I have too often set forth in search of will-o'-the-wisps. For example, I had in mind a certain new kind of dictionary. I talked with a few people who dealt in words and they were enthusiastic about my target. I set myself to the task and spent hundreds of hours working out the first 100 words. Then I talked to a dictionary publisher. It soon became obvious that it would take 10 men almost a lifetime to complete my work, the cost would be too great and the market would be too limited. Had I analyzed that aim in time, I could have invested those creative hours in something of greater promise.

* * *

This chapter has had to do with definition of problems which call for creative processing. But let's bear in mind that there are other types of problems; and these call for other types of treatment. This distinction was brought out in this statement by Colonel Kelso G. Clow, Commandant of the U. S. Army Armor School:

It must be remembered that while every problem for creative attack is expressed as a question, not every question poses a problem for creative attack. One type of question calls for a factual answer, such as the question, "How much money do we have to complete this project?" A second type of question calls for judgment or decision, such as, "Should we try to get more money for this project?" Possible answers are "Yes," "No," or even "Maybe." A third type of question is one that calls for ideas, such as, "In what ways can we profitably utilize available excess funds?" A question worded in this manner is a problem for creative attack. Although facts and judgment are involved in the solution of the problem, the problem is so expressed as to demand a maximum of ideas.

TOPICS

1. What separate functions were performed by Dr. Stine and Dr. Carothers in the creation of nylon?
2. On what problem did Dr. Walter Reed set his aim, and how did he narrow his target?
3. If you were given the job of designing a better mousetrap, under what specific heads would you break down that general problem?
4. Why should an ideational problem be written out? Discuss.
5. "What is wrong with the younger generation?" Do you consider this a good statement of a problem for creative attack? Why or why not?

EXERCISES

1. Think up at least six creative problems to which a group might profitably seek solutions.
2. Describe an idea for a television show which you think would attract a large audience but which, to your knowledge, has never been tried.
3. Large flocks of starlings have created a public nuisance in many a city. Think up six possible solutions to this problem.
4. Name at least three "Inventions Wanted" which you believe would be most useful to the world.
5. "How would you improve your local government?" List the subtopics into which you would dissect this problem in order to attack it creatively.

REFERENCES

ARMSTRONG, E. H., "Vagaries and Elusiveness of Invention." *Electrical Engineering.* April 1943, pp. 149–151.

ARMSTRONG, FRANK A., *Idea Tracking*. New York. Criterion, 1960.

CARREL, ALEXIS, *Man the Unknown*. New York. Harper & Brothers, 1935.

DEWEY, JOHN, *How We Think*. New York. D. C. Heath and Company, 1933.

GHISELIN, BREWSTER, ed., *The Creative Process*. Berkeley. University of California Press, 1952.

GIBSON, JOHN M., *Physician to the World—the Life of General William C. Gorgas*. Durham. Duke University Press, 1950.

GILFILLAN, S. C., "The Prediction of Invention." *Journal of the Patent Office Society*. September 1937, pp. 623–645.

INSTITUTE OF CONTEMPORARY ART. *Proceedings* of conferences on the creative process held 1956–57. Boston.

KOGAN, ZUCE, *Essentials in Problem Solving*. New York. Arco Publishing Co., 1956.

LANGNER, LAWRENCE, *The Magic Curtain*. New York. E. P. Dutton Company, Inc., 1951.

REID, JOHN W., "An Experimental Study of 'Analysis of the Goal' in Problem Solving." *Journal of General Psychology*. 1952, pp. 44, 51–69.

ROKEACH, M., "The Effect of Perception Time upon Rigidity and Concreteness of Thinking." *Journal of Experimental Psychology, 40*, 1950, pp. 206–216.

SCOTT, JAMES D., ed., *The Creative Process*. Ann Arbor. Bureau of Business Research, University of Michigan, 1957.

SPEARMAN, C., *Creative Mind*. New York. Appleton-Century-Crofts, Inc., 1931.

TAYLOR, JACK, *How to Create New Ideas*. Englewood Cliffs, N. J. Prentice-Hall, Inc., 1961.

WEAVER, H. E., and MADDEN, E. H., " 'Direction' in Problem Solving." *Journal of Psychology*. April 1949, pp. 331–345.

WHITE, W. L., *Bernard Baruch—Portrait of a Citizen*. New York. Harcourt, Brace and Company, 1950.

Chapter VIII

Preparation and analysis go hand in hand

THE PREVIOUS CHAPTER dealt with problem-definition—one phase of the fact-finding portion of the creative problem-solving process. Now we come to preparation, the phase that calls for gathering and analyzing data relevant to the problem we seek to solve.

No sharp distinction should be made between problem-definition and preparation. We often shift back and forth from one phase into the other. In fact, scientific fact-finding may sometimes result in the optimum form of problem-definition. For example, the Gluecks of Yale have made a magnificent investigation of juvenile delinquency. They have even developed a formula which makes it possible to predict, with high probability, whether or not a boy of six will turn out to be a delinquent. The Gluecks have narrowed the determining factors down to these five: 1) The father's discipline. 2) The mother's supervision. 3) The father's affection. 4) The mother's affection. 5) The family's cohesiveness.

Strangely enough the Glueck study ruled out poverty as a significant factor. As Bruce Morgan has said, the same slum can turn out an Al Capone and an Al Smith.

The Glueck research is cited to illustrate how fact-finding can define the problem as well as supply the needed knowledge. But why stop there? For instance, why not think up 100 ways in which a father could discipline better? By thus adding idea-finding to fact-finding, we could do more than *predict*—we could help reduce juvenile delinquency.

Getting back to preparation, this calls for two kinds of knowledge—that which we have previously stored and that which we gather anew to bear upon our creative problem.

Memory serves as a fuel tank. The octane of the contents depends on how we have taken them in. The fuel which we have stored up by active striving and by firsthand experience is likely to be far richer than that which has come in through idle spectating, listless reading, and lazy listening.

There is disagreement about the extent to which one should gather material at the start of a creative project. Many successful creativists believe in saturating themselves with facts. One writer recently remarked: "I seem to be unable to turn out anything worthwhile without the attendant agony of boning up interminably at first." This is especially true in science, according to Nobel Prize winner Ivan Pavlov: "Perfect as is the wing of a bird, it never could raise the bird up without resting on air. Facts are the air of a scientist. Without them you never can fly."

Henry J. Taylor once described Bernard Baruch's creative thinking as following this pattern: "He gets the facts. He studies them patiently. And then he applies his imagination." But in talking with Mr. Taylor later, I found he agreed that Mr. Baruch's imagination must work in all three steps—that after he gets his basic facts, he has to think up what further information he needs, and in seeking those new facts, he likewise has to use his imagination.

Many, including Charles Kettering, believe that fact-gathering should be limited—that we can get too many facts at the wrong stages of our creative projects. As John Livingston Lowes has pointed out, "Facts may swamp imagination."

I found that out when, in one week, I had to create two plans—one for an enlistment drive, another for a money-raising campaign. In preparation for the former plan I spent day after day digging into what others had done along similar lines. My exhaustive study of comparable programs lulled me into a willingness to adapt, and thus shut me off from thinking up anything really new. In preparing the other plan, I lined up the salient facts and then deliberately ignored what others had done. Thus I found I could make my imagination work more radically. The latter plan turned out to be far better than the former.

Such experiences indicate that, instead of doing an exhaustive job of digging before starting to create, we might well line up a few fundamental facts and then start thinking up all the hypotheses we possibly can. After listing 50 or 100 such ideas, we could go back to our fact-finding, gather all facts which might be helpful, and then turn on our imagination again. It is more than possible that an early idea, thought up by us while still shy on factual knowledge, might turn out to be the best idea in the end—and yet might have been drowned at the start in a premature and excessive flood of facts.

2. *Kinds of data best sought*

Sometimes we realize that we want new facts, but are at sea as to just what or where they might be. In this event, we can well prospect at random. For example, if our problem is to think up a new package, we might profitably meander through stores and just look over package after package. Or we might turn to some source that could serve as a checklist. For instance, in contemplating a package, or even the creation of a gadget, a good field for prospecting is a Sears, Roebuck catalog.

Good prospecting calls for an open mind and for wide exposure; and our prospecting should dig deeper than mere sensing. We should delve into the how and the why. Merely seeing a new type of fountain pen will add but little ore to our creative mill. But, by finding out how the pen works and why people are buying it, we may strike a vein of thought which our imagination can turn into gold. Our prospecting should also cover duds, for good ideas are often uncovered by digging into causes of failure.

Related facts are sometimes more helpful than facts directly in point and readily at hand. Before Doctor George R. Minot could establish a cure for anemia, he had to devise a way actually to watch the cells of bone-marrow as they busily created new red corpuscles. Only thus could he lay his hands on the essential facts attendant on his problem. It took plenty of new facts for him to find that folic acid was what anemia needed. And then it took more new facts, plus imaginative effort, to arrive at liver as the best source for this purpose.

New facts as to *cause* are often all-important. When Doctor Robert Koch was challenged to find a cure for diphtheria he is said to have expostulated, "How can I cure diphtheria when I do not even know what causes it?" Personal problems are far simpler, but even these often call for new facts as to causes. For example, a boy is doing badly at school. It is up to his parents to think up a solution. Through talks with the teacher and the family physician, they could list a score of possible causes. One might concern the child's eyesight. In many such cases, eyeglasses have turned out to be the simple solution.

Medical analysis lays stress on contributory facts. A good

doctor, in seeking a treatment to cure an ailment, often goes deeply into his patient's habits. Life insurance examinations may show a man to be a good risk, and yet his application may be turned down because of some facts in the history of his parents.

A conscious search for extraneous material may be well worthwhile, as was demonstrated by a lawyer friend of mine who was defending a wealthy old man who had been charged with incompetency by his relatives. My friend knew that his opponents could bring in just as much or more expert testimony than he could. So he asked himself, "What could we get that they couldn't have?" Then he remembered that his client had had a housekeeper. He wondered what *she* would say about the old man. So he went to see her to find out.

"I am surprised you would ask me such a question," was her indignant reply. "You ought to know that if he weren't 100 per cent I wouldn't have stayed on as his housekeeper for all these 17 years." At the trial, her testimony turned the tide. The lawyer had won by reaching out beyond the obvious.

The need for new facts may be so far-reaching that it calls for a new and complete education, as illustrated in the story of Alexander Graham Bell. "As a young, unknown man," said Doctor Bell, "I went to Washington to talk with Professor Henry, an authority on electricity, about an idea I had conceived for transmitting speech by wires. He told me he thought I had the germ of a great invention. I told him, however, that I had not the electrical knowledge necessary to bring it into existence. He replied, *"Get it!"* Doctor Bell had studied sound all his life. More than any man, he knew the shapes of vibrations that pass through the air when we talk. But he had to—and did—absorb a new subject, electricity, in order to transform his notion into a telephone.

Paul Ehrlich had to go almost as deep into other fields to dig up what he needed to find his famous "606" cure for venereal diseases. His pursuit of new facts was less orderly than Doctor Bell's, but almost as exhaustive. He read book upon book in search of clues as to the kind of microbes he was fighting, and what might kill them without killing the patient. In poring over the detailed reports of Alphonse Laveran, who himself had isolated the malaria microbe, Ehrlich finally got the information which ultimately led to his "606." The name is said to have come from the number of ideas he had thought up on his way to the final answer.

When Glenn Martin was at work on his first airplane model, he studied the engineering of stationary bridges in order to get new facts on strains and stresses that might apply to flying. In search of similar new facts, Wilbur Wright built a crude glass-covered box at the end of which he installed a fan to create winds. From their effect on the miniature wings inside the toy tunnel, he could see just what happened. This was the world's first wind tunnel. From it, the Wright Brothers got the needed new facts—true facts, even though they were at variance with the scientific tables in the textbooks of that day. And that day was only about 50 years ago.

3. *The importance of analysis*

Analysis plays an indispensable part in problem-definition—especially in clarifying our objectives, and in making our targets more specific. In these ways, preparation can be better directed—time and effort can be saved by limiting our fact-finding to that which will serve best to further our creative thinking.

Analysis also plays a vital part in preparation, as well as in synthesis and evaluation. In fact, analysis can be quite as helpful to creative thinking as to judicial thinking.

One use of analysis in attacking a problem is to separate those parts which call for ideas from those parts which call for adjudication. By doing this we may avert a confusion which sometimes blocks creative thinking.

A case in point was that of a Protestant girl who married a Jew. By the time their first son was three years old, her marriage was almost wrecked by religious disharmony. When she determined to attack this problem creatively, she soon found that she first had to face a question which called solely for decision—the basic question as to whether or not her boy *should* be brought up as a Jew.

After judicial analysis, she found that the pros overwhelmingly outweighed the cons. Having settled that confusing factor, she then was able to attack the remaining parts of the problem creatively, by thinking up programs of action she might take along these lines:

1. What to do to enhance her knowledge of, and appreciation of, Judaism.
2. What to do to help teach her son Judaism at home.
3. What to do to create a religious harmony between her husband and herself.

Under these heads, she thought up over 50 constructive ideas, most of which called for special preparation. According to her true story, the problem of religious difference was thus largely eliminated from her family life within less than a year's time.

4. *Analysis can provide clues*

Analysis of any kind can of itself uncover clues which speed up our power of association and thus feed our imagination. And, in turn, imagination plays a guiding part in analysis. In fact, in *any* form of thinking, "imagination supplies the premises and asks the questions from which reason grinds out the conclusions as a calculating machine supplies answers." Doctor R. W. Gerard of the University of Chicago is the authority for that statement.

Just as effort is the core of creativity, so questions are the bone-and-sinew of analysis. "Why?" is almost always the main question, since cause and effect are usually the most important facts to find. So we have to delve into the *why-so* and the *what-if;* and in doing this, let's not forget our pencils and pads. Let's heed the advice of Doctor Norman Vincent Peale—list on paper every fact and every factor in the problem. "This," said Doctor Peale, "clarifies our thinking, and brings various elements into orderly system. The problem thus becomes objective instead of subjective."

In setting up a creative procedure, initial analysis is important. On this point, Doctor William Easton stressed the need of what he called "framework"—a natural term for a great engineer such as he was. In outlining plans of attack for creative projects, he first covered "clearly defined objectives," and as to the next steps he commented:

"These steps will necessarily vary with circumstances; but in all cases, one of the first is to use the imagination to construct, out of data supplied by memory and observation, a framework of ideas that will serve as a foundation for further work. Thus the writer uses imagination to outline the composition he will write. The inventor uses it to determine the details of the device he is developing. The scientist uses it to draw inferences that will form the basis of a hypothesis. Without imagination, there would be no framework, and the thinker would never get started on his project." And, to that we might well add: Without analysis, no framework can be constructed.

As John Dewey pointed out, our creative thinking will improve as we relate the new fact to the old, and all facts to each other. That's why, in addition to finding new facts, we need analysis to discover *relationships.* For instance, digging for *likenesses* can sometimes unearth a common factor which can serve as a *principle* in guiding our creative thinking.

Differences should be likewise analyzed. And to arrive at both contrary and similar relationships, the laws of association can serve as guides. Logically so, because the very process of relating facts and impressions is an almost automatic function of our associative power.

For example, let us take cognizance of the law of contiguity. (This can well include sequence and therefore cause and effect.) Let's ask these questions of any facts we have sought out: "This is *next* to what?" . . . "What does this *go with?*" . . . "What happens *before* or *after?*" . . . "This is *smaller* than what, or *larger* than what?" . . . "What would *cause* this effect?"

Similarity, the second law of association, covers likeness, sameness, composition and the common factor. Thus, under similarity we could relate our data by asking: "What is this *like?*" . . . "What attribute has this in *common* with that?" . . . "Isn't this the *same* as that?" . . . "What about the *component parts?*"

The third law of association is contrast. Accordingly we

should relate our facts through queries such as: "What is this *un*like?" . . . "What is the point of *difference?*" . . . "What about the *opposite?*" . . . "How about *vice versa?*"

And so it is that in preparation for a creative project, analysis can help us to relate our facts and thus enhance our ability to form a *pattern*—a pattern which can serve as a map in our search for solutions of the problem in hand.

TOPICS

1. Is it possible to marshal too many facts before starting to solve a creative problem? Why or why not?
2. What are the advantages of check-lists in preparation for a creative problem?
3. When salient facts are arrived at through analysis, should their interrelationships be studied? Why?
4. How does analysis tend to reveal clues to possible solutions? Discuss.
5. In analysis, should special attention be given to the causes behind the facts? Why or why not?

EXERCISES

1. Imagine you are the parent of a teen-age boy. What arguments can you think of which might convince him he should be in bed by ten o'clock every weekday evening?
2. Most neighborhood shopping centers attract their customers by publicizing the variety and quality of their facilities, plus easy parking. What other features could they offer to make themselves even more attractive to shoppers?
3. Think of at least five things which today operate basically on the principle of the simple lever.
4. Name five things that a thermos bottle is like—and in each case tell in what way.

5. Describe at least five improvements which might be made in the ordinary snow shovel.

REFERENCES

BUROCK, BENJAMIN, "The Nature and Efficacy of Methods of Attack on Reasoning Problems." *Psychological Monograph, 313,* 1950.

CONANT, JAMES B., "Scientists, Inventors, and Executives." *Chemical and Engineering News.* June 4, 1951, pp. 2262–2264.

CONNELLY, A. G., "Library vs. Laboratory Research." *Journal of Chemical Education.* November 1943, pp. 531, 533.

COULSON, T., "Neglected Aspect of Research; Preliminary Library Research." *Journal of the Franklin Institute.* March 1946, pp. 187–193.

DAVIS, A. S., JR., "Library in Research." *Special Libraries.* April 1950, pp. 129–132.

FLESCH, RUDOLF, *The Art of Clear Thinking.* New York. Harper & Brothers, 1951.

GEORGE, WILLIAM H., *The Scientist in Action.* New York. Emerson Books, 1938.

INDUSTRIAL RESEARCH INSTITUTE, *Bibliography on Creativity* (almost 2000 references). Prepared by Creativity Sub-Committee of Research Personnel Committee, 1955.

JOHNSON, D., "Role of Analysis in Scientific Investigation." *Science.* June 16, 1933, pp. 569–576.

MACKENZIE, CATHERINE, *Alexander Graham Bell.* Boston. Houghton Mifflin Company, 1928.

POLYA, G., *How to Solve It.* Princeton. Princeton University Press, 1945.

VAN ZELST, R. H. and KERR, W. A., "Some Correlates of Technical and Scientific Productivity." *Journal of Abnormal and Social Psychology.* October 1951, pp. 470–475.

Chapter IX

The basis of idea-finding— "association of ideas"

FOR THE SAKE of perspective, let's again consider the creative problem-solving process in terms of these procedures:

1. FACT-FINDING

Problem-definition: Picking out and pointing up the problem.

Preparation: Gathering and analyzing the pertinent data.

2. IDEA-FINDING

Idea-production: Thinking up tentative ideas as possible leads.

Idea-development: Selecting from resultant ideas, adding others, and re-processing by means of modification, combination, et cetera.

3. SOLUTION-FINDING

Evaluation: Verifying the tentative solutions by tests and otherwise.

Adoption: Deciding on and implementing the final solution.

Having covered both of the phases of fact-finding, we now come to idea-finding—the part of problem-solving that is most likely to be neglected.

In almost all idea-finding activity the talent that plays the leading part is that which is known as association of ideas—

sometimes referred to as "associationism" or "re-integration."

This phenomenon gears imagination to memory and causes one thought to lead to another. Its power has been recognized for over 2,000 years. Plato and Aristotle stressed it as a cardinal principle of human psychology.

Association works harder for those whose imaginative urge is more intense and whose minds are better stocked. The more vivid the memory, the more it lends itself to the associative process. For example, I recently said to the wife of a lifelong friend, "This reminds me of that Sunday supper at your house when Richard Washburn Child told us what Woodrow Wilson had privately said to him about the Versailles treaty." That caused nothing to click in her mind. Having entertained so many famous people, Mr. Child had been just another guest to her, and she had forgotten the occasion. But, since I had never before broken bread with an ambassador, I had been so thrilled by the event that 30 years later it was brought back to my mind by something similar.

Association plays a big part in the *accidental* factor of creativity. While pondering the workings of chain-thinking, I went to the dentist's. As he drilled, I let my left hand rove around, and it touched the little tube that carries gas to the Bunsen burner. "What smooth delicate rubber," I thought. "It feels like a baby's cheek."

That touch of rubber reminded me of how the Nazis, on the eve of the Normandy invasion, had been fooled by balloons in the shape of full-size ships, tanks and big guns. This association of ideas between those decoys in England and the little tube in my hand flashed across my mind in less than a second flat.

A few days before, I had gone to a shop specializing in

models for window-displays. Later I had visited an apparel shop where I had run across the store's display manager. Thus quite naturally, as the dentist drilled, there flashed across my mind: "babies . . . rubber . . . giant toys . . . clothing models." All this made me then ask myself: "Instead of making manikins out of heavy plaster, so costly to ship and so easy to break, why not make them out of rubber to be shipped flat and then inflated for use in a window?"

Even as my mind worked in that roundabout way, I analyzed my mental gyrations, and, within the same hour I started to write down the above report. My son, just home from college, dropped in. "What are you working on?" he asked. I told him. A few minutes later he said, "Say, Dad, you remember those inflated figures we saw in Macy's parade on Thanksgiving Day 10 years ago, don't you?" Of course I did. Thus, that which I had thought might be a "new" idea had come out of the sub-soil of my mind—from a seed planted 10 years before.

Production of ideas depends upon the contents of your mind and how you "mix" these ingredients. Association of ideas serves as a catalyst in this process.

Dr. Sidney J. Parnes likens the mixing function to the use of a kaleidoscope. "When you look into a kaleidoscope," he says, "you see a pattern. If you manipulate the drum of the kaleidoscope, you begin to get countless patterns. If you then add a new piece of crystal to the kaleidoscope, and hold the drum still, you get a slightly different pattern. Now if you manipulate the drum, with the new stone included, you have a multitude of new possible patterns.

"The mind operates in a similar way. If you 'look into the brain,' you find millions of bits of knowledge and experience stored there—like the information stored in the memory drum of a computer. If you manipulate, 'turn on the computer,' you get countless patterns—*ideas* produced by combination and recombination of the existing elements. If you add a new fact or experience, as in adding a new piece of crystal to the kaleidoscope, you add one new pattern. However, as soon as you begin to *manipulate*, combining and rearranging the new fact with the old, you get an even greater number of new possible patterns of ideas."

2. *The laws of association*

The ancient Greeks laid down as the three laws of association: contiguity, similarity, and contrast. By *contiguity* they meant nearness, as when a baby's shoe reminds you of the infant. By *similarity* they merely meant that a picture of a lion will remind you of your cat. By *contrast* they meant that a midget might remind you of a giant. Many other principles of association have been suggested, but the original three are still regarded as basic.

Association can work in many ways. Our figures of speech provide a parallel that may throw light on its diverse actions. Similarity, of course, is the prime law of association, and a simile is the simplest of the figures based on similarity. A graceful lily might remind you of your little daughter. As a simile, you might say, "Helen is like a flower."

The metaphor *implies* similarity. You see a play where everything happens from birth to death, and it reminds you of the world. "The world is a stage," might be your metaphor. You see a wizened old man who reminds you of death. You add a scythe and, by personification, you call death "the grim reaper." Allegories, fables and parables are likewise founded on similarity. These hit home mainly by causing us to bring other thoughts to mind, either directly or by way of a moral.

Association works through partial identity, and this, likewise, is the basis of at least two figures of speech. When a part suggests the whole, as in "the hand that rocks the cradle rules the world," it's synecdoche. When we see a cradle and think of a mother, this is association by partial identity. When one word suggests another as in "the pen is mightier than the sword," that's metonymy.

Association likewise works through sounds rather than words, and in this way parallels onomatopoeia. You hear a melody your wife played during your courtship, and you think of your wedding day. Not that there is any connection, but you hear the whir of a vacuum cleaner and think of a dentist's drill.

Other figures of speech are founded on contrast, listed by Aristotle as the third law of association. In irony we use the opposite of what we mean to convey, such as: "A loud mouth is never wrong." By the same token, association works by contrast, as when I meet a noisy lout, and am reminded of my nice quiet brother. Antithesis, another contrasting figure, couples opposite words, such as: "What's mine is yours, and what's yours is mine." In the same way, a snowstorm in the Laurentian Mountains may remind me of a drought in the Arizona desert.

Hyperbole calls for deliberate exaggeration. The biographer of Baron Munchausen sought to picture a snowfall ludicrously deep. "Snowbanks as high as a church spire," he may have thought to himself. "But where, then, could the Baron tie his horse?" And his answer was, "To the top of a steeple, of course." Thus, through exaggeration, the author's chain-thinking led him to a delightfully preposterous word picture.

"The tyranny of words" stems from association of ideas. "Communism" meant Christian living in the days of the old Oneida community, whereas now the European version of the same word spells Godlessness. On the other hand, when 645 students were asked to put down the greatest word in our language, the majority chose "mother." Nearly all the rest chose "home." No two other words can arouse so many memories.

Even smells can invoke chains of thought. The aroma of boiling coffee can take some of us back to a camp in the woods, even though the odor may come from a mammoth urn in a downtown cafeteria.

As an exaggerated illustration of why laws of association cannot be pinned down, here's a weird passage my daughter loved to quote while at college:

"What is a double petunia? A petunia is a flower like a begonia. A begonia is a meat like a sausage. A sausage-and-battery is a crime. Monkeys crime trees. Tree's a crowd. A crow crowd in the morning and made a noise. A noise is on your face between your eyes. Eyes is opposite from nays. A colt nays. You go to bed with a colt, and wake up in the morning with a case of double petunia."

3. *Steps in a creative process*

Although physical facts are easier to unseal than psychic facts, nobody yet knows *exactly* how babies are born. No wonder, then, that we are still at sea as to exactly how ideas are born. Perhaps neither of these mystic processes will ever be fully comprehended. For this reason it is unlikely that creative procedure can ever be strictly formulated.

About 50 years ago, Henri Poincaré set forth the mental processes of mathematical creation. He could do that quite precisely, since he mainly dealt with elements which were tangible and constant. Nearly every non-mathematical problem, however, is fraught with intangibles and variables. This is another reason why creative procedure cannot be rigidly methodized.

And so it is that those who have studied and practiced creativity realize that its process is necessarily a stop-and-go, catch-as-catch-can operation—one which can never be exact enough to rate as scientific.

In actual practice, we may start our guessing even while preparing. Our analyses may lead us straight to the solution. After incubation, we may again go digging for facts which, at the start, we did not know we needed.

All along the way we must change pace. We push and then coast, and then push. By driving our conscious minds in search of additional facts and tentative ideas, we develop a concentration of thought and feeling strong enough to accelerate our automatic pump of association, and make it well up still more ideas. Thus through strenuous effort we indirectly induce "idle" illumination.

The piling up of tentative ideas is an indispensable part of any problem-solving project, whether it be in creating a new drug, or in correcting the behavior of one's child. Almost always we have to think up a number of unusable ideas in order to arrive at one that may work.

Nor can analysis be slighted in any creative process. In many a case, the mere breaking down of the problem has revealed the answer, or has shown that the real problem is other than the one we had set out to attack.

As to other phases of the creative process evaluation calls

for realism. As Luigi Galvani warned, "It is easy to deceive oneself into believing that he has found just that which he had set out to discover."

When applying our own judgment, we might well analyze our solution by setting down on paper all of its pros and cons. And, of course, we should also enlist the judgment of others. The surest method of evaluation, however, is to put our ideas to test. And the task of thinking up the best way to test is a creative challenge in itself.

4. *Setting the "working mood"*

In any idea-finding effort, the first step is to *get set*—to establish a "working mood."

To do this may be akin to pulling ourselves up by our bootstraps; but there are ways to do just that, and highly creative people consciously use these ways.

Even self-confidence can be self-induced to some extent. When it comes to physical effort, there is scientific proof that, within limits, we can if we think we can. For instance, psychologists Muller and Schumann in Germany proved that our minds can even make a heavier weight seem lighter. They had people lift a light weight—then a weight three times as heavy—and then a medium weight. Although this last one was about 30 per cent *heavier* than the first, nearly all the people thus tested thought it to be much *lighter* than the first weight.

Just as baseball players swing two bats before stepping to the plate, we need to flex our imaginations when approaching a creative task. I have watched ad-writer Alan Ward day by day for 20 years. Time upon time I have felt amazement at how many creative jobs he can start and carry through. You'd hardly believe that he has to wrestle with himself whenever he undertakes a project, but that's what he claims. When I asked him how he goes at it, he explained:

"I have no sure way of uninhibiting myself for creative thinking, but I have found that one good way to get into a working mood is to close my door and try to forget everything but the job before me. Then I pull my typewriter to me, wrap my legs around it, and start to write. I write down every line that comes into my head—crazy, dull, or however it sounds. I find that if I don't, it may linger there and block others. I write as fast as I can. Then, after a long while, some cogs that haven't worked start to whir, and something striking begins to tap itself out on the yellow sheet before me—like a telegraph massage. That's the hard way and about the only way I know."

Open-mindedness is so essential to creativity that we sometimes have to ward off influences which might close our minds while in quest of ideas. It would have been easy for Pasteur to have taken for granted the cause of silkworm disease when he went to the south of France to save it from ruin. The local silkworm-growers tried to tell him just what the disease was and what caused it. Had he heeded their theories, he might never have found the answer that meant so much to France.

We sometimes have to keep our minds open by shutting out environment, as does the ingenious head of a big manufacturing company. He built his success out of an ability to cut costs by reducing the number of operations on a product. He has decided never again to tackle such a problem while in his plant. Instead he takes it home. "When I tried to do that kind of thinking in the factory," he told me, "I heard the machinery purring so beautifully, and saw the product flowing out so smoothly, it tended to close my mind. As long as there is anything in the shop that we could produce with at least one less operation, I'm going to work on it at home where my mind can see more clearly."

Doctor Suits of General Electric lays great stress on being open-minded to one's hunches. "Aim to keep an open mind," he urged. "Be on the alert for hunches, and whenever you find one hovering on the threshold of your consciousness, welcome it with open arms. Doing these things won't transform you into a genius overnight. But they're guaranteed to help you locate the treasure chest of ideas which lies hidden at the back of your own brain."

5. *No formula possible*

In some cases, the so-called steps in the creative process as listed earlier in this book have been erroneously regarded as a scientific formula—even to the extent that some teachers have had their students learn that list by heart.

Those steps are neither "scientific" nor are they a "formula." They are presented merely as an aid to the understanding of the several phases of creative problem-solving.

Many different lists of such steps have been worked out by others. And those lists are just as "authoritative" as mine. In fact, one such series of steps devised by C. F. Hix, Jr. and D. L. Purdy of General Electric is obviously preferable to mine for use in teaching creative engineering—the specific purpose for which that list was designed. Perhaps the most significant feature of my list is that it points up the two phases of the creative process which are most generally in need of greater emphasis—problem-definition and idea-finding.

Ideation has been the most subject to neglect. Heretofore, most people have tended to think up far too few tentative ideas as possible keys to solutions. The desirability of multiple alternatives has recently gained wide recognition.

As to why the ideation part of the process has been so neglected, one reason is that concurrent intrusion of judgment has usually been permitted to throttle the generation of ideas. Another reason is that it takes extra effort to think up enough tentative ideas. Preparation and analysis are comparatively easy. Such functions—as well as evaluation—come naturally. Being relatively habitual, they require less effort than does adequate ideation.

* * *

This chapter has largely dealt with the instinctive and more-or-less automatic phases of idea-finding. This leads us to the *deliberate* phases—the conscious effort to follow the principles and procedures which have been developed and clarified during the past decade—principles and procedures which have been validated by scientific research, as well as by actual application in countless cases.

TOPICS

1. Should you have confidence in your hunches? Why or why not?
2. How would you describe the phenomenon known as association of ideas?
3. Name three laws of association and give an example of each.
4. Discuss the analogy between laws of association and figures of speech.
5. What should be the first steps in ideational procedure?

EXERCISES

1. Think up an original metaphor or simile on each of the following subjects: love; life; death; football; thinking-up.
2. Write down the word "MOTHER." Under it, put down the first word it makes you think of. Repeat the process with the second

and succeeding words until you have a list of six. Identify the law of association by which you were guided to each.

3. Which advertising slogans come most readily to mind? With which product or service is each associated?
4. List all the ways atomic energy might be useful in a peaceful world.
5. You are the minister of a church where attendance of young people is dwindling. Describe at least six things you might do to correct this trend.

REFERENCES

ALBRIGHT, R. W. and ALBRIGHT J. B., "Chain associations of pre-school children to picture stimuli." *Pedagogical Seminary.* September 1951, pp. 77–93.

BENTLEY, M., "Where Does Thinking Come In?" *American Journal of Psychology.* July 1943, pp. 358–380.

CRAWFORD, ROBERT P., *How to Get Ideas.* Lincoln, Nebraska. University Associates, 1950.

EPSTEIN, R. C., "Industrial Invention: Heroic or Systematic?" *Quarterly Journal of Economics.* February 1926, pp. 232–272.

HARTER, R. S., "Study of Individual Differences in Associative Capacity." *Pedagogical Seminary.* March 1934, pp. 139–153.

KOHLER, W., "On the Nature of Association." *Proceedings of the American Philosophical Society, 84.* 1941, pp. 489–502.

MAY, MARK A., "The Mechanism of Controlled Association." *Archives of Psychology, 39,* 1917.

ROBINSON, EDWARD S., *Association Theory Today.* New York. Century Company, 1932.

SCHAEFER, R., "Study of Thought Processes in a Word Association Test." *Character and Personality.* March 1945, pp. 212–227.

THURSTONE, L. L., *The Nature of Intelligence.* New York. Harcourt, Brace and Company, 1924.

TILTON, J. W., *The Relation Between Association and the Higher*

Mental Processes. Contributions to Education *218.* New York. Teachers College, Columbia University, 1926.

WARREN, HOWARD C., *A History of the Association Psychology.* New York. Charles Scribner's Sons, 1921.

WESCHLER, IRVING R., *The Leader Looks at Creativity.* Washington, D. C. Leadership Resources, Inc., 1961.

Chapter X

Principles and procedures of DELIBERATE idea-finding

UNTIL RECENTLY it was customary to leave the idea-finding part of creative problem-solving largely to chance. Now it is realized that you can *deliberately* increase production of good ideas by following two basic principles. These are summed up as follows:

1. DEFERMENT OF JUDGMENT: You can think up almost twice as many good ideas (in the same length of time) if you defer judgment until after you have created an adequate check-list of possible leads to solution.

2. QUANTITY BREEDS QUALITY: The more ideas you think up, the more likely you are to arrive at the potentially best leads to solution.

Some scientists refer to tentative leads to solution as "hypotheses." Lewis Walkup of Battelle Memorial Research Institute advocated a deliberate and methodical effort for hypothesis-formulation, and commented as follows: "This step is so important that it might be called the tail that should wag the whole dog. Many times it is relatively easy to carry out the remainder of the process once an inspired hypothesis has been created."

One or more of our tentative thoughts and theories may turn out to be the very keys we seek. More likely our output of ideas may lead to other ideas, which in turn may reveal even better leads to solution. Often, too, each new idea may suggest a line of further investigation, which in turn may prove to be a new road to solution.

The use of inductive reasoning can be a primary factor. To discover the underlying ideas in the material with which we are working, we need to integrate the specifics into the general; and in doing this we may well pay heed to the principle which Professor C. Spearman of the University of London has described as the "educing of correlates."

We can build up hypotheses better by detecting the relationship of facts to facts and of thoughts to thoughts. When we think of this instead of that; when we think of making that larger or smaller; when we think of changing attributes or relocating constituents—in all these mental thrusts we are "educing the correlates," and thus, through induction, we can produce more and likelier hypotheses.

Our less logical surmisings may often be the keys to progress in a creative project. By this process, we can pile up far more alternative ideas. But, we can do much to make our conjecturing even more productive by adhering to the deferment-of-judgment principle throughout our idea-finding effort.

There are many who claim that in a search for ideas there can be no techniques—and rightly so, if technique means a rigid set of rules. Any attempt to lay down hard-and-fast methods would be naught but terminology masquerading as technology. But, as stated, there can be, and are, certain *principles* in the form of guides to procedure.

Variation is one of the supplementary principles that makes for better understanding of the idea-finding process. This principle defies any straight-line procedure. We have to weave our imaginations hither, thither and yon, uphill and downhill; and almost always into blind alleys.

How does the principle of plentiful variation fit in with *correlation* and *combination*—the two principles most frequently espoused by students of creativity? A partial answer is that variation includes both—and more, too. Although most new ideas are combinations of old ideas, if we limit our creative effort to the field of combination, we cannot help but restrict our idea-finding and thus curtail our resultant crop of alternatives.

In seeking alternatives, we should never overlook the obvious; for our best answer may sometimes be as plain as a planet. Beyond that, the more uninhibitedly we search for tentative ideas, the better. "No one rises so high as he who knows not whither he is going," said Oliver Cromwell; and this is largely true in the imaginative soaring which is called for when seeking to pile up hypotheses.

The "ideas" of the insane are mainly the result of the functioning of associative mechanisms, with the associations of the most superficial sort—frequently nothing more than connections based on word sounds. But maybe we could take a cue from the insane to improve our own creative thinking. If, when we are in quest of tentative ideas, we were to do our thinking out loud—holding back none of our "crazy" associations—we might hit upon something eminently sane.

Scientists seldom fail to pay attention to the preposterous. Many a wild seed has reaped a harvest. Of Pasteur, Paul de Kruif said, "This man was a passionate groper whose head was incessantly inventing right theories and wrong guesses —shooting them out like a display of village fireworks going off bewilderingly by accident."

2. *The deferment-of-judgment principle*

Much has been done in recent years to develop and clarify the deferment-of-judgment principle. Nevertheless, this aid to ideation has long been recognized. For example, in 1788 Friedrich Schiller ardently advocated this principle in a letter to a friend who had bemoaned his own ability to think up enough good ideas. Here's what Schiller wrote:

"The reason for your complaint lies, it seems to me, in the constraint which your intellect imposes upon your imagination. Here I will make an observation and illustrate it by an allegory. Apparently it is not good—and indeed it hinders the creative work of the mind—if the intellect examines too closely the ideas already pouring in, as it were, at the gates.

"Regarded in isolation, an idea may be quite insignificant and venturesome in the extreme; but it may acquire importance from an idea which follows it. Perhaps, in a certain collocation with other ideas which may seem equally absurd, it may be capable of furnishing a very serviceable link. The intellect cannot judge all these ideas unless it can retain them until it has considered them in connection with these other ideas.

"In the case of a creative mind, it seems to me, the intellect has withdrawn its watchers from the gates, and the ideas rush in pell-mell, and only then does it review and inspect the multitude. You worthy critics, or whatever you may call yourselves, are ashamed or afraid of the momentary and passing madness which is found in all real creators, the longer or shorter duration of which distinguishes the thinking artist from the dreamer. Hence your complaints of unfruitfulness, for you reject too soon and discriminate too severely."

In idea-finding we instinctively tend to judge too soon. And yet, in other matters, we defer. For example: When we look for a synonym in the Thesaurus, we don't stop at the first word or two or three. We look over the entire list, and *then* we go back and evaluate. That's the natural thing to do in this case because, in the Thesaurus, we have a ready-made check-list.

For some of our other problems we likewise have ready-made check-lists. For example, you face the problem of re-decorating your bedroom. What do you do? Your borrow a check-list in the form of a book of wallpaper samples. This takes care of the imaginative phase of your problem-solving. All you need to do is judge and decide. Likewise the yellow pages of your telephone book can readily serve as a check-list, even for a problem of vocational guidance. And what a check-list a Sears, Roebuck catalog can be in a gift-giving problem!

But there just are no ready-made check-lists for most of our problems. Therefore we have to create our own lists of alternatives.

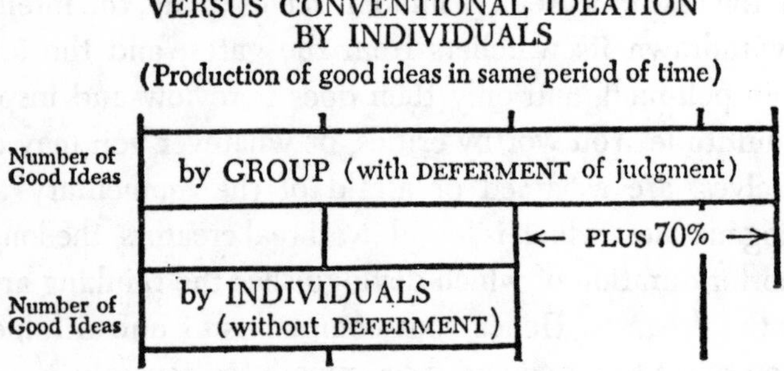

Several research projects have confirmed the potency of the deferment-of-judgment principle. For example, in one of the Meadow-Parnes studies a group brainstormed the assigned problem while an equal number of ideators individually attacked the same problem, but did so in the ordinary way—*without* deferring judgment during the ideative effort. The chart on page 128 shows that the group produced 70% more good ideas in the same period of time.

What if those individual ideators *had* adhered to the deferment-of-judgment principle, instead of allowing judgment concurrently to intrude? Would they then have produced more good ideas?

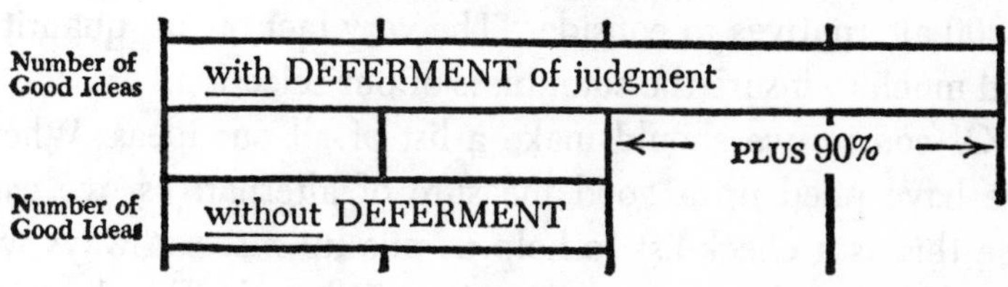

As the chart above shows, when individuals adhere to the principle of deferred judgment they generate almost twice as many good ideas as when they allow judgment concurrently to interfere.

3. *How quantity yields quality*

Quantity, quantity and more *quantity!* This should be the order of the day when building up hypotheses. "As in navigation, the more sights we take, the more likely we are to hit port." That is the analogy used by naval officer John Caples. The principle of the machine gun is another parallel.

Alfred North Whitehead summarized the wisdom of copious ideation in these words: "We need to entertain every prospect of novelty, every chance that could result in new combinations, and subject them to the most impartial scrutiny. For the probability is that nine hundred and ninety-nine of them will come to nothing, either because they are worthless in themselves or because we shall not know how to elicit their value; but we had better entertain them all, however skeptically, for the *thousandth* idea may be the one that will change the world."

The Mayor of Buffalo asked me to head a committee to name a new $25,000,000 bridge over the harbor. If we had had only 100 suggestions from which to choose, the most desirable names may not have been on that list. But we had 3,800 alternatives to consider. The very fact of this quantity did much to insure the soundness of our selection.

Of course, we should make a list of all our ideas. When we have piled up a good measure of alternatives, we can use this as a check-list to help us pile up *more*. Always we should keep asking our imagination: "What *else?*" and again, "What *else?*"

Industry believes in piling up alternatives galore in the conception of new products. For example, here is what happens when Community Plate brings out a new pattern of silverware. In the first place, the artists turn out hundreds of sketches of all possible new designs. Finally, one of these sketches is chosen as a starter. Hundreds of more sketches are then made within a narrow range, with slight changes in this and that little detail. Actual models of spoons are then made by hand. Scores of these are then changed in this and that way until the final model is chosen.

In seeking a name for Community's newest pattern, over 500 suggestions were considered and checked against names registered in the U. S. Patent Office. And in another industry, some 70 people thought up and wrote down a list of over 5,000 possible names for a new product. By scientific testing, one of these was ultimately chosen. But, alas, it was then found that this name was owned by a small company, and it had to be bought out in order to acquire proprietorship of that one word. Even on so trivial a project as finding a title for a recent book of mine, 611 alternatives were listed and tested.

We think of Irving Berlin as turning out one masterpiece after another. But the fact is that in between hits he makes scores of mediocre stabs. He is a demon for quantity, according to Alexander Woollcott, who said: "In his early days, he poured songs out so fast that his publishers thought it best to pretend that he was several persons. At least one song was thus launched under the name of Ren G. May. If you meditate on the letters of that implausible name, you will see that they spell Germany, of which nation Berlin was the capital."

And when it comes to writing, the good author thinks up endless alternatives. For a headline for a short editorial, I saw one editor write down over 100 possible captions. A century ago, a French novelist put the case for quantity in a nutshell. "I require," said Stendhal, "three or four cubic feet of new ideas per day, as a steamboat requires coal."

It is almost axiomatic that quantity breeds quality in ideation. Logic and mathematics are on the side of the truth that the more ideas we produce, the more likely we are to think up some that are good. Likewise it is true that the best ideas seldom come first. As Herbert Spencer said, "Early ideas are not usually true ideas."

Scientific research has confirmed the fact that the first ideas are unlikely to be the best ideas. This same investigation further indicated the soundness of the quantity-breeds-quality principle. The findings showed that those who thought up twice as many ideas thought up more than twice as many good ideas in the same length of time.

Still another study further confirmed this principle. In these tests, the first half of the ideas produced during a sustained effort were compared to those in the second half. As the chart below shows, the second half provided 78% *more* good ideas than did the first half.

QUANTITY BREEDS QUALITY

(Relative number of good ideas produced in *later* versus *earlier* stage of effort)

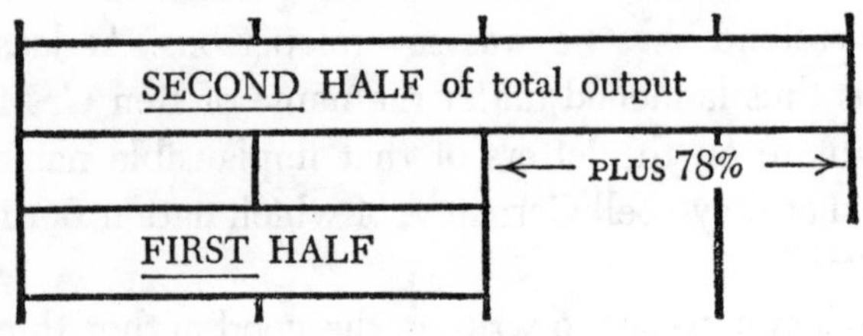

The need for quantity was demonstrated in an idea-finding session we conducted for a group of Air Force officers. The problem presented for their joint attack was unusual in the fact that the answer was already known. This was the problem:

If 700 miles of outside telephone wires were so coated with frost that long distance calls could not be made, how would you restore normal service as fast as possible?

This emergency actually arose in the State of Washington

in November, 1952. Local telephone men solved the problem by flying helicopters over the wires. The downdraft from the blades quickly blew off the frost, and long distance service was restored in record time.

We were fearful that the officers might know about this actual case. Luckily they did not. They started shooting ideas as fast as could be stenographically recorded. As airmen, they would be most likely to hit upon the helicopter solution. And they did. BUT—and here's the point: They suggested 35 *other* ideas *before* they hit upon the proven answer. The helicopter suggestion was their 36th. They would have missed the proven solution if they had stopped at 5, or 10, or 20 or even 35 ideas.

4. *Creative science calls for quantity*

The principle of plenty of variation is of the essence in scientific experimentation. The Edisonian theory called for trying everything. No progress was made in alleviating allergies until the medical scientists started to scratch the skin with this dust and that pollen and countless other things to find the cause and thus find the treatment.

When experimentation calls for making models, the same principle applies. My friend Doctor C. W. Fuller was busy on his newest invention when I asked him, "How do you go at this kind of work?" "Oh," said he, "if I have any technique at all, it simply consists of my making one new model after another until I happen to hit on the one that seems likely to work best."

Leeuwenhoek, famous for his invention of microscopes and his blood discoveries, believed not only in piling up alternatives, but in shooting wild. In one series of experiments he lost himself trying to find out what makes pepper taste as it does. One idea he hit upon along the way was that each speck of pepper has points which prick the tongue and thus make the pepper taste sharp. Even this fruitless experimentation turned out to be of help to one of his later achievements. And every modern scientist of whom I know is strong for plenty of alternatives or "tentative stabs," as one research director calls them.

Charles Kettering told about a man who came to see his new Diesel engine. "I would like to talk to your thermodynamics expert about it," said the visitor. "I am sorry," Kettering replied, "we don't have anyone here who even understands the word 'thermodynamics,' much less is an expert on it. But if you want to know how we developed this engine, I'll be glad to show you."

He led the man to the dynamometer room and showed him a single-cylinder setup. Kettering's explanation included this remark: "We tried one thing after another for about six years until the engine itself finally told us exactly what it wanted."

Six years of trying one thing after another, endless piling up of alternatives—that, said Kettering, "is the only way we know."

Proverbially, nearly every history-making triumph of creative scientists is credited to a single inspiration; whereas, in truth, that "inspiration" usually came from trying this and that—by building up a huge pile of hypotheses.

One reason so much is made of brilliant flashes is that they can be dramatized, while the hard truth behind such flashes is usually dull. Charles Goodyear found a new way to make rubber useful, and did so at his kitchen stove. That's about all the public knows in regard to his discovery. Only a few realize how many years of searching for ideas preceded his moment of triumph.

"Watt invented the steam engine—he thought it up on a fine Sunday afternoon while taking a walk." That is what most of us believe. How true is it? In the first place, he did not invent the engine—he invented a condenser which made steam power more widely usable. And what's the truth about Watt's Sunday flash? As a matter of history, he had not only been thinking of the problem, but working on it—piling up hypotheses—for a long time before he took his historic walk.

The neatest summary of the cold truth about inspiration was written by Henri Poincaré: "This unconscious work is not possible, or in any case not fruitful, unless it is first preceded and then followed by a period of conscious work."

When blocked in the course of a creative project, we need to stop and review. We should analyze the problem anew, should think up still other alternatives, and then proceed all over again. We may find that we were on the right road, but had taken a wrong detour. As Joseph Jastrow said, imagination can easily "run off the track and wreck the train of thought."

When, at the end of a creative project, we find we have failed, it usually pays to reprocess from start to finish. We should review the relevant data, and even recheck the aim; but, above all else, we should pile up more alternatives. Here again we should seek *quantity*, with wildness wilfully allowed. We should get in step with Edison, who said: "I'll try *anything*—I'll even try Limburger cheese!"

* * *

The last two chapters have discussed the type of thinking which Dr. J. R. Killian, Jr. of M.I.T. has called "free-wheeling." But, as pointed out, we can produce more good ideas if we consciously and deliberately *steer* our free-wheeling, guided by the principles and procedures that have just been outlined.

Please bear in mind that in stressing idea-finding, we mean in no way to belittle the value of judgment. In fact, imagination-without-judgment is more deplorable than judgment-without-imagination. But, in problem-solving, we need to use *both* talents—preferably one at a time.

We fully recognize that idea-finding is only a part of the problem-solving process. If imagination *does* seem to be over-emphasized, it is for two reasons: 1. Idea-finding is the function most likely to be neglected. 2. Imagination must also be used *throughout* the solution-finding phases of the process, even in decision-making.

Some educators and management men have glorified fact-finding as the be-all and the end-all of this final phase of problem-solving. But, idea-finding can do much to insure correct decisions. On this subject, Lt. Gen. Thomas L. Harrold, Commandant of the National War College, has stated as follows: "In the Army we train our leaders to draw up what we call an 'Estimate of the Situation.' First, they must know their objective. Unless you know what you want, you can't possibly decide how to get it. Second, we teach them to consider alternative means of attaining that objective. It's not often that a goal, military or any other, can be realized in only one way."

The pertinent words in General Harrold's statement are these: "We teach them to consider *alternative* means of attaining that objective." The only question is how many alternatives should be considered—two? ten? twenty? *more?*

In view of the findings of scientific research, it would seem wiser to seek too many ideas rather than too few.

TOPICS

1. What part does power of association play in building up hypotheses? Discuss.
2. Should we let ourselves "shoot wild" in reaching for tentative ideas? Why or why not?
3. Why does quantity tend to insure quality in thinking up hypotheses? Discuss.
4. To what extent does scientific research depend on "free-wheeling" thinking? Discuss.
5. What is the Edisonian theory? Discuss.

EXERCISES

1. If your neighbor's dog used your favorite tulip bed as a shortcut, how would you go about stopping this?
2. Men's canes have gone out of style. What would you do to try to re-popularize them?
3. What new stunts could you think up to try out if you were your school's cheer leader?
4. Apply "free-wheeling" thinking to the problem of making a dining room table more useful. Write down the first 10 ideas that occur to you, no matter how wild.
5. What can you think up by way of possible new features for new homes of the future?

REFERENCES

Ashley, C. M., "Ideas, the Essence of Development." *Product Engineering*. November 1940, pp. 511–512.

Chamberlain, T. C., "The Method of Multiple Working Hypotheses." *Scientific Monthly*. November 1944, pp. 357–362.

DURKIN, HELEN E., "Trial-and-error, Gradual Analysis, and Sudden Reorganization." *Archives of Psychology, 210,* 1937.

HAHN, ARNOLD, *Use Your Mind.* New York. Henry Holt and Company, 1931.

JASTROW, JOSEPH, *Managing Your Mind.* New York. Greenberg, Inc., 1935.

KNOWLSON, T. S., *Originality.* Philadelphia. J. B. Lippincott, 1918.

MEARNS, HUGHES, *Creative Power.* New York. Doubleday and Company, 1930.

MIDGETTE, E. L., MACDUFF, J. M., and MODROUSKY, J., "On Teaching Creativeness in Design." *Journal of Engineering Education.* 1949–1950, pp. 57, 122–126.

MORGAN, J. J. B., "Value of Wrong Responses in Inductive Reasoning." *Journal of Experimental Psychology.* April 1945, pp. 141–146.

PARNES, SIDNEY J. and MEADOW, ARNOLD, "Effects of Brainstorming Instructions on Creative Problem-Solving by Trained and Untrained Subjects." *Journal of Educational Psychology.* August 1959, pp. 171–176.

POINCARÉ, H., "Mathematical Creation." *The Foundations of Science.* New York. The Science Press, 1929, pp. 383–394.

SARGENT, S. S., "Thinking Processes at Various Levels of Difficulty." *Archives of Psychology, 249,* 1940.

TAYLOR, C. W., "A Factorial Study of Fluency in Writing." *Psychometrika.* December 1947, pp. 239–262.

TAYLOR, C. W., ed., *Research Conference on the Identification of Creative Scientific Talent.* Salt Lake City. University of Utah Press, 1959.

WALKUP, LEWIS E., "Individual Creativity in Research." Columbus, Ohio. *Battelle Technical Review.* August, 1958.

Chapter XI

Individual ideation and team collaboration

Most of the best ideas are now being produced by laboratory staffs through organized research. That kind of joint effort was started only a few centuries ago. The early investigators were lone workers. They were mostly amateurs who collaborated, or rather co-operated, in "scientific societies." In 1651 several Italians banded together and later founded the Academia del Cimento, which outshone the British Royal Society of that day in both brilliance and continuity of effort.

That kind of loose organization was about all there was until about 50 years ago, when organized research, as we now know it, came into being; and in this half century such research has grown to be the fountainhead of most new ideas.

Basically, the staffs of modern research laboratories are made up of teams. For example, in the new B. F. Goodrich Research Center, where hundreds of workers are hard on the hunt for ideas every hour, every day, the personnel is divided into specialized groups—one for each major phase of chemistry, one for each major phase of physics, and so on. Each of these teams is made up of about a dozen scientists, directed by a research supervisor.

2. *Solo thinking still essential*

Despite the advances in organized research, the creative power of the *individual* still counts most. This truth is recognized by heads of all the great research departments. The usual procedure is to assure even the youngest researcher that his own brain-child will be credited to *him.* On other matters he reports to his group head; but he is authorized to go straight to an executive in charge of patents and register ideas directly with him as custodian.

"In this way," said Doctor Howard Fritz, "we always know who started what and on what date; but even more important, this system encourages each individual to do his best on his own—to keep his creative power turned on not only during working hours but all the time."

To the far-flung research staffs of Du Pont, the late Doctor Ernest Benger spelled out this philosophy: "No idea has ever been generated except in a single human mind. . . . No matter how you toss this thought around or how you add to it by consideration of the effect of getting people into a co-ordinated organization, the fact still remains that every idea is the product of a single brain."

In proof of that point, history sparkles with names of solitary thinker-uppers. Paul de Kruif rightly called Robert Koch a "lone-wolf searcher who knew nothing whatever about the art of doing experiments." A lowly medical practitioner with a high creative urge, he even lacked experimental apparatus. All alone, against his wife's snarling protests, he fought his way from one idea to another until he isolated bacteria by types. "I beg leave," wrote de Kruif, "to remove my hat and make bows of respect to Koch—the man who really proved that microbes are our most deadly enemies."

A. Atwater Kent was a one-man research laboratory. Against the competition of the biggest companies, he won first place in the radio industry. Even after he had a well-staffed laboratory, he still designed each new model almost singlehanded.

Just as there are those who, temperamentally, can do their best creative work by themselves, others have to work on their own through the very nature of their calling. Ministers are among them. Many lawyers are likewise on their own, especially in the country. In a rural district near my summer home, a local attorney showed how solitary creativity can win cases. A woman was being tried for murder. Her lawyer timed his plea to the jury so that he ended at exactly noon—just as the chimes from the church across the street were ringing *Rock of Ages* into the jury's ears. The lawyer gave credit to that hymn for his client's acquittal.

Individual idea-finding effort can be more productive if done deliberately and methodically. For one thing, the problem should be clearly defined. The simplest way to do this is to state the general problem on paper, make a written list of its component phases, and then select the sub-problem or sub-problems most suitable for creative attack.

The idea-finding process should be systematized by making a written list of alternatives by way of possible leads to solution. In doing this, of course, the two basic principles of ideative efficacy should be followed:

1. Defer judgment.
2. Reach for quantity.

These principles are also the essence of the procedure called group brainstorming which will be more fully covered in the next chapter.

3. *Collaboration serves as supplement*

At this point it might be well to clear up a misconception about group brainstorming. Some have erroneously thought that this collaborative effort is meant to *replace* individual effort. The fact is that group brainstorming is recommended solely as a *supplement* to individual ideation.

This point was covered by Professor John Arnold of Stanford University in an address he made at Stanford's Creative Engineering Seminar:

"One of the most useful *tools* of organized creative activity, especially for organized *group* activity, is that of 'brainstorming'. . . . A great many companies are now using brainstorming in one form or another to help them pile up alternatives that can, at a later date, be evaluated and eventually implemented and then verified.

"I believe brainstorming is so successful because it is a form of group therapy. Here you have an ideal environment for being yourself. You set up an artificial environment that contains most of the essentials required for what the psychologists call 'psychological safety' and 'psychological freedom.' External standards of evaluation are completely absent. You have no fear of being called a fool. Even internal evaluation is effectively ruled out because you are specifically asked to think up as wild ideas as you possibly can, and as many as you possibly can. To meet the speed and quantity demands, you don't have time to evaluate your own ideas. . . .

"I am convinced that it is possible, for I can do it and I know many others who can also do it, that an individual can form a brainstorming group with himself as the only member. In this case, the elimination of the internal as well as external standards of judgment and evaluation and the proper use of check-lists, area thinking or attribute listing, or what have you, can result in a great many ideas and alternatives that can, at a later time, be evaluated as possible solutions for some problem that is facing you. Some people don't need (though they may be helped by) a group to spark them into thinking up a long list of different approaches to solving a problem. Individual brainstorming should be encouraged and developed, not as a substitute for, but as a supplement to group brainstorming activity. Morphological analysis might be considered as a kind of individual 'brainstorming.'

"In the same way, the brainstorming rules can be applied and should be extended to a much larger group than the original six or ten. There is no reason why a modified form of these rules can't be applied to a whole research section or even to a whole company. If all members of an organization were encouraged to think as daringly as possible, without fear of immediate evaluation or possible ridicule, and without fear of making a mistake, I can't see but how the company would benefit. The ideas suggested would eventually be individually evaluated, the wholly 'crack-pot' schemes would be eliminated before damage was done, but the resultant activity would be much more daring and imaginative than that which occurs in many organizations today. . . .

"While brainstorming was originally proposed for group activity, it should be extended to the extremes of the organization. An individual can brainstorm and so can a company. The rules that were essential to the well being of the small group can be modified to fit the individual or the total organization."

Dr. Jere Clark has also helped clear up some of the misconceptions concerning the applicability of the deferment-of-judgment principle. Speaking of this principle he said:

"It does not reduce the importance of judicial thinking, but rather tends to increase the need of judgment because of the greater number and variety of ideas from which to choose.

"Its value is not limited to the idea-creation stage of the

problem-solving process. It is often just as helpful in problem-definition and in the development and implementation of the chosen ideas.

"Its applicability is not limited to collaborative effort, although it can be even more valuable in group sessions because it tends to minimize fear of ridicule and to prevent loss of time in discussing each idea."

Let's bear in mind that scientific research has shown that when individual ideators adhere to the deferment-of-judgment principle they generate almost twice as many good ideas as when they allow judgment concurrently to interfere.

4. *Two-headed teamwork*

One way to get started creatively is to make a date—to go somewhere to concentrate, or to team up with someone to collaborate. The latter was what Irving Berlin did. While still waiting on tables in Chinatown, he thought up the first line for a new song. He went to his musical neighbor Nick and asked him to help. Together they wrote the words and music of *My Sweet Marie from Sunny Italy*, a hit which started Irving Berlin on his brilliant career of creativity.

Most of us can work better creatively when teamed up with the right partner because collaboration tends to induce effort, and also to spur our automatic power of association. On this latter point, Thomas Carlyle wrote: "The lightning spark of thought, generated in the solitary mind, awakens its likeness in another mind."

Men's doubles are common in comedy-writing. Two congenial fellows working in a spirit of fun can be so mutually contagious that they spark each other. Criticism is likely to be less of a blight, because it is usually so spontaneous—a fair gag will get only a faint smile, but a good gag will get a hearty laugh out of one's teammate.

Writers of radio and television nearly always team up to create scripts. Bob Hope has almost a dozen people turning in ideas each week. From this material, his head writer, like a managing editor, selects a joke here and a situation there. He then sits down with the star and the producers, and together they work up the show.

For many years, Robert Tallman wrote radio all by himself; but he now admits that with a congenial partner, he can create even better. "We tried several kinds of collaboration," said Tallman, "and found one that really works." The chosen method is jointly to prepare an outline—a "beginning-and-end treatment" which enables both to know where they are heading. After mutual discussion of each scene, they then split up the job of writing first drafts of the actual lines.

John Winthrop Hammond wrote about a famous trio in General Electric: "These three constituted a team whose fame penetrated into every corner of the electrical realm. Together they originated a complete line of alternating-current equipment, announced and advertised as the 'SKC' system—Stanley, Kelly, Chesney. They were an aggressive triumvirate, and their work greatly accelerated the development of the alternating current."

A high tribute to man-and-woman relationship is the brilliant list of creative teams made up of married couples. There are many such partnerships in the writing field—teams like the Lockridges, authors of "Mr. and Mrs. North," and the Goetz team of playwrights. Other examples include the distinguished historians, Doctor Charles A. and Mrs. Mary Ritter Beard. She worked hand in hand with him on at least a dozen histories bearing his name, and was co-author of at least five others.

In scientific research, there have been more than one

mixed team like Madame Curie and her husband. The David Bruces stood out as creative pioneers. David Bruce could not have thought through to the cause and cure of sleeping sickness without his wife's help. But what a contrast she was to Mrs. Robert Koch! The latter was always badgering her husband, trying to get him to give up his dissection of animals because it made him so smelly; whereas Mrs. Bruce not only cheered her husband on, but did much of the dirty work.

About 12 years after Doctor Fleming had got track of penicillin mold, the Nazis were sending to their death thousands of British people whom penicillin could have saved. But there was none of it to be had, except a handful in the London laboratory of Doctor Howard Florey. To get it into production fast and on a large scale, Doctor Florey had to prove its efficiency on enough humans. His wife, a doctor, did this almost singlehanded and almost overnight. She used it successfully in 187 cases; and that started the flow of penicillin in time for its wartime miracle. Howard and Ethel Florey surely deserve a place in the man-and-wife hall of fame.

5. *Technique for twosomes*

To insure maximum creativity in teamwork, each collaborator should take time out for solitary meditation. By working together, and then alone, and then together, a pair is more likely to achieve the best in creative thinking.

To illustrate that point, let's consider the *modus operandi* of a family physician and a specialist when a patient's case calls for consultation. The two medical men would go over the symptoms together, jointly study the X rays, and finally agree on the *diagnosis*. This phase of their collaboration mainly requires *judgment.* But the question of *treatment,* often calls for *imagination;* and, whereas two minds are always better than one judicially, they may warp each other creatively at times.

It would be better in such a case for the family physician to say to his patient: "Doctor Specialist and I agree on the diagnosis. As to treatment, we are going to ponder that overnight. Each of us will separately concentrate on the question as to what to do to effect the fastest cure. We will meet in his office tomorrow morning and will each bring a list of ideas that seem promising. We will compare these and then try to arrive at a still better plan. A combination of the best of our ideas is likely to be the answer. I will be back here at 10 tomorrow to put our treatment into action."

In that hypothetical case, the team utilizes the deferment-of-judgment principle by having each member work as an individual after mutually defining the problem and establishing the facts.

Incidentally, this type of procedure helps insure against the danger that one member of the team may slow down the creativity of the other. The more faith one has in his teammate, the more his instinct is likely to say to him: "What's the use of my trying too hard? He'll think up the answer." But, this danger is averted when each collaborator brings in a list of his own ideas.

Intensity of effort is the without-which-nothing in thinking up solutions to difficult problems—we must have a feeling of "mustness" to be at our creative best. If we were on a ship and someone asked, "What would you do if we crashed into an iceberg?" most of us would reply: "I have no idea. What would you do?" But if you were alone in your cabin, heard a deafening crash, looked out of the porthole and saw an iceberg, felt the floor sinking beneath you—your intensity of interest would drive you so hard and so fast that it would *force* you to think up something to do. On the other hand, if there were two of us in that cabin, we might just look at each other blankly and wait for the other to suggest something.

Such hazards of teamwork can be avoided by simple procedures. For one thing, during certain periods in a creative quest, each member of a team should go off by himself and do some idea-finding on his own. When the partners come together after such solo thinking, they will find that they have piled up more worthwhile alternatives than if they had kept on collaborating all the time.

Above all, teammates should refrain from destructive argument. This was brought out by David Victor. He and Herbert Little are authors who keep regular office hours and make a business of their joint writing. After they discuss and settle on a plot, they outline it in writing. Then they talk as much as they write; but they never argue. When one of them disapproves of a certain line or idea, they drop the matter immediately and set about thinking up something better. "If we let ourselves argue, we'd both get stubborn and could not collaborate," David Victor explained. Thus they deliberately avoid the mutual discouragement which so often kills ideas in the embryo.

* * *

This chapter has sought to suggest some of the ways by which we can produce more good ideas both in solo effort and in team collaboration.

The main thing to remember is that we can hinder or help our flow of ideas, depending upon what we consciously do.

Of the many ways in which we can guide our thinking, the most important is to guard against being both critical and creative at one and the same time.

Inevitably, if we let our judgment intrude prematurely, we tend to abort ideas which could prove to be the most valuable of all. Therefore, we should consciously defer evaluation until a later period. Thus, we can think up more and better ideas. Thus, we can later screen and weigh our ideas more judicially.

The next two chapters will deal with collaboration by a group—especially when following the procedure which has become known as brainstorming.

TOPICS

1. What are the advantages of teaming up on a creative project? Discuss.
2. What are the dangers to be avoided in creative teamwork? Discuss.
3. What are the advantages of "changing roles"? Discuss.
4. Why is solo thinking still vital, even in joint creative effort? Discuss.
5. Name pairs of partners whose collaboration brought success in the following fields: (a) Stage and screen. (b) Science and medicine. (c) Literature. (d) Business.

EXERCISES

1. Think up titles for six new songs.
2. Map out an outline of editorial features for a new monthly magazine to be called "Idea Doublers."
3. A Sports Booster Club would help stimulate adult interest in your local high school. What steps would you take to get one started?
4. What interesting new events might be added to a track meet?

5. Pick a partner and together think up additional problems like the ones listed in Exercises 1–4.

REFERENCES

ARNOLD, JOHN, ed., *Creative Engineering Seminar.* (Speeches at summer session program) Stanford University, 1959.

BOUTERLINE, ROSENBERG, *et al., Individual Creativity and the Corporation.* Boston. Institute of Contemporary Art, 1959.

DEKRUIF, PAUL H., *Microbe Hunters.* New York. Harcourt, Brace and Company, 1926.

HAMMOND, JOHN W., *Men and Volts—the Story of General Electric.* Philadelphia. J. B. Lippincott Company, 1941.

HUSBAND, R. W., "Cooperative versus Solitary Problem Solution." *Journal of Social Psychology, 11,* 1940, pp. 405–409.

KITTREDGE, J. W., "Is It Good-Bye to the Attic Genius?" *Mechanical Engineering.* April 1947, pp. 302–305.

OSBORN, ALEX F., *How to Think Up.* New York. McGraw-Hill Book Company, Inc., 1942.

PALUEV, K. K., "How Collective Genius Contributes to Industrial Progress." *Advancement Management.* June 1948, pp. 76–83.

RATCLIFF, J. D., *Yellow Magic, the Story of Penicillin.* New York. Random House, 1945.

SHAW, M. E., "Comparison of Individuals and Small Groups in the Rational Solution of Complex Problems." *American Journal of Psychology.* 1932, pp. 44, 491–504.

STEIN, MORRIS I. and HEINZE, SHIRLEY J., *Creativity and the Individual.* Illinois. The Free Press of Glencoe, 1960.

WOOLLCOTT, ALEXANDER, *The Story of Irving Berlin.* New York. G. P. Putnam's Sons, 1925.

Chapter XII

Creative collaboration by groups

It was in 1938 when I first employed organized ideation in the company I then headed. The early participants dubbed our efforts "Brainstorm Sessions"; and quite aptly so because, in this case, "brainstorm" means using the *brain* to *storm* a problem.

Brainstorming has become so much a part of the American scene that the verb brainstorm, in the sense of creative effort, is now included in Webster's International Dictionary and defined as follows: "To practice a conference technique by which a group attempts to find a solution for a specific problem by amassing all the ideas spontaneously contributed by its members."

This kind of conference is not entirely new. A similar procedure is known to have been used in India for more than 400 years as part of the technique of Hindu teachers while working with religious groups. The Indian name for this method is *Prai-Barshana. Prai* means "outside yourself" and *Barshana* means "question." In such a session there is no discussion or criticism. Evaluation of ideas takes place at later meetings of the same group.

The modern brainstorm session is nothing more than a creative conference for the sole purpose of producing a checklist of ideas—ideas which can serve as leads to problem-solution—ideas which can *subsequently* be evaluated and further processed.

No conference can be called a brainstorming session unless the deferment-of-judgment principle is strictly followed.

In the early 50's brainstorming became too popular too fast, with the result that it was frequently misused. Too many people jumped at it as a panacea, then turned against it when no miracles resulted. Likewise, too many have erroneously regarded group brainstorming as a complete problem-solving process, whereas it is only one of several phases of idea-finding; and idea-finding is only one of the several phases of creative problem-solving.

The principal value of group brainstorming is the fact that a brainstorming session, properly conducted, can produce far more good ideas than a conventional conference—and in less time. A striking example of time-saving was reported by Dr. Fred C. Finsterbach. He conducted a session at American Cyanamid which produced 92 ideas in 15 minutes—more than six ideas per minute—an average of over eight ideas per person.

The usual kinds of conferences have always been noncreative. Even at the council-fires of the Mohawks and Senecas, there were but few burning embers in the form of ideas and much cold water in the form of judgment. Our forefathers used their town hall meetings mainly as occasions for debate, rather than for thinking up ideas while in session.

According to James L. Wright, ex-president of the National Press Club, our federal cabinets have been good or bad according to the degree to which they have encouraged ideas. "A President's cabinet is at its best when all members are encouraged to express ideas on any national problem and when no member is confined to the particular portfolio on which he is working, such as agriculture or interior," was Mr. Wright's conclusion.

But cabinets have too much to decide and must therefore concentrate on judicial thinking almost to the exclusion of sparking new ideas; whereas a brainstorm group devotes itself *solely* to *creative* thinking.

One such permanent panel in our government was the "Advanced Study Group" created by General Eisenhower in May, 1947. The sole function assigned to those young officers was to imagine warfare in the future and to think up suggestions accordingly. General Eisenhower stipulated that this group was to be "divorced of all practical and mundane things of today." According to the editor of the *Army, Navy Journal*, "This is the only service unit in history that is solely an idea-thinking organization."

That was true at the time. But, ever since 1954, group brainstorming has been used as an idea-finding procedure in the Armed Services and in several federal departments. The Veterans Administration, for example, has made such extensive use of this method that it has published a 12-page report of case histories. Free copies of this are available from the Creative Education Foundation, 1614 Rand Building, Buffalo 3, N. Y.

2. *Group fluency explained*

The quantitative results of group brainstorming are beyond question. One group produced 45 suggestions for a home-appliance promotion, 56 ideas for a money-raising campaign, 124 ideas on how to sell more blankets. In another case, 15 groups brainstormed one and the same problem and produced over 800 ideas.

There are several reasons why group brainstorming can be highly productive of ideas. For one thing, the power of association is a two-way current. When a panel member spouts an idea, he almost automatically stirs his own imagination toward another idea. At the same time, *his* ideas stimulate the associative power of all the *others*. This contagion was described by Fred Sharp as follows: "When you really get going in a brainstorm session, a spark from one mind will light up a lot of bang-up ideas in the others just like a string of firecrackers." Another man called this same phenomenon "chain reaction."

In an effort to determine the extent to which ideas are sparked by ideas, one organization analyzed the cross-fertilization which occurred in 38 sessions. It was found that 1,400 of the 4,356 ideas produced could be identified as "hitch-hikes"—suggestions which had been triggered by suggestions voiced by other panelists.

Social facilitation is a principle which has been proved by scientific experiments. Tests have demonstrated that "free associations" on the part of adults are from 65 to 93 per cent more numerous in group activity than when working alone. This same fact was confirmed by the Human Engineering Laboratory of Stevens Institute. According to its director, Johnson O'Connor, men and women show greater creative imagination in groups than individually.

Another explanation of the productivity of group brainstorming is the stimulative effect of rivalry. As early as 1897, psychological experiments indicated the power of pace-making. Later psychologists have proved that competition will increase accomplishment in mental work by adults or children by 50 per cent or more. Such motivation counts more in ideation than in almost any other mental function, because true creativity more largely depends on application of effort.

The effectiveness of group brainstorming is further explained by the fact that this procedure includes an incentive known to psychologists as "reinforcement." This stimulating factor is particularly stressed by Dr. B. F. Skinner of Harvard, nationally recognized authority on teaching-machines. Nearly all educators now agree that the learning process is far more effective when "correct" answers are "reinforced" by "rewards" in the form of immediate corroboration.

Group brainstorming provides "reinforcement" by "rewarding" all suggestions with receptiveness. Conversely, the conventional type of conference often penalizes suggestions with deprecation. This type of deterrent is called "negative reinforcement"—a factor which cannot help but militate against desired behavior. Premature criticism is a "negative reinforcer." Deferment-of-judgment is a "positive reinforcer." And, deferment-of-judgment is the essence of group brainstorming.

Nathaniel Hawthorne spelled out the essential virtue of group brainstorming in these words: "The best things come, as a general thing, from the talents that are members of a group; every man works better when he has companions working in the same line. Great things, of course, have been done by solitary workers; but they have usually been done with double the pains they would have cost if they had been produced in more genial circumstances."

3. *Guides for panel sessions*

Idea-producing conferences are relatively fruitless unless certain rules are understood by all present, and are faithfully followed. Here are four basics:

(1) *Criticism is ruled out.* Adverse judgment of ideas must be withheld until later.

(2) *"Free-wheeling" is welcomed.* The wilder the idea, the better; it is easier to tame down than to think up.

(3) *Quantity is wanted.* The greater the number of ideas, the more the likelihood of useful ideas.

(4) *Combination and improvement are sought.* In addition to contributing ideas of their own, participants should suggest how ideas of others can be turned into *better* ideas; or how two or more ideas can be joined into still another idea.

Those are the guides. The leader of the brainstorm panel should explain them in his own words, because a brainstorm session should always be kept informal. Here's how one leader interpreted the first rule to one of his groups:

"If you try to get hot and cold water out of the same faucet at the same time, you will get only tepid water. And if you try to criticize *and* create at the same time, you can't turn on either *cold* enough criticism or *hot* enough ideas. So let's stick solely to *ideas*—let's cut out *all* criticism *during* this session."

A few incurable critics will still disregard that rule and will belittle what others suggest. At first, such a transgressor should be gently warned; but if he persists, he should be firmly stopped. In one of our sessions, when one man kept on criticizing, the leader blasted him with: "*Think* up or *shut* up!"

Surreptitiously breaking up into little groups is another hazard; and this, too, may call for a bit of discipline. The leader must make sure that the session is always a single meeting, with all minds working together.

The only strictly formal feature should be a written record

of all ideas suggested. This list should be reportorial rather than stenographic. At times, the ideas will tumble out so fast that even a shorthand expert could hardly record them verbatim.

The *spirit* of a brainstorm session is important. Self-encouragement is needed almost as much as mutual encouragement. A perfectionism complex will throttle effort and abort ideas. One of the ablest members kept mum throughout one of our sessions. I button-holed him afterward and begged him to spout whatever ideas might come to his mind at our next meeting.

"All right, I'll try," he said, "but here's what happened. *After* our last meeting I jotted down about 15 ideas, with the thought that I would bring them to our next session; but when I looked them over I decided that they were worthless, so I just tore up the list."

It took quite a while to make him realize that one of his "worthless" ideas could be better than most of ours, or could be improved on or combined into one which might become the best of all our ideas.

"When I can make my brainstorming team feel they are *playing*, we get somewhere," said one of our most successful leaders. "Each session should be a game with plenty of rivalry, but with complete friendliness all around." Paradoxically, we can think up more ideas when trying hard but in a relaxed frame of mind. A good device is to create the atmosphere of a picnic. Some of our best sessions have been sandwich-luncheons in the office. After coffee and cake we convene, the group rules are laid down, the problem is assigned. Suggestions begin to flow. Every idea, crackpot or crackerjack, is written down.

The entire crop will serve as a check-list of possible leads to solution. In subsequent selection and evaluation, most of the ideas will probably be discarded, some will stand up as worthwhile leads, and others will merit re-processing by means of modification, combination, and similar methods which will be set forth in later chapters. This re-processing is most important because it may often transform mediocre ideas into sterling ideas.

4. *Subjects and personnel*

As to which *subjects* lend themselves best to group brainstorming, the first rule is that the problem should be *specific* rather than general—it should be narrowed down so that the panel members can shoot their ideas at a single target.

A manufacturer wanted ideas on a name, a package and an introductory plan for a new product. We made the mistake of trying to brainstorm this multiple problem. Soon after our session started, one of us suggested a few names. We were just beginning to click with still more, when someone suggested a packaging idea. Before we built up momentum along that line, someone switched us to marketing ideas. The session was so ineffective that we decided never again to tackle a complex subject in a single session but to break it down and devote a separate session to each specific problem.

Group brainstorming is indicated only for problems which primarily depend on idea-finding—*not* for problems which primarily depend on judgment. Nor is it indicated for any problem for which there are only two or three alternative solutions.

For example, if the problem is whether or not to marry, the best methodology is first to list the pros and cons. That takes analytical judgment. Then, the pros and cons should be weighed. This takes comparative judgment.

Even in this judicial process, imagination will probably play a part. And rightly so because some important pros and cons may not come to mind unless visualized by imagination. In some cases, imagination may unduly intrude on judgment. A college-mate of mine told me he would never marry because he couldn't get out of his mind's eye the picture of unruly brats with raspberry jam all over their faces.

Leo Nejelski, speaking of the launching of any kind of conference, said this: "Meetings drift aimlessly when a clear statement of the problem is lacking. By stating the goal of the meeting, a framework is established within which all thought can be directed."

Such initial statements can be much briefer for creative conferences than for judicial conferences. Facts are the brick and mortar out of which judgments are built; but in idea-finding, facts serve mainly as springboards. Too many facts can stifle the spontaneity needed in group brainstorming. Factual justification can come later when the ideas are evaluated.

As to the size of a brainstorming group, the ideal number is about a dozen. As to caliber of minds, there is no rule—panels have done well when made up of neophytes alone, and of neophytes and veterans. And panels can be either all male, or all female, or mixed. It usually helps if a group includes a few self-starters; and they should begin to spark the moment the problem is stated. But they should carefully refrain from dominating the session once it is under way.

Probably the most difficult panel members are executives who have been over-trained in the usual kind of non-creative conference. I found this out when I organized 10 of our community's business leaders for the purpose of brainstorming civic problems. Even after our first 10 sessions, some of them still could not get themselves to shoot wild at our luncheons. One was a vice-president in a huge corporation. After he got into the swing, he told me:

"It was hard to get through my head what you were trying to do with us. My 15 years of conference after conference in my company have conditioned me against shooting wild. Almost all of us officers rate each other on the basis of *judgment*—we are far more apt to look up to the other fellow if he makes no mistakes than if he suggests lots of ideas. So I've always kept myself from spouting any suggestions which could be sneered at. I wish our people would feel free to shoot ideas the way we have been doing in these brainstorm sessions."

5. *Versatility of application*

Group brainstorming has been effectively used in many fields of endeavor, including social service, traffic problems, civic affairs, federal affairs, military affairs, hospitals, churches, education, broadcasting, retailing, marketing, promotion, product design, packaging, personnel problems, safety, cost-cutting, transportation, accounting, engineering and journalism. The Creative Education Foundation has published two reports covering 100 case histories in these fields. Free copies are available on request to the Foundation.

As to the applicability of group brainstorming to technology, here is a statement from *The Next Hundred Years*, the coauthors of which are Harrison Brown, James Bonner and John Weir of the California Institute of Technology:

"There is still a further avenue for increasing the output of our technical manpower, an avenue that may be the most important one of all. This has to do with creative imagination. There is, for example, the technique known as 'brainstorming.' In this procedure a group meets under conditions designed to make it easy for its members to express their ideas without fear of ridicule or criticism. It is quite effective in increasing the output of new ideas from people brought together for the purpose."

The same technique can be applied to personal and family problems. One example comes from a movie producer who lived with his parents and five unmarried brothers. Theirs was quite an explosive family, susceptible to squabbles. It took courage on his part, but he organized a creative group consisting of his parents, his brothers and himself. They held regular meetings and tackled one family problem at a time. "Some of our ideas worked and improved the harmony of our home," he reported. "Much to our surprise, we all had a lot of fun in these sessions."

Even a club group or a church group might well devote an occasional evening to that kind of ideation. David Beetle was president of an outing club. The officers had always thought up the plans for excursions. But he decided to divide the whole membership into 10 groups to think up ideas. The result? "We have more and better plans than ever before," reported Mr. Beetle. "And what fun these 10 committees have had—not to mention the good they got out of limbering up their imaginations."

Even in public affairs, the possible applications of group brainstorming are almost limitless. For example, the United States ambassador to Brazil might well organize a brainstorm group of five Brazilians and five Americans to meet with him once a month to produce ideas as to how Brazil and the United States could be made to feel more and more friendly to each other. There are hundreds of similar opportunities for concentrated creative thinking on our international front.

And in public matters of domestic import, group brainstorming has been successfully applied time after time. For example, New York State wanted ideas on how to stimulate more interest in the fine arts. Dr. Lee H. Bristol, Jr. conducted a session of 10 panelists in a half-hour period. As a result the State received 65 ideas, selected from the 110 that were suggested. These ideas served as springboards—as planks for the creation of a comprehensive plan.

Group brainstorming has been widely used in educational circles. A striking example is the way it was employed in the revision of the curriculum of the School of Pharmacy at Columbia University.

Webber College in Florida has probably made the greatest use of group brainstorming. Ever since 1957 the students have regularly employed this technique in operating the Student Council, and in rendering service to the community. They even brainstormed a helpful list of ideas for the architect of Webber's new auditorium. And, the faculty regularly uses this method in its meetings.

Group brainstorming is used more and more in the classroom as a part of teaching methodology. The University of Texas offers a striking example of this in a course in report-writing which has been developed by Dr. Jessamon Dawe. The students continually brainstorm problems such as: "What could Chrysler do to meet the small-foreign-car invasion?" Dr. Dawe sums up her teaching plan in these words: "The search for the significant, the anticipation of all possible alternatives—these are the features of the brainstorming which our classes do prior to writing reports."

The versatility of group brainstorming has been pointed up by Dr. Robert Wilson of Portland State College in Oregon in these words: "Brainstorming may be used on almost any type of problem. It is especially useful on school and classroom problems such as: What can we do to make our school more interesting and more comfortable? How can we develop better discipline in the playground? How can the line in the lunch room be speeded up? What questions would be most interesting to study in this unit?"

TOPICS

1. What are the basic rules of group brainstorming?
2. Which is the most important rule for a successful brainstorm meeting? Why?
3. What is meant by "social facilitation"? How and why does it induce ideation? Discuss.
4. What types of subjects lend themselves best to group brainstorming? Discuss.
5. To what other uses could the group brainstorm technique be put?

EXERCISES

1. Think up three talking points which the Voice of America could use favorably to impress its audience behind the Iron Curtain.
2. If there have been "flying saucers," and if they have come from Mars, for what "useful" purposes could they have been commissioned? Name three.
3. "A man's mother is his misfortune; his wife is his own fault." Think up three similar epigrams on domestic relations. (Problem suggested by *The London Spectator*.)

4. In what three ways might graduation ceremonies be changed for the better?
5. Suggest at least three changes that might have improved this course.

REFERENCES

BALES, R. F. and STRODTBECK, F. L., "Phases in Group Problem-Solving." *Journal of Abnormal and Social Psychology*. October 1951, pp. 485–495.

BRISTOL, LEE H., JR., "The Application of Group Thinking Techniques to the Problems of Pharmaceutical Education." *American Journal of Pharmaceutical Education*. Spring 1958, pp. 143–146.

BROWN, HARRISON, and OTHERS, *The Next Hundred Years*. New York. Viking Press, 1957.

CARTWRIGHT, DORWIN, "Achieving Change in People: Some Applications of Group Dynamics Theory." *Human Relations, 4*, 1951, pp. 381–392.

COON, ARTHUR M., "Brainstorming—A Creative Problem-Solving Technique." *Journal of Communication*. 1957, pp. 111–118.

HANNAFORD, EARLE S., *Conference Leadership in Business and Industry*. New York. McGraw-Hill Book Company, Inc., 1945.

HEISE, G. A. and MILLER, G. A., "Problem-Solving by Small Groups Using Various Communication Nets." *Journal of Abnormal and Social Psychology*. July 1951, pp. 327–335.

MAIER, N. R. F. and SOLEM, A. R., "The Contribution of a Discussion Leader to the Quality of Group Thinking: The Effective Use of Minority Opinions." *Human Relations, 5*, 1952, pp. 277–288.

PETERSON, E. I., "Cost-Cutting Conference Brings Out an Idea a Minute; Bigelow-Sanford Carpet Company." *Factory Management*. May 1948, pp. 94–96.

ROYCE, JOSIAH, "Psychology of Invention." *Psychological Review*. March 1898, pp. 113–144.

SOUTH, E. B., "Some Psychological Aspects of Committee Work." *Journal of Applied Psychology, 11*, 1927, pp. 348–368, 437–464.

STEWART, I., *Organizing Scientific Research for War.* Boston. Little, Brown and Company, 1948.

"The Dynamics of the Discussion Group," *Journal of Social Issues.* Spring, 1948.

"The National Training Laboratory in Group Development," a report to the adult education profession in *The Adult Education Bulletin.* February 1950.

WATSON, G. B., "Do Groups Think More Efficiently Than Individuals?" *Journal of Abnormal and Social Psychology.* October 1938, pp. 328–336.

"What Is Group Dynamics?" *The Adult Education Journal.* April 1950.

WOLF, JACK L., *The Production Conference.* Boston. Houghton Mifflin Company, 1944.

Chapter XIII

Detailed procedures of group brainstorming

EXPERIENCE has brought to light further knowledge in regard to the principles, procedures and applicability of group brainstorming. Much of this new light has come from the practical use of group brainstorming by all kinds of organizations.

Educational institutions have done much to develop a deeper understanding of the working of group brainstorming. Starting in 1955, Creative Problem-Solving Institutes have been conducted at the University of Buffalo and other universities. The hundreds of educators, executives and military officers who have attended these institutes have practiced group brainstorming to an extensive degree. The resultant experience has helped develop a better understanding of methodology and has helped confirm these findings of scientific research:

1. *Ideation can be more productive if criticism is concurrently excluded.* Education and experience have trained most adults to think judicially rather than creatively. As a result, they tend to impede their fluency of ideas by applying their critical power too soon. By deferring their judgment during a brainstorm session, they find they can think up substantially more good ideas.

2. *The more ideas the better.* Practically all the experience with group brainstorming confirms the principle that, in

ideation, quantity helps breed quality. In case after case, the last 50 ideas produced at a brainstorm session have averaged higher in quality than the first 50.

Some enrollees at recent institutes have shown a tendency to attribute to brainstorming an undue psychological significance. Although the underlying principles seem to be clear enough and relatively simple, one of the institute leaders offered this theory:

"Scientists recognized 'synergistic action' as meaning that two or more things can be combined to yield something greater than the sum total of the individual parts—like $2 + 2 = 5$. Group brainstorming can provide similar synergistic action, too."

And a federal official suggested that group brainstorming induces extra-normal perceptions of a psychically intuitive nature (as in Tecla, Newton, Ouspensky). "At least, in my experience," he said, "brainstorm sessions have occasionally produced what appeared to me as intuitive solutions to a relatively fundamental problem."

Dr. Richard Youtz of Columbia University made an exhaustive survey of psychological experiments significantly relevant to brainstorming principles. Several of the tests he reported had to do with two of the blocks which tend to curtail ideation in the conventional type of conference—frustration and functional fixation.

Professor S. M. Moshin's research revealed "the effect of frustration on problem-solving behavior." For one thing, this indicated how seriously a sense of inferiority can hamper creative output. Since brainstorming excludes factors which tend to induce such an emotion, this method not only reduces frustration to a minimum, but also breeds self-confidence.

Several of the experiments covered in the Youtz report dealt with factors which tend to increase "functional fixedness" and "rigidity." These blocks to ideation are reduced to a minimum by the "free-wheeling" rule which indispensably governs each braïnstorm session. In summarizing the research that had been done in the areas outlined above, Dr. Youtz commented: "These experimental findings support the contention that the judicial process should be reserved until after the tentative solutions have been achieved."

Although psychological evaluation of group brainstorming is important, the author of this book recommends that it be judged comparatively and pragmatically—simply as a workable way of jointly producing more and better ideas than is possible through the usual type of conference in which judicial judgment jams creative imagination.

2. *Composition of brainstorm panel*

The question as to what should be the size of a brainstorm panel has been subject to a wide variety of experiments. An extreme example was a session of over 200 training directors of federal agencies in Washington, D.C. Well over 100 promising ideas came out of this group in less than 30 minutes. Then, too, the American Association of Industrial Editors secured over 400 ideas from four brainstorm panels averaging about 50 men each. Likewise, Professor Dan Pursuit of the University of California has reported that, in his course for police officers attending the Delinquency Control Institute, panels of as many as 40 have successfully used brainstorming.

The consensus of opinion, however, favors the division of such groups into smaller sections. A strong advocate of this is an educational consultant, Dr. F. C. Finsterbach. He conducted brainstorming in one company for 28 members of the staff. But, first he divided this personnel into four groups of seven each.

He employed a two-session technique. The first session brainstormed the problem, "What are the specific problems of our company most in need of solution?" This produced 51 targets for the ensuing session to shoot at. Over 200 ideas resulted from the second brainstorm which creatively attacked two problems selected as a result of the first session.

When group brainstorming is used as a continual operation, the desired number of panelists can be pre-determined. Based on the preponderance of experience, the optimum size is indicated as being about a dozen.

An even number such as 12 might seem to be at variance with one of the principles advanced by Professor Robert F. Bales of Harvard as a result of his research on conferences. The main reason he recommends an odd number is to assure the availability of a majority, and thus avoid the danger of a split between two cliques of equal number. This reason is obviously sound in regard to decision-making conferences, but it need have no bearing on ideation conferences from which evaluation is excluded for the time being.

The ideas produced by group brainstorming should always be screened and otherwise processed at later conferences —preferably by conferees other than those who had thought up the ideas. Since such follow-up conferences would judge and sometimes decide, an odd number of conferees would then be indicated. The optimum number in such cases would be five in accordance with Professor Bales' findings.

Experience has likewise indicated that the ideal panel

should consist of a leader, an associate leader, about five regular or "core" members and about five guests. These "core" members serve as pace-setters. They should be people who have proved themselves to possess above-average facility in offering suggestions.

In most cases, a different group of guests should be invited for each brainstorm meeting. But they, of course, should be expected actively to participate, not merely to observe.

Rotation of guest-panelists is strongly recommended by Dr. Merle Ogle, Educational Consultant of the Air Force ROTC. Here is his conclusion: "The same group left together over a long period of time tends to develop a rigid pattern of thinking, so that one member can almost anticipate the reactions of another. Therefore, we try to keep changing the make-up of our groups for brainstorming sessions."

The nature of the problem to be brainstormed should help determine the type of guests to be invited. For example, if the subject deals with shotguns, people with hunting experience should be invited to participate; if it concerns hotels, the preferred guests would be those who have traveled extensively.

Several organizations have found it helpful to include females on each brainstorm panel. The girls try to "out-ideate" the men, and vice versa. This tends to induce an extra rivalry which stimulates the flow of ideas.

Experience justifies a word of warning to the effect that a panel should consist of people of substantially the same rank. If superior officers are present, they tend by facial expression or otherwise to induce an inferiority complex on the part of panelists, and thus to discourage "free-wheeling." A case in point occurred in a telephone company. A "big boss" sat in on the session. The ideas began to flow at an inordinately slow rate. After 10 minutes the executive left. About four times as many suggestions were forthcoming in the last 20 minutes as in the first 10.

Although the preponderance of experience indicates that brainstorm sessions tend to be less productive when a ranking officer is in attendance, General Electric has reported successful sessions with high-ups present—but not as participants, solely as observers. This is another indication that the procedures set forth above should not be regarded as inflexible. Except for the basic brainstorming rules (as set forth in the previous chapter), all other phases of the methodology should be adapted to circumstances.

By way of summary, the following is a condensation of the pertinent part of the University of Chicago's "Group Brainstorming Manual":

Each panel should consist of a chairman, an assistant chairman called "idea collector" and about 10 others.

If guests are included they should be invited from various departments, a different group for each meeting. This rotation helps spread a creative spirit throughout an organization.

The nature of the problem to be brainstormed should help determine the type of guests to be invited.

It is often helpful to include two or three women on each brainstorm panel. For problems of a feminine nature, at least half of the participants should be women.

Since panelists who have attended no previous sessions are unfamiliar with group brainstorming, a fairly thorough orientation is recommended. The ideal is a 30-minute presentation which covers the basic principles of ideation as well as brainstorming procedures. (Scripts, slides, and sound movies for this purpose are available from the Creative Education Foundation.)

3. *Preliminary procedures*

The panel leader should be trained in advance for his function. Ideally, he should have taken a course in creative problem-solving. At least, he should have assiduously studied the principles and procedures set forth in this book.

Some industries have engaged professional educators to train creative leaders. One instance of this was at Bridgeton, N. J., where the Owens-Illinois Company enlisted Dean B. B. Goldner of LaSalle College for such a purpose. He conducted an intensive course for nine staff-members of that plant, before they assumed their leadership duties.

Having become grounded in the basics of brainstorming, each panel leader should develop in advance of each session his own list of suggested solutions to the problem. Then, if the stream of ideas slows down, the leader can prime the joint flow by interpolating suggestions of his own. On the other hand, he should always hold back whenever any of his panelists are waiting to be heard.

The leader should also be prepared to suggest leads by way of certain classifications or categories. For example, a chairman may say, "Let's look for ideas on this problem in such-and-such an area." For the purpose of thus pointing out directions in which to look for ideas, the questions listed in Chapter XVI have been frequently and fruitfully used.

The leader's first job in setting up a session is to process the problem. The objective should be to make sure that it is particular, not general. A problem like "How to introduce a new synthetic fibre" is too broad. This should be broken down into at least three sub-problems, such as: (1) "Ideas for introducing the new fibre to weavers and mills." (2) "Ideas for introducing the new fibre to dress houses and cutters." (3) "Ideas for introducing the new fibre to retailers."

The guiding principle is that a problem should be simple rather than complex. Failure to narrow the problem to a single target can seriously mar the success of any brainstorm session. On the other hand, sessions have been successfully devoted solely to breaking down a broad problem into its specific components. Subsequent sessions are then held to produce ideas on the sub-problems, with one session devoted to each of these.

In other words, definition of aim is often half the battle. First of all, we should try to split our problem into its components. Then, we should coin each sub-problem into a perfectly definite question. These and other factors in the proper processing of problems were previously stressed in this book. They apply even more vitally to group brainstorming than to individual ideation.

As already stated, the panel leader should also arrange for the conditioning of new participants for their initial session. For this purpose, "warm-up" practice is usually used at the start of the meeting. Some exercises call for some simple problem unrelated to the subject of the brainstorm session —a problem such as: "In what ways could men's pants be improved?"

The panel leaders first select the personnel. Then, at least two days in advance of the session, the participants are invited, and they are simultaneously supplied with copies of a "background" memo of not more than one page in length.

The double purpose of this memo is to orient the panelists

and to let them "sleep on the problem," thus allowing incubation to enhance the workings of association. In a typical memo for this purpose, issued over the signature of the panel leader, the first paragraph would name the time and place. The second paragraph might read like this: "The problem we will brainstorm is this: '*What new products not now available are needed for the home?*' Here is your opportunity to dream up all those gadgets, appliances, etc. which you believe would make home life more enjoyable."

Such a memo should include a few examples of the type of ideas desired. In this case, leads like these might be mentioned:

1. BEDROOM—Sheets with double-strength weave in the center where the wear shows first.
2. KITCHEN—Suction cups on bottom of egg-beaters to prevent skidding in bowl.
3. LIVING ROOM—Venetian blinds so constructed that the slats in the upper or lower half may be opened or closed independently of each other half.
4. DOORWAY—Switches for door bells so you can turn them off when children are asleep or when you don't want to be disturbed.

The brainstorm session for which that memo served as "background" was actually held. Within 40 minutes, 12 men and women produced 136 ideas.

In that case the problem was of a somewhat multiple nature. It would have been better if each of four or five subproblems had been brainstormed separately. Although this would have taken more time, the results would have been relatively superior.

By way of summary, the following is a condensation of the pertinent part of the University of Chicago's "Group Brainstorming Manual":

The chairman's first job in setting up a session is to go over the problem and make sure that it is simple and specific—not an "umbrella" problem like "How to win the cold war."

The basic aim of brainstorming is to pile up a quantity of alternative ideas. Therefore the problem must be one that lends itself to many possible "answers." Brainstorming should not be used on problems requiring value judgments like "What's the best time to start to teach algebra?"

After a single specific problem has been determined, the panel leader should prepare a one-page memo which highlights the background of the problem, states the problem in its simplest terms, and spells out at least two examples of the type of ideas which are sought. (When possible this should be accompanied by exhibits in further illustration of the problem.)

The chairman or the assistant chairman then selects the panelists. At least two days in advance of the session, the participants are invited by phone or otherwise; and they are simultaneously supplied with copies of the "background" memo.

The panel leaders should develop in advance their own list of suggested solutions to the problem. If and when the session slows down or gets off the track, the leaders can then prime the joint flow of ideas by contributing some of their own.

The panel leader should also be prepared to suggest leads by way of certain classifications or categories. Many chairman have found that idea-spurring questions like these can be helpful: *Put to Other Uses?* (New ways to use as is?

Other uses if modified?) *Adapt?* (What else is like this? What other ideas does this suggest?) *Modify?* (Change meaning, color, motion, sound, odor, taste, form, shape? Other changes?) *Magnify?* (What to add? Greater frequency? Stronger? Larger? Plus ingredient? Multiply?) *Minify?* (What to subtract? Eliminate? Smaller? Lighter? Slower? Split up? Less frequent?) *Substitute?* (Who else instead? What else instead? Other place? Other time?) *Rearrange?* (Other layout? Other sequence? Change pace?) *Reverse?* (Opposites? Turn it backward? Turn it upside down? Turn it inside out?) *Combine?* (How about a blend, an assortment? Combine purposes? Combine ideas?)

As previously stated, these questions will be fully developed in subsequent chapters.

4. *Conduct of session*

The session should start with a further explanation of the problem and with answers to questions.

The leader should then present the four basic rules (as spelled out in the previous chapter). A placard is usually used to display these rules.

The leader then calls for suggestions. He quickly recognizes those who raise their hands to signify that they have ideas to offer. Sometimes so many hands are raised that he simply goes around the table and lets each person present one idea in turn. Participants should never be allowed to read off lists of ideas which they may have brought to the meeting. These can be handed to the leader before the session. Only one idea at a time should be offered by any brainstormer. Otherwise the pace would be badly impeded because the opportunity for "hitch-hikes" would be precluded.

The leader especially encourages ideas that are directly

sparked by a previous idea. This chain-reaction is so worthy of full play that panelists are asked to snap their fingers as well as raise their hands whenever they have such "hitch-hikes" to offer. If several hands are up at the same time, the leader gives priority to the finger-snappers and thus makes the most of the power of association.

When several hands are raised there is danger that the last panelist called upon may have become so absorbed in the ideas of the others that he will have forgotten what he was about to suggest. Therefore, it is recommended that each panelist make notes of ideas he plans to offer when his turn comes.

To record the ideas brought out by the brainstorm session, a secretary should be appointed. This person should sit next to the leader so as to be in direct line of conversation between him and the others. The ideas should be taken down reportorially—not word for word. Some organizations have found it helpful to have two secretaries make notes. Greater accuracy and clarity are thus achieved. In this case, one secretary takes the even-number ideas and the other records the odd-number ideas. Sometimes a session is tape-recorded. This enables the secretary to recheck the list of ideas which has been reportorially recorded during the meeting.

In any case, each idea is consecutively numbered during the session. This enables the leader to know how many suggestions have come forth up to any point in the meeting, at which time he might apply pressure of this type: "Let's get just 10 more ideas," or, "Let's break 100," or, "Let's each of us come up with just one more idea before we close." This kind of drive often uncovers new ideas which set off a chain of other and better ideas.

No idea is identified by the name of its suggestor. The

very same idea may have been previously thought up by another panelist. Or it may have resulted directly from a suggestion made by someone else a few minutes before. The need for group congeniality far outweighs the good of granting individual credit.

As to how long the idea-finding activity should last, experience indicates that the optimum is about 30 minutes. However, some successful leaders advocate 15 minutes or less, while others keep their sessions going until the flow of ideas begins to trickle too slowly.

Dr. Sidney J. Parnes has probably had the widest experience in the conduct of brainstorm sessions. He says: "I have found 30 to 45 minutes best. If more time might be needed, it is a good idea to break up the problem into smaller questions that can be handled in a 45-minute session. If the time is too short, panelists are prone to present only the superficial and more obvious suggestions. It is usually in the later stage when they begin to dig deeper and present ideas which are relatively more unique and potentially more usable."

In the usual type of continuous ideation it has been found that the speed of flow tends to accelerate. For example, the Armstrong Cork Company brainstormed an employment problem for its Macon, Georgia, plant. The first 10 minutes produced 27 ideas. The next 15 minutes produced 86 ideas.

In closing the meeting the leader expresses his appreciation, and then asks participants to keep the problem on their minds until the next day when they will be asked for their afterthoughts.

That's the usual type of program for brainstorm sessions. Of course, there are many variations. For example, Harold E. Schmidhauser of the American Management Association operates on a "stop-and-go" basis by using an egg-timer to measure a three-minute drive period for ideas. Then he stops and gives the panelists a five-minute period of silence for incubation. Then he puts on another three-minute drive, then allows another five minutes for incubation, and so on.

So much for the methodology of the brainstorm session. The follow-up procedures will be covered in the next chapter.

5. *Further evidence of productivity*

As to use of brainstorming by business, here are a few cases among the many: Aluminum Company of America, Armstrong Cork, Bristol-Myers, Christmas Clubs of America, Corning Glass Works, Du Pont, Ethyl Corporation, General Electric, International Business Machines, New York Telephone, R.C.A., Reynolds Metals, Rexall, Scott Paper Company, Taylor Instruments, Union Carbide, U. S. Rubber, United States Steel.

In most companies, the use of brainstorming has tended to spread. For example, early in 1954, the U. S. Rubber Company started this practice in its Naugatuck, Connecticut, plant. Based on the results in that one branch, the head office, in November, 1955, issued a bulletin to the managers of all plants advocating the adoption of similar activity.

The Armstrong Cork Company likewise started brainstorming in just one plant. A year later, an executive was especially assigned to help install brainstorming in the 20 other plants of this company.

In some industrial organizations brainstorming is being used as an adjunct to Suggestions Systems. One panel in General Electric attacked the problem of "ways to improve our Suggestions System so that we will get more and better ideas from our employees." Within 35 minutes, 131 ideas were thought up for that purpose.

Group brainstorming has been adopted by scores of industries in technological phases of operations. A typical example was reported by C. M. Sinnett of the Advanced Development Section of the R.C.A. Victor Television Division. The panel consisted of research scientists. One brainstorming session yielded 200 different ideas for the improvement of TV receivers. According to Mr. Sinnett, "Some of the ideas were excellent, some good, some impractical for the moment." Mr. Sinnett rated this group method of ideation as an improvement over any previous attempt to obtain ideas.

Joseph G. Mason of Minneapolis has been a leader in the application of group brainstorming to technological problems. His manual entitled "Suggestions for Brainstorming Technical and Research Problems" is available on request to the Creative Education Foundation.

In government circles the productivity of group brainstorming has been demonstrated in countless cases. Starting in 1954, several federal departments in Washington, D. C. have adopted this form of organized ideation. All-told over 200 training directors in the national capital have grounded themselves in the principles and procedures involved. At one session of the Training Officers Conference, the problem chosen for brainstorming was: "What can federal employees do to give visitors to Washington a truer and better impression of their government?" Within 30 minutes, 121 ideas were elicited.

At a session of U. S. Treasury personnel, three problems were brainstormed. The first was: "How can we get more federal employees to sell more U. S. Savings Bonds?" Result: 103 ideas in 40 minutes. The second problem was: "How to reduce absenteeism?" Result: 89 ideas in 30 minutes. The third problem was "How to free bond-selling employees from office duties?" Result: 61 ideas in 30 minutes.

The armed services have likewise made increasing use of group brainstorming. Chief John E. Ehrmantraut of the U. S. Air Force Headquarters reported these two sessions, dealing with educational matters: One panel attacked the problem, "What can Headquarters Civilian Personnel Division do to further the growth of Executive Development Programs throughout the Air Force?" This session produced 57 ideas in approximately 45 minutes. Another panel brainstormed this problem: "What can be done to gain and maintain top-level support, at all levels of command, for the new Air Force Management Course for Supervisors?" This panel produced 75 ideas in approximately 30 minutes.

In a course in creative thinking at the Adjutant General's School at Fort Benjamin Harrison, two classes separately brainstormed these two problems: "How can a recruiter improve his prospecting technique?" "What is the best way to develop centers of influence?" In each class approximately 12 minutes were devoted to each question. The results were as follows: One class produced 91 ideas on the first problem and 85 on the second. The other class produced 89 ideas on the first problem and 83 on the second.

Institutes at universities have further demonstrated the productivity of brainstorming. At one of these at the University of Buffalo, Dr. James E. Gates of the University of Georgia presented a problem based on a new type of household tool. Four panels devoted a 15-minute period to each of three specific problems and produced a grand total of 1,322 possible leads to solution.

At the same institute, specific instances were brought out

concerning the soundness of seeking quantity in ideation. One case was that of a young engineer in Union Carbon and Carbide. Having taken an evening course in creative thinking, he asked his superiors to let him brainstorm some plant problem. They assigned him one which had long baffled the senior engineers. He organized a group of six associates. Within 30 minutes they jointly thought up 46 possible solutions. When these suggestions were evaluated by the management, only *six* out of the 46 ideas were rejected as unworthy of exploration. Four of these ideas led to the final solution of the problem.

The productivity of brainstorming has been substantially confirmed by classroom experiments in creative problem-solving courses. One series of tests sought to determine the extent to which premature intrusion of judgment tends to inhibit the flow of ideas. For this investigation the class was divided into two groups: (1) A creative, or positive section. (2) A judicial, or negative section. Whenever the creative group suggested solutions to the problem, the judicial group freely voiced its criticism. With half the class thus pouncing on the ideas offered by the other half, the number of suggested solutions averaged less than five per 15-minute session.

For the second part of the test, the judicial half of the class then left the room. The remaining students were forbidden to express any criticism whatsoever. These purely creative groups averaged nearly 50 ideas per 15-minute session.

Repeated results from this type of experimentation have further indicated that, in the same length of time, the average group can produce substantially more helpful ideas when ideation is unhampered than when judgment is allowed concurrently to stifle imagination.

6. *Case histories of results*

Some educators have raised this question about group brainstorming: "Granted that this procedure can produce a maximum of ideas in a minimum time, how usable are the ideas?"

The basic answer is that the usefulness of the tentative ideas largely depend on what is done with them—how effectively they are evaluated and how creatively they are developed. As a rule, the resultant ideas serve only as ore—ore that must be milled and refined. And, by way of analogy, the average gold mine has to dig up four tons of ore to produce one ounce of gold.

However, there are plenty of case histories of tangible resultfulness. The following are a few.

The Richmond, Virginia, chapter of the National Association of Social Workers held a brainstorm session which produced over 200 ideas. Professor Joseph H. Bunzel of William and Mary College reported that at least 50 of these suggestions had been put into operation.

The Greater Lawrence Chamber of Commerce ran a brainstorm session on ways to improve and increase downtown bus service. Paul J. Greeley, Executive Manager, reported that of the 29 ideas developed, 12 were practical and workable. Said Mr. Greeley, "Traffic on the bus lines has steadily increased as a result of using the brainstorm ideas."

A group of members of the Cleveland Advertising Club brainstormed the problem: "Ways to Publicize Opera Week and get as many people as possible to buy tickets." Of the 124 ideas suggested, opera executive Rodney Sutton developed 29 of them with seat-filling success.

At the Rockland State Hospital, a brainstorm session was

held to produce ideas for a new in-service course of training for occupational therapists throughout the state. Martin W. Nearly, Maine's Supervisor of Occupational Therapy, reported that, within 30 minutes, the brainstorming generated enough ideas for the resultant manual.

At the Veterans Administration Hospital in Buffalo, one of the many problems brainstormed was this: "How to increase employee participation in the Hospital blood donor program." General Howard Fuller, Hospital Manager, reported: "Many of the ideas were adopted. As a result there was a marked increase in the number of employee donors at this Hospital."

The elders, trustees and deacons of Buffalo's Westminster Presbyterian Church brainstormed four problems. Over 100 suggestions resulted. One idea called for enabling office workers in the neighborhood to make better use of the church. This resulted in a new series of noon services during Advent, with an inexpensive luncheon following each service. These services are now an annual event.

The Catholic Community Church in Neuilly Sur Seine, Paris, France, brainstormed the problem: "How to make our community more livable?" Fifteen panelists produced 276 ideas. Through individual ideation after the session, 82 more suggestions were added. Out of the total of 385 ideas, 70 were found to be usable.

At Harrisburg, Pennsylvania, a series of brainstorm sessions were conducted by Right Rev. Msgr. Robert J. Maher, Superintendent of the Schools of that Diocese. About 120 elementary school teachers participated. The subject was: "How to improve the art of our teaching." Monsignor Maher reported this brainstorming as "highly successful." He added:

"I would recommend it for use by other school administrators."

At Denver, Postmaster T. G. Hefner and his management staff brainstormed the question, "What can be done to reduce man-hour usage?" The panel of 12 produced 121 suggestions in 60 minutes. According to an official publication of the Post Office, some of the resultant ideas helped to effect a saving of 12,666 man-hours within the following nine weeks.

When a Pittsburgh department store was unable to move a quantity of embossed chair-covering material, employees brainstormed "other uses" for the fabric. Advertising was then concentrated on these "other uses." As a result, the entire stock was sold out within one week.

Derek Castle of Sydney, Australia, while conducting a class for store executives at Melbourne, had his students brainstorm an urgent problem. "In 40 minutes we amassed 163 ideas. The Managing Director told me afterward that 16 of these ideas were immediately practicable," Mr. Castle reported.

The Rexall Drug Company has been a consistent user of group brainstorming. In one year 58 resultant ideas were successfully put to use.

An H. J. Heinz plant brainstormed the problem: "How can we, as a group, help to increase the sale of products made at this factory?" W. A. Stockfield, of the Heinz organization later reported as follows:

"In less than one hour, over 100 good suggestions were made—not only more but better ideas than our special committee had come up with after holding 10 ordinary conferences."

Another Heinz problem which was brainstormed by two

different groups had to do with "ways to get sales promotional materials to our consumers more quickly." One group developed 82 ideas and the other group came up with 103. After evaluation, eight of the suggestions were immediately put to work.

At the Garden Supply Merchandising Convention in Chicago, a brainstorm session on power equipment produced the idea of a trailer with which distributor salesmen and dealers could transport lawn mowers and tractors to prospects' locations for demonstration. This idea was subsequently adopted by Musgrave Manufacturing Company, Springfield, Ohio, manufacturers of power riding mowers. According to D. Murray Franklin, this manufacturer's new bumper-hitch trailer closely follows the idea that came out of the brainstorm session.

At the annual Convention of the Christmas Club Corporation, a group of salesmen asked if they could conduct a brainstorm session instead of indulging in the entertainment program which had been planned for that evening. The bosses acquiesced; but they were barred from the session. The salesmen brainstormed this problem: "New items to be added to the line sold to banks." As a result, after investigating and developing the screened ideas, the company added 12 new products.

With the purchase of a new "Univac," Bristol-Myers needed additional calculation jobs to keep its original IBM equipment profitably in use. A group from the Market Research Department attacked this problem: "What further uses could the Market Research Department make of the IBM machines?" The panelists developed 251 job ideas in an hour.

As part of its creative selling service, Reynolds Metals

brainstormed this problem: "New and more convenient ways to package Aunt Jemima Cornmeal Mix." Cloyd S. Steinmetz of Reynolds has reported that the resultant ideas were used in the prize-wining sales-winning package. Reynolds then brainstormed this problem: "Ways to sell this revolutionary improvement to Quaker Oats executives." The result was a new sales plan of comparison demonstrations.

The Swiss Society of Life Insurance at Berne brainstormed the problem of: "How to find new salesmen." The panel produced 225 ideas in one hour. Evaluation determined that 25 were worthy of immediate adoption and that 125 were potentially usable.

Steel Magazine reported that a panel of Chicago-area executives brainstormed the problem: "What can we do about the engineering shortage?" From the 110 suggestions which resulted in the 25-minute session, six recommendations were found to be worthy of adoption.

A panel of Utah Power & Light employees, led by Vice President Joseph E. Cushman, brainstormed the problem of how to make storm-emergency operations more effective and less dangerous. The panelists attacked the sub-problems one at a time—specific problems of emergency operations such as weather forecasts, communications, trouble-desk operation, et cetera. The *Electrical World* reported that nine of the brainstormed suggestions were put into immediate effect and that these ideas "are now bolstering emergency procedures."

An insurance firm in Mexico City brainstormed the problem of improved economy of operations in its new offices. This was done before construction began. Gary Pickard, the manager, reported that, within 30 minutes, the panel produced 109 ideas. Of these, 23 were put into use.

Purchasing Magazine reported that Argus Camera had conducted brainstorm sessions with the entire buying staff to find potential areas of savings in purchasing, and that these sessions turned up practical suggestions which could eventually save as much as $112,000 annually. The magazine estimated that the ideas which were immediately usable would result in savings of $46,000 a year.

A series of sessions at Westinghouse was directed at the solution of engineering and sales-feature problems. Harold F. Simmonds, Westinghouse Project Engineer, says that one result of this procedure was the development of a process which saved the company $32,000.

The New York Times reported as follows: "An East Coast electronics company that regularly brainstorms at every production impasse has cut production time 37% on its last *six* problems . . . A Pennsylvania chemical company recently held a six-minute brainstorming session for tax-saving ideas and wound up with 87. Two of these survived critical evaluation by company tax specialists and resulted in a tax saving of $24,000."

In an effort to economize, the U. S. Navy's Bureau of Supplies wanted to make "one supply ship do the work of three" in the Pacific Fleet's electronic, ordnance and ship repair work. The solution, arrived at through brainstorm sessions, resulted in the de-commissioning of two ships. According to the official report, "The *U.S.S. Castor* was transformed to do the work of three, with a total saving of three million dollars a year in salaries and operating costs."

The Berkeley Heights, N. J., School Board anticipated trouble in getting a bond issue approved for a proposed $850,000 school building. So a group led by Dr. Fred Finsterbach brainstormed this problem: "Ways to cut costs of a new school building, without cutting quality of education nor quality of building materials." Resultant ideas cut the estimated costs down to $735,000—a saving of $115,000.

7. *Indirect values—and limitations*

After teaching many courses in creative thinking at the University of Pittsburgh and at the University of Buffalo—and after conducting many brainstorm sessions—Dr. Sidney Parnes compiled a list of 47 benefits from participation in this type of group effort.

The multiple values were likewise pointed out in an intra-company bulletin of the Ethyl Corporation: "While the main purpose is to generate ideas which it definitely accomplishes, the by-products of such sessions can be many. They can be tools for improving morale; they can provide a method of discovering what people think about supervisory problems; and they can help supervisors gain a better understanding of each other. As one man said after a meeting, 'I gained a new respect for each man in the session. It was a novel and elevating experience to me.' "

One by-product is enjoyment. Here's what a panelist reported, following a strenuous session: "I had a wonderful time. At the end I felt exhilarated; but an hour later I felt tired. It is a fatiguing experience, and yet it's fun. The usual conference is far less tiring. It's about the same difference as between golf and tennis. In golf, you just amble along, but in tennis you sweat. I like strenuous effort—that's why I enjoy brainstorming."

A most valuable effect on participants is improvement in initiative. In most cases, they come into their first brainstorm session with their imaginations flabby from disuse. As a result of their brainstorming experience they become inclined to tackle problems more enterprisingly as well as more creatively.

Such personal development is a common reward of brainstorming effort. On this point, the administrative head of a large firm reported: "Three of our panel leaders have been advanced to far higher posts—posts for which they probably would not have qualified, at least for some time to come, if it had not been for the personal development which resulted from their brainstorming activity."

Another indirect value is that the systematic use of group brainstorming can help insure against failure to think up improvements—improvements which obviously should be made. This point was inferentially brought out by the "I've Got a Secret" television show which featured the Quartermaster General of the Army. His secret was that he had saved $1,600,000 for the taxpayers within the last two years. How? By thinking up an idea. The idea was to eliminate watch pockets from Army uniforms. Asked how he got the idea, he said that it came to him by accident, while chatting with some cronies.

In all probability, that idea could have started to save money for taxpayers many years ago—if the operational plan had included a systematic use of group brainstorming. In that event an obvious problem would be, "What could be done to make army pants more cheaply without sacrificing quality?"

If this problem had been assigned to a panel under a well-trained leader, he would undoubtedly have spurred the session with questions from M.I.T.'s check-list—including this question: "What could be eliminated?" When asked a question like that, any group would have been almost certain to hit on the idea which accidentally came to the Quartermaster

General 25 years after pocket watches had given way to wrist watches.

* * *

Despite the many virtues of group brainstorming, individual ideation is usually more usable and can be just as productive. In fact, the ideal methodology for idea-finding is a triple attack: (1) Individual ideation. (2) Group brainstorming. (3) Individual ideation. And, of course, each of these procedures can be far more productive if the deferment-of-judgment principle is consistently followed.

And it must be admitted that the adoption of a program of group brainstorming sometimes turns out to be a flash in the pan—usually for these reasons:

1. *Faulty Operation*—failure to follow the procedures based on 33 years of experience.

2. *Exaggerated Expectation*—failure to realize that miracles are not in the wood.

In summary, let's put group brainstorming in its place. For one thing, it is only one of the phases of idea-finding which, in turn, is only one of the phases of the creative problem-solving process.

And let's bear in mind that group brainstorming is meant to be used—not as a substitute—but as a supplement, and especially in these three ways:

1. *As a supplement to individual ideation:* Individual effort is an indispensable factor in creative problem-solving. Brainstorm sessions should never be considered as a substitute for such effort. Group brainstorming serves solely as a supplemental source—a means of generating a maximum number of potentially usable ideas in a minimum of time.

2. *As a supplement to conventional conferences:* The

usual conference is necessarily judicial, both in spirit and in function, and therefore relatively unproductive of ideas. This does not mean that brainstorm sessions should supplant conventional conferences. It merely means that conventional conferences can be profitably supplemented by an occasional brainstorm session—if and when creative thinking is the primary purpose.

3. *As a supplement to creative training:* In over 1,000 courses in creative thinking, group brainstorming has been used as one of the teaching methods. This type of self-demonstration does much to induce a more creative attitude and to develop fluency of ideas. By the same token, participation in brainstorm sessions can help improve the average person's creative ability, not only in group effort, but also in individual effort.

And let's bear in mind these further limitations about group brainstorming:

1. *Some sessions can produce final answers*—but only if the problem is simple enough. One example of this was finding names for Armstrong Rugs.

2. *Some sessions can provide planks for plans.* An example of this was the new program for the School of Pharmacy at Columbia University. In that case, a complete plan came out of the 350 ideas which brainstorming produced.

3. *Some sessions can produce check-lists.* Such check-lists can serve as working guides to stimulate further constructive thinking. For example, 500 suggestions for teaching American history more creatively came out of brainstorming at the University of Buffalo, with 60 teachers of American history as the panelists. The resultant check-list has served many a teacher as a working guide.

4. *Some sessions can provide approaches* to subsequent

solution of problems. This is especially true when the problem is necessarily complex—as in technological research. In such cases, brainstorming can supply enough ideas by way of leads so that the most promising paths to ultimate solution can be more quickly found in advance, thus saving time and money.

In contrast to occasional cases of short-lived use of group brainstorming, let's look at the record of Dr. Dan Pursuit of the University of Southern California. He started over seven years ago to use this procedure on problems of his university, his community and his state. He has kept this up ever since to an extent that speaks for itself in a letter he recently wrote:

"During the past year I have brainstormed before a wide variety of groups, including a high-school student council, four Federal Management Seminars, a number of professional associations, several groups of government officials from Pakistan, and various service clubs. Next week I will be conducting brainstorming for the City Manager and department heads of the city of Beverly Hills. And at our Youth Studies Center we are constantly using brainstorming to develop new research projects for us to conduct under grants from the Ford Foundation."

Dr. Pursuit's record is presented as time-tested proof that, when properly conducted, group brainstorming can be used on almost any problem—and profitably so, within the limits that this chapter has indicated.

TOPICS

1. Why is a combination of group ideation and individual ideation desirable?
2. "In what ways can we combat juvenile delinquency?" Wouldn't this be a good problem to brainstorm? Discuss.

3. How can brainstorming be used as an adjunct to a company's suggestion system?
4. What is the usual result of the controlled experiment in which a purely creative idea group competes against a group where criticism is allowed?
5. "Mixed brainstorm groups are usually doomed to failure because of the inherent rivalry between the sexes." Do you agree? Why or why not?

EXERCISES

1. Write a pre-brainstorm memo (as suggested in this chapter) for the following problem: "What new improvements could be made on the modern kitchen sink?"
2. List the different types of guests you feel would add most to the productivity of a brainstorm session on the above problem.
3. Make up a list of 10 "category" hints which the panel leader might use during said session.
4. Break down the following general problem into sub-problems suitable for brainstorming: "In 1954, French Prime Minister Pierre Mendes-France's efforts to promote the drinking of milk throughout his country met with limited success. What might he have done to achieve maximum results?"
5. Brainstorm one of the sub-problems developed from the foregoing exercise.

REFERENCES

Adamson, R. E., "Functional Fixedness as Related to Problem-Solving." *Journal of Experimental Psychology, 44,* 1952, pp. 288–291.

Advertising Age, "Don't Try to Create Idea and Judge It at Same Time." February 27, 1956, p. 188.

Birch, Herbert G., "The Relation of Previous Experience to Insightful Problem-Solving." *Journal of Comparative and Physiological Psychology,* 38, 1945, pp. 367–383.

BIRCH, H. G. and RABINOWITZ, H. S., "The Negative Effect of Previous Experience on Productive Thinking." *Journal of Experimental Psychology, 41,* 1951, pp. 121–125.

Business Week, "How to Keep New Ideas Coming." October 22, 1955, pp. 112–118.

Business Week, "Teaching of Creative Thinking Added to Executive Training." August 6, 1955, p. 158.

CLARK, CHARLES H., *Brainstorming.* Garden City, N. Y. Doubleday and Company, Inc., 1958.

CLARK, CHARLES H., "Visual Spur to Wild Ideas." *Life.* June 11, 1956, pp. 20–21.

COWEN, EMORY L., "Stress Reduction and Problem-Solving Rigidity." *Journal of Consulting Psychology, 16,* 1952, pp. 425–428.

CREATIVE EDUCATION FOUNDATION, "Available Materials for Teaching and for Group Brainstorming." Buffalo. 1960.

CREATIVE PROBLEM-SOLVING INSTITUTE, University of Buffalo. *Proceedings* of annual Institutes, beginning in 1955.

GEHMAN, RICHARD, "Train Your Own Inventors." *Nation's Business.* February 1955, pp. 28–100.

GIBSON, E. J. and MCGARVEY, H. R., "Experimental Studies of Thought and Reasoning." *Psychological Bulletin.* June 1937, pp. 327–350.

HIX, C. F., JR. and PURDY, D. L., "Creativity Can Be Developed." *G-E Review.* May 1955.

Industrial and Engineering Chemistry, "Freedom to Dream." March 1955, pp. 7A–9A.

JOHNSON, DONALD M., "A Modern Account of Problem-Solving." *Psychological Bulletin.* 1944, pp. 201–229.

LUCHINS, A. S., "Mechanization in Problem-Solving. The Effect of Einstellung." *Psychological Monograph, 54,* 1942, whole No. 248.

MAIER, N. R. F., "Reasoning in Humans. Part I. On Direction." *Journal of Comparative and Physiological Psychology, 10,* 1930, pp. 115–144.

PARNES, SIDNEY J., *Student Workbook for Creative Problem-Solving Courses and Institutes.* Buffalo. The University of Buffalo Bookstore, 1959.

PARNES, SIDNEY J. and HARDING, HAROLD F., eds., *A Source Book for Creative Thinking*. New York. Charles Scribner's Sons, 1962.

PRATT, C. C., "Experimental Studies of Thought and Reasoning." *Psychological Bulletin*, 25, 1928, pp. 550–561.

UNIVERSITY OF CHICAGO, Industrial Relations Center, "Group Brainstorming Manual," 1961.

Chapter XIV

Processing of tentative ideas

THE LAST SEVEN chapters have dealt with problem-definition and idea-finding. We will now consider some of the steps in solution-finding, including the selection of ideas resulting from group brainstorming, and the evaluation, development and implementation of ideas gathered from all sources.

Although creative imagination is essential to the solution-finding phases of the creative problem-solving process, judgment must play an even larger part. This point was summed up in these words by Colonel Kelso G. Clow, head of U. S. Army Armor School:

"Judgment, analysis, and criticism are exercised in the selection of the problem to be solved, in the selection of the statement of the problem, in the evaluation of the ideas developed by creative attack, in the preparation of the plan of action regarding the problem, and in presenting the plan of action to the individual who has authority to take the action indicated. Judgment is suspended only in those steps of the process in which ideas are produced and developed."

I concur with Colonel Clow. And I agree with this statement by Professor John Arnold of Leland Stanford: "Few ideas are in themselves practical. It is for the want of active imagination in their application rather than in their means of acquisition that they fail of success. The creative process does not end with an idea—it only starts with an idea."

In most courses in creative problem-solving, more time is devoted to teaching students what to do with ideas than how to think them up. This weighting is largely the result of the "Instructor's Manual," the author of which is Dr. Sidney J. Parnes, Director of Creative Education, University of Buffalo. Copies of this 140-page book are available free to educators (only) on request to the Creative Education Foundation, 1614 Rand Building, Buffalo 3, N. Y.

2. *Supplementation and evaluation*

After a brainstorm session is over, time should be allowed to enable incubation to help the panelists think up still more ideas by way of supplementation to those produced during the brainstorm session. Accordingly, the panel leader or an assistant should phone or see the participants on the following day and secure their subsequent suggestions.

After brainstormers have slept on a problem, they sometimes generate the most valuable of all the ideas. This was indicated by the experience of one of the federal bureaus. A brainstorm session developed 105 ideas in 33 minutes. Then the harvesting of the afterthoughts added 23 more. Four of the latter turned out to be better than any of the first 105 suggestions.

Some brainstorm leaders use a more thorough method of supplementation. For example, Douglas Thomson of the U. S. Rubber Company has reported as follows: "To gather more ideas, we send the typed minutes of each brainstorm session to each participant, with plenty of blank space for additional ideas. We also circulate a round-robin ideas folder, to be passed along within a limited time, for new ideas to be added in handwriting. Also, we sometimes set up a subsequent reminding system to re-enlist participants for further ideation on the problem."

For evaluation and selection the usual brainstorm procedure calls for these preparatory steps:

1. The panel secretary prepares a triple-spaced, typewritten list of all ideas suggested both during the session and afterwards.

2. The panel chairman then edits the list, making sure that each idea is succinctly but understandably stated. At the same time he classifies the ideas within logical categories. A glance over the full list usually indicates from five to ten classifications. Under each classification are placed the individual ideas which should be included in that section.

The resultant list is then screened so that the most promising of the ideas may be selected. By whom? In some cases this is done by all or part of the brainstorm panel. In other cases this is done by a smaller group composed partly of panelists and partly of non-panelists. In many cases, the panel's function ends with the preparation of the list of ideas, and others take over the evaluation and further re-processing.

One of the leading authorities on creative follow-up is Professor Leo B. Moore of the Massachusetts Institute of Technology. In citing one of his personal experiences he said this:

"The question we raised was whether the brainstorming technique which created the list of ideas could be used to evaluate these ideas. The manager raised the issue first as to whether the creative group should be the evaluative group. For human relations reasons I felt that the same group should perform the two tasks. I take issue with the proposition that two different groups perform these two activities unless there is very definite reason for this separation and only then if full and complete communication is provided the creative group on the evaluation process and its results. Not only do I have concern here for the human aspects but if we remember the linkage of evaluation with development and use of the output of the evaluation process, more often than not the same group should perform the two activities."

Others who have made extensive use of group brainstorming hold to the opinion that the final screening should *not* be done by the panelists, but by another group—people better posted on feasibilities, as well as being more judicial and objective. "Otherwise," said one educator, "it's like a beauty contest being judged by the mothers of the would-be Miss Americas."

It is usually wise to have the final evaluation done by those directly responsible for the problem. This may or may not be the group that did the brainstorming. In any event, the brainstormers should eventually be informed of the disposition of their ideas.

Further steps are often indicated in order to insure a more accurate evaluation. For example, a sales manager sought a name for a new product, the best market for which was among young women. Brainstorming sessions produced over 300 suggestions. A screening group then picked the 10 best. These 10 were then submitted to 100 young women. When 61 of this consumer jury picked out one name as the best by far, the final decision was automatic.

Let's bear in mind that, in most cases, a list of tentative ideas should be considered solely as a springboard for further action—as a *check-list*—as a pool of ideas to be screened, evaluated and further developed before solution can be arrived at.

To facilitate the evaluation process, it often pays to create a check-list of criteria. Here's one example of such a guide:

1. Is the idea simple enough?
2. Is it compatible with human nature?
3. Is it timely?
4. Is it feasible?

And here is a more complete check-list of criteria as used in the U. S. Navy:

1. Will it increase production—or improve quality?
2. It is a more efficient utilization of manpower?
3. Does it improve methods of operation, maintenance, or construction?
4. Is it an improvement over the present tools and machinery?
5. Does it improve safety?
6. Does it prevent waste or conserve materials?
7. Does it eliminate unnecessary work?
8. Does it reduce costs?
9. Does it improve present methods?
10. Will it improve working conditions?

Professor Leo B. Moore of M.I.T. cites this case in an industry:

A brainstorming group produced 22 promising ideas. As basic criteria the evaluators chose: (1) The amount of probable cost. (2) The degree of likely improvement. Under cost, the question of cost of time was translated into degree of difficulty. One phase of the task therefore called for scoring each idea as "simple," "hard" or "difficult." Roman numerals I, II and III were assigned to each of these three indices.

As a result the group was able to go through the 22 ideas quite quickly and score each of them appropriately on this point.

3. *Development of screened ideas*

As to the development phase of the follow-up procedure, the best ideas are usually combinations of other ideas. Therefore, even during a brainstorm session, every effort should be made thus to produce more and better ideas. This principle applies just as importantly to the processing of ideas which have subsequently been selected as most promising.

For example, General Electric's Advanced Electronic Center at Cornell University operated a highly organized ideation program, under the direction of Professor S. G. Trull. His manual of procedure required the screening committee to do far more than merely judge and select. One of its prescribed functions was creatively to reprocess the ideas through combination, elaboration, and other means.

C. Frank Hix of General Electric has warned against screening out the far-fetched ideas too quickly. He believes that from a list of brainstorm suggestions, it is sometimes possible to pick the seemingly silliest and, by probing in and around it, to develop it into the best idea of all.

That type of procedure has led to the successful solution of several problems at General Electric. In one case, a panel brainstormed the problem of more economical ways to house and suspend the copper rods which conduct power through factories. One of the many ideas that came out of the session was, "Hang them with ropes." When all the suggestions were submitted to the management executive, that one made him laugh—more disdainfully than heartily. The panel chairman immediately asked for more time. Then he held another session solely to brainstorm some way of hanging those conduits "with ropes, or something better." And out of that the final solution was developed.

4. *Verification of value of ideas*

The verification process seeks to confirm what looks likely to be true about the worth of an idea.

At this stage a chosen idea should be fairly well developed. For example, if it concerns a new food, a rough dummy of a package should have been prepared. In any case, known facts should have been marshalled, including data from previous surveys. Then, too, consultation should have been held with those who have had most to do with similar kinds of problems. And, of course, the verification process could well include new surveys or tests, or both.

Ideation (either individual, or group, or both) should here again be brought into play in order to devise the forms of testing which could do most to confirm or repudiate the value of the idea.

One problem would be *where* to test. The least obvious place might be the best answer. This was true in regard to a telephone company which wanted to verify the idea that colored telephone sets could be profitably marketed to women. The sets come in eight different colors. One suggestion was that a supermarket would be just the place to test their salability. A display was accordingly arranged in one such store. The many-hued hand sets were exhibited, along with curlycords, extensions and jacks. A representative from the telephone company was present to answer questions and take orders. The test ran for three days. Of the 3,700 customers who came into the store, 325 stopped at the telephone exhibit, and 19 bought the colored sets.

This and many other cases tend to indicate that practical testing is a most desirable method of verification.

5. *Presentation of ideas*

Where others need to be persuaded of the worth of an idea, its proponents face a creative challenge. This is especially true in a sizable organization where the destiny of new ideas lies in the hands of higher-ups.

In preparing a presentation, we should heed the advice of Benjamin Franklin to this effect: "The way to sell an idea to another is to state your case moderately and accurately. This causes your listener to be receptive and, like as not, he will turn about and convince you of the worth of your idea. But if you go at him in a tone of positiveness and arrogance, you are likely to turn him against your idea, no matter how good it is."

Another point is to watch your timing. Even a little aging may help. Dr. William J. Reilly has put this advice into these words: "The time to discuss an idea with others is *after* you have thought it through."

For certain purposes it is well to visualize an idea with charts, models and exhibits. And pictures are often persuasive. For example: When Calvin Coolidge was President, I thought up the idea of getting William J. Donovan into the Federal Government. I prepared a scrapbook, with many photos of the General—as an athlete, as a lawyer, and as an army officer, as head of the American Legion. In this way I was able to sell my idea to the Administration, whereas without creative preparation I would probably have failed.

An important point is to plan the proper sequence for your presentation. Here's the framework recommended by Daymond Aitken:

1. Prepare the way by developing the problem or the situation. Show a need. If practical, do this by using some visual means.

2. Organize your recommendation around key points. Use sketches, pictures, diagrams, models, or whatever is best suited for the purpose. Show and explain simply. Waste no words. Give the general picture, stressing the important features. Many of the little details can be left for the discussion phase.

3. Sum up the points you have made. Tersely state the results and advantages. Re-emphasize the need. If appropriate, end with an appeal for action, if only by way of testing.

In connection with that last point of Daymond Aitken's, an executive of a large firm recommends this tactic when presenting an idea to superior officers:

"Be sure to facilitate at least tentative acceptance by suggesting easy actions to take. For example, suggest the appointment of a committee for further study; or suggest that a small appropriation be made to secure more facts; or suggest that an estimate of costs be prepared; or suggest that a patent search be made; or suggest some kind of limited test."

One advantage of a small company is its ability to act fast when considering a new idea. One case in point was that of a large corporation in which a brainstorm panel thought up a promising idea for a new store display. A dummy was made and submitted to management. The recommendation was passed around among the executives. After several months, they decided to adopt the idea. But, before the display could be put into production, a small competitor came out with virtually the same design.

Zippers on men's trousers are a classic example along the same line. When the men in management were approached with that same idea, they subjectively decided that it was impracticable. It wasn't until three years later that any action was taken. How simple it would have been to devise a test—to engage a local tailor to make a few pairs of trousers with zippers and try them on some men not connected with the company. By doing that, a most profitable market could have been opened up at least three years sooner.

Based on his own experience, Professor Leo Moore has summarized as follows:

"In review, it seems to me that we should delay evaluation and let time seep into the process. In sequence (after the creativity list is well along), we should manage the process by successively (1) Calling for natural groupings. (2) Introducing criteria. (3) Calling for decision on use. (4) Reaching agreement on plan of action. (5) Deciding on form of recommendation to the boss. (6) Highlighting what was accomplished by the group. During these changing activities we should continue the creative thinking mood to the degree that we are able."

The Creative Education Foundation has published Professor Moore's 16-page brochure entitled "Creative Action—Evaluation, Development and Use of Ideas." Copies are available on request.

6. *Alternating types of thinking*

In Professor Moore's summary he recommended that throughout the creative problem-solving process "we should continue the creative thinking mood."

Even on relatively simple problems, a "one-two" type of procedure is usually helpful—an alternation between creative thinking and judicial thinking. For example, suppose you are chairman of a committee to line up the main speaker for the opening dinner of your Community Chest campaign. The usual method would be to call your committee into a session to think up and knock down names. Perhaps a dozen possibilities would thus be considered.

But, suppose you hold two meetings—one to think up names, the other to select. For the first conference each member would be asked to come with a list of his own. At this meeting you, as Chairman, would read all these names aloud, without comment. Then you would ask for additional suggestions. The names brought in, plus those added at this session, would probably total around 100 instead of only 10 or so.

You could then send a list of the nominations to all the members, and ask each of them to come to the second conference with his first 10 choices marked. A composite list of preferences could be quickly arrived at in this meeting. The members could then discuss these names pro and con, and decide upon the 10 most wanted speakers in the order of their desirability. The chances are that some of the names on this chosen list would never have been suggested in the usual form of conference.

Further to illustrate the principle of separating our two major types of thinking, the several steps in problem-solving might follow an alternating sequence something like this:

1. *Think up all phases of the problem.* Vital angles of a problem are often so obscure that their detection calls for imagination. Therefore we might well start with a solely creative approach.

2. *Select the sub-problems to be attacked.* Then, having

created a copious list of possible phases of the problem, scrutinize them judicially and pick out the single targets.

3. *Think up what data might help.* Having clarified the problem, we now need facts. But let's first devote a creative period to thinking up the kinds of material that might help most. (Dr. Walter Reed did just that in solving the mystery of Yellow Fever. Many scientists had gone bleary-eyed peering through microscopes at bacteria and blood. Dr. Reed suggested that insects be investigated, and this led to the solution.)

4. *Select the most likely sources of data.* Having free-wheeled the question of what information is needed, then let's go into a decision session and determine just what items on that list should first be researched.

5. *Dream up all possible ideas as keys to the problem.* This part of the process obviously calls for full play of imagination, without concurrent intrusion of critical thinking.

6. *Select the ideas most likely to lead to solution.* This screening process calls mainly for judicial thinking, with emphasis on comparative analysis.

7. *Think up all possible ways to test.* Here, again, we need creative thinking. Some brand new way of testing is often called for.

8. *Select the soundest ways to test.* Having decided on how best to test, let's keep on being judicial and verify what seems to have been proved.

9. *Imagine all possible contingencies.* Even though our final solution has been corroborated by experiment, we might well envision what might happen as a result of its adoption. For example, every military strategy has to be finally processed on the basis of what the enemy may do.

10. *Decide on the final answer.* To do this right we must

weigh all the pros and cons. And, of course, this calls for nothing but the coldest judgment.

All of that nets down to this: When it comes to thinking, we should try to act as if we were two people—at one time, a thinker-upper; at another time a judge. Figuratively speaking, just as the voltage of electricity can be stepped up by alternating current, so we can step up our mental power by alternating our thought processes.

TOPICS

1. "The creative process does not end with an idea—it only starts with an idea." Do you agree? Discuss.
2. What preparatory steps should be taken to facilitate evaluation?
3. "Since they know more about their ideas than anyone else, the members of the brainstorm panel are the logical ones to perform the final screening process." Do you agree? Discuss.
4. What might be the danger of screening out the far-fetched ideas too quickly? Discuss.
5. What is the most worthwhile method of verifying the choice of an idea for possible adoption? Discuss.

EXERCISES

1. Select the most "far-fetched" idea from a recent brainstorm session and through further creative attack develop it into a more workable solution.
2. Think up ways in which panel leaders could gather more post-session ideas.
3. Brainstorm a community problem. Then present the best ideas to the proper authority with your recommendations as to testing.
4. Small businesses by the hundreds fail every year. Select one of such and think up ways the owner might have pre-tested his chances for success.

5. Conduct an experiment in your household. Think up a new idea to present to your wife, husband, or parents. Before presenting the idea, list all the possible objections that might be raised. Then think up an answer to each objection. Then present the idea and find out how many additional objections were raised.

REFERENCES

Air Force Personnel Newsletter, "Problem Solving Techniques." December 1955, pp. 12–13.

Chemical Digest, "Adventures in Imagination." Number 2, 1955.

Chemical Digest, "Tomorrow Is in Creative Minds." Number 2, 1955.

Chemical Week, "New Creativity Gambits: How Management Can Fish for Dollar Ideas." July 23, 1955.

Factory Management and Maintenance, "How to Make Good Ideas Come Easy." Vol. 114, Number 3, March 1956, pp. 84–90.

Foreman's Letter, "Applied Imagination." National Foremen's Institute, December 5, 1955.

General Food's News, "Brainstorming." November 1955, pp. 3–4.

GILMORE, FORREST E., *How to Invent.* Houston. Gulf Publishing Company, 1959.

GOODMAN, WALTER, "Brainstorming." *The New Republic.* February 20, 1956, pp. 8–10.

HARVARD, Critical study entitled "Imagination—Undeveloped Resource." Prepared under direction of Professor George F. Doriot, 1955.

HEIDBREDER, E. F., "Reasons Used in Solving Problems." *Journal of Experimental Psychology.* August 1927, pp. 397–414.

LARSON, J. W., "Products of More Creative Thinking Sought by Society." *Dallas Times Herald.* Sec. 8, February 19, 1956, p. 2.

Monitor, The, "Brainstorming." Associated Industries of New York State, Inc., January 1956, pp. 5–28.

PARNES, SIDNEY J., *Instructor's Manual For Semester Courses in Creative Problem-Solving* (Including Adaptations for Abbreviated Courses, Integrated Courses, Institutes, and Conferences). Buffalo. Creative Education Foundation, 1959.

Reader's Digest, "Brainstorming for Ideas." April 1956, pp. 137–138.

Stillman, Donald G., "Creative Problem Solving." The Clarkson Letter. Clarkson College of Technology, April 1956.

Thompson, A. Stewart, Jr., "Brainstorming to Success." *The Business Quarterly.* Spring 1956, pp. 47–52.

Thompson, A. Stewart, Jr., "How To Spark an Idea." *Supervisory Management.* American Management Association, January 1956, pp. 42–44.

Wall Street Journal. December 5, 1955, p. 1.

Williams, Frank E., *Foundations of Creative Problem Solving.* Frank E. Williams, San Jose State College, 1960.

Chapter XV

Devices designed to help activate idea-production

THIS AND FOUR subsequent chapters will mainly deal with tactical devices which can activate idea-production, especially in individual effort.

But, first, here's an outline of some other methods that have been devised to stimulate idea-production in problem-solving.

THE GORDON METHOD: In William J. J. Gordon's "Operational Creativity," the group discussion first explores every conceivable aspect of the broadest possible approach to the problem. For example, if a new can opener is to be devised, the Gordon group will discuss openness. The group would first discuss all possible meanings of the word, and all possible examples of openness in physical things, in nature, etc. This process tends to reveal unusual approaches which would not ordinarily be associated with the problem of devising a new can opener. Later in the session, the group explores and develops approaches thus uncovered.

For further information about the Gordon method write to William J. J. Gordon of Cambridge, Massachusetts.

ATTRIBUTE-LISTING: The previous chapter discussed check-lists of criteria. Subsequent chapters will discuss check-lists of idea-spurring questions.

Another check-list method of idea-stimulation is that of "Attribute-Listing," developed by Professor Robert P. Crawford. The problem-solver lists the various attributes of an object or idea. He then turns his attention specifically to each one of these attributes, using them as a check-list to force him to look at all aspects of the problem. For example, if we were to consider the attributes of the usual wooden-handle screwdriver, we might list such items as (1) Round (2) Steel shank (3) Wooden handle, riveted thereon (4) Wedge-shaped end for engaging slot (5) Manually operated (6) Torque provided by twisting action.

To devise a better screwdriver, we could then focus on each of these attributes separately. For example: The round shank could be changed to a hexagonal shank, so that a wrench could be used to increase the torque; the wooden handle could become a plastic handle, etc. Many variations could thus be thought up in regard to each of the attributes.

For further information about Attribute-Listing write to Professor Robert P. Crawford, P.O. Drawer 1231, Lincoln 1, Nebraska.

FORCED RELATIONSHIPS: Charles S. Whiting defines his "Forced Relationships" as "techniques for inducing original ideas which rely upon the creation of a forced relationship between two or more normally unrelated products or ideas as the starting point for the idea-generation process." One example of this method involves consideration of each idea on a list as associated with each other idea on the list.

In illustrating how to produce new product ideas for a manufacturer of office equipment, Mr. Whiting lists the following items the company already manufactures: Desk, Chair, Desk lamp, Filing cabinet, Bookcase. The first relationship to be considered would be between the desk and the chair. From this starting point, the ideator would seek to start a chain of free associations which might lead to new product ideas. A number of suggestions might arise such as calling for a combined unit, for storing or recessing a chair in the desk, etc.

As to relationship between desk and desk lamp, most of the ideas would probably concern various ways to integrate the desk lamp into the design of the desk—such as recessed desk lamps and lamps that could be adjusted by pushbutton. Later evaluation would determine which, if any, of these ideas might deserve further consideration.

For further information about the Forced-Relationship method write to Charles S. Whiting, Creative Training Associates, P.O. Box 913, Grand Central Station, New York 17, New York.

MORPHOLOGICAL ANALYSIS: This method pertains to analysis of structure. Once the structure is analyzed, forced-relationship techniques are used in order to produce countless idea possibilities.

Dr. Fritz Zwicky and Dr. Myron S. Allen are two of the scientists who are outstanding in this procedure. Dr. Parnes simplifies morphological analysis for his students by applying this process to the non-technical problem of developing a sales promotion campaign for a downtown candy shop. In this case, three of the independent variables would be: (1) The occasion or appeal for the promotion (2) The types of prospects (3) The medium or method of informing.

"We could think up about 10 ideas under each of these three headings," says Dr. Parnes. "In other words, about 10 occasions or appeals for a promotion, about 10 kinds of prospects, and about 10 media or methods of informing.

"Each idea under 'occasion or appeal' can then be related to each 'type-of-prospect' idea and to each 'medium-or-method-of-informing' idea. With 10 ideas in each of the three lists, 1,000 possible combinations or specific ideas could thus be produced."

In this case, for simplification purposes, Dr. Parnes uses only three variables. However, there might be any number of independent variables which could be cross-related and thus converted into many more ideas or approaches.

Dr. Parnes sums up by saying, "It is obvious that the more imagination we use in thinking up the list of independent variables and in thinking up ideas under each independent variable, the more possible combinations we can conceive by means of morphological analysis."

Those wishing further to investigate the Morphological method should write to Dr. Myron S. Allen, President, Technical Service Research, Inc., 4701 Village Road, Long Beach 8, California.

2. *Making a start, note-making and check-lists*

Regardless of procedural method, the principle of deferment-of-judgment can do most to augment idea-production. This is true of individual effort and team effort as well as group collaboration.

Imagination can likewise be activated by the conscious use of several devices, sometimes called "techniques." These will be set forth in the next five chapters.

One of the basic devices is to *make a start*. To shove off on a creative voyage is not so easy—our brains are so prone to drift. As William James pointed out, "In the dim background of our mind we know what we ought to be doing, but somehow we cannot start. Every moment we expect the spell to break, but it continues, pulse after pulse, and we float with it."

A handyman learned that I, when over 50, had started

to paint in oils, and he showed me some of his pencil sketches which, to my eye, revealed real talent. He was a widower and lived alone. I felt that painting could brighten his life, so I gave him a complete equipment, plus a book on how to get started. A few months later I asked him, "How are you getting along with your painting, Frank?" He replied that he had not "started yet." And even two years later, I found he had yet to squeeze a tube or pick up a brush.

Professionals know that they can't create unless they make a start. The favorite device of melody writers is to sit down at a piano and cold-bloodedly get going by picking a tune, any tune. George Meyer, when asked how he turned out *For Me and My Gal,* snapped back, "I just sat down and went to work." Most authors find that their best starting device is to collar themselves at a set hour each day and chain themselves to their creative tasks. In Phoenix, after a meeting at which we both spoke, I asked Clarence Budington Kelland how he could produce as much as he does. He confessed that he would turn out hardly anything if he did not force himself each morning after breakfast to start tapping his typewriter, whether he felt in the mood or not.

Another simple but effective way to induce imaginative effort is to *make notes.* For the purpose of moving our minds, pencils can serve as crowbars. Note-taking helps in several ways. It empowers association, it stores rich fuel that otherwise would trickle out through our "forgettery"; but, above all, note-taking of itself induces a spirit of effort. It is amazing how few of us take advantage of this device. One week I went through six conferences in which, all told, about 100 men took part. Only three of them put down any notes.

Robert Updegraff wrote a book about William H. Johns whom he called *Obvious Adams.* Although Mr. Johns was never regarded as "brilliant," the ideas he laboriously brought to American business made his creative record shine. His secret weapons were pencils; and they were so important to him that he went to great ends to choose them. He even had some of them made to his personal specifications.

Then, too, Mr. Johns considered the usual memo book too hard to pull out and too cumbersome to use. Likewise, he regarded the usual 3 x 5 cards as not "reachable" enough. So he designed a form of his own, 8″ long and only 2½″ wide, made of cardboard stiff enough to stand up and almost stick out of his inside pocket.

My own habits of note-taking might easily mark me as a "nut." Even while listening to a sermon, I sometimes surreptitiously make notes. Sitting in the dark on a veranda, I have often pulled out my card and scribbled without seeing what I wrote. While playing golf, I carry no note cards, but, whenever I hear or think of something that might lead to an idea, I put it down on my score card. Once, when without a score card, I caught and saved an idea on the inside cover of a match folder.

The use of *check-lists* can likewise help creative thinking. A would-be writer of articles, for instance, could well look over index after index of many magazines. In a few hours he could probably bring to his mind at least 50 ideas for possible subjects, none exactly the same as covered by the indices. And there are scores of other such check-lists by which we can consciously prod imagination. One of these pump-primers is the classified section of the telephone directory. I have found this to be especially helpful when faced with a problem of vocational guidance.

Clement Kieffer, in charge of window displays for a big store, has won more prizes for ideas than any man in his line. In addition to cash awards, he has garnered over 350 medals and cups. He has 33 windows to fill each week. It is his stint to think up at least one new idea every day of the month including Sundays. For his "check-list" he uses a big box into which he has thrown 3,000 idea-starters in the form of clippings and other printed matter, together with notes and sketches he has dashed off himself. He finds this grab-bag to be his best priming device.

3. *Setting deadlines and quotas*

Many creative people are driven by automatic deadlines. Most columnists face one such whip each day. A minister's weekly deadline badgers him into creative action. At Sunday dinner we are likely to say "Wasn't that a wonderful sermon this morning?" We seldom stop to think how tremendous was the creative effort that went into that message. The basic idea of each sermon—just that alone—requires more creative juice each week than most of us generate in a month. And, beyond the theme, some 50 other ideas have to be thought up to give power and sparkle to each sermon.

A deadline was the turning-point in Walter Chrysler's career. As a boy apprentice in the Union Pacific shops, he loved locomotives, and learned the purpose of every bolt and nut. One day an engine pulled in with a cracked cylinder-head. The superintendent of motor power called young Chrysler into his office. "Boy," he said, "we haven't any other locomotive to take the place of this one. This has got to be fixed in two hours. Can you do it?" After he had it fixed, Chrysler remarked; "Believe me, that was some whale of a job. If I *hadn't* said I could do it in two hours, I wouldn't have put in so much mental sweat, and we would have *failed.* I got myself in a spot where I had to finish it on time. And I did."

So another device we can use to spur imaginative effort is to *set a deadline*—even to thrust one upon ourselves—even to the point of issuing an I.O.U. by promising in writing that we will submit our ideas by such-and-such a time. Our wills are apt to bow to such self-commitments. When we fix deadlines, we intensify our emotional power because we expose ourselves to the fear of falling down.

Another device is to *set a quota* of ideas to be thought up. Suppose we first give ourselves a stint of only five ideas. In thinking up those five, others will occur; and the first thing we know we will be on our way to 25. And the more ideas, the more likely it will be that one or more of them will provide the answer we seek.

For example, a chairwoman of a church supper, alone in her boudoir, could write down at least 10 suggestions to make the event more successful. She could then say to her committee: 'Let's think up everything we can to liven up this supper. Here are 10 ideas of mine. Gertrude, I want you to come to our next meeting with a list of 10 ideas for the entertainment part. Adele, I am going to ask you to do the same thing on food. And Maude, there must be lots of ways to better the service—you bring in 10 ideas on that. And Kay, you have a taste for making things look attractive—will you take the subject of decorations and bring in 10 ideas on that? Lighting can do a lot to liven up a supper, so I am going to ask you, Joan, to bring in 10 ideas on that." Together with her own 10 ideas, that chairwoman could probably end up with 60 or 70, from which her committee could then choose the most usable.

Fluency is becoming a common term among psychologists; and the value of it is receiving an ever greater recognition. But it is admittedly not easy to think up more and more alternative ideas. To keep myself going to that end I thought up a trick to play on myself. Having found that the first alternatives come easily, I wanted an incentive to make me strive for the next and the next and the next. So I wrote out a table of prices, all imaginary, of course. By this calculation, my first idea would be worth one cent, my second two cents, my third four cents—and so on, doubling the price for each alternative. Thus, when I list my 24th idea, I look at my table and see how much, on that basis, my 25th idea would be worth. Its theoretical value would be $167,772. This sounds puerile; but it tends to dramatize the worthwhileness of reaching for still another idea.

4. *Setting a time—picking a place*

If we set aside a definite period for creative thinking, we can best lure the muse. This rule should govern those who are in business. "We should take time out for thinking up ideas—*nothing else,*" said Don Sampson. Too many business men tackle routine first, usually because it is easier. Sampson rightly recommends mornings for thinking, afternoons for routine.

But we can also use our nights for creative chores. We can go to bed to awaken our imaginations. A bed can also be a good place for creative thinking, even when we take to it to go to sleep. By sleeping on ideas, we often hatch out better ones. This can be far more productive if, before we turn out the lights, we actually jot down the best thoughts we have been able to dream up while awake. The very making of these notes tends to free our minds and thus enable us to fall asleep sooner. And those notes tend also to engrave our minds with thoughts which may lead to worthwhile ideas, even while we sleep.

In the dark hours when our army first landed in North Africa, a great help was the series of emergency landing fields which our men were able to set up almost overnight—magic carpets smooth enough for planes to take off from and to land upon. These landing-field mats were the brain-child of Walter E. Irving. When I asked him how, when and where he got his best ideas, he paid tribute to beds as creative cradles.

"The bed, the bedside pad and pencil," said Mr. Irving, "are great aids to ideas and schemes. Only last night I scrawled over four sheets of paper in the pitch dark. But my notes were easily deciphered this morning, and they contain possible solutions to a current problem. A few months ago in a Washington hotel I awakened from a dream about 2:30 A.M. Then and there I sketched a simple idea that I believe will soon start an important new product. Had I just turned over and gone to sleep, I am sure I never would have thought of it again." Another who believes that bed can be a hothouse for ideas is Alfred Hull. The creator of more new types of electron tubes than any other inventor, Hull has said that most of his best ideas have crept up on him "in the middle of the night."

Insomnia is a vicious circle. When we find we cannot get to sleep, we begin to worry over our wakefulness. We try harder to get to sleep, and new fears flit through our squirrel-cage. Instead of counting sheep, we might well select something for which we want ideas, and then let our minds roam around that hunting-ground. It can be fun. It may be profitable. It may bring sleep. And, strangely enough, insomnia may even intensify our creativity. According to Ernest Dimnet, unless sleeplessness saps us to the point of exhaustion, it can sometimes make our imaginations more than normally lucid.

We can likewise make dates with ourselves to combine creative thinking with walking. Since the days of Thoreau, hiking in lonely places has been a favorite way to court ideas. I asked an M.I.T. graduate: "Who was the most creative of all your professors?" He said Doctor Warren K. Lewis. I asked if he knew whether Doctor Lewis consciously did things to make himself more creative. "I don't really know," said my cautious friend, "but he is a great man for hiking through the woods. It is common belief that he does this partly for exercise, but mainly as a help to his creative thinking."

If you know what ideas you are hunting, a lonely walk may help a lot. But if you have no set creative aim, and want only to expose your mind to ideas, a walk through busy marts may likewise help. I asked a friend of mine why he wore a cane when visiting New York. "I come to New York to get ideas," said he, "I don't want to think about my own business while here, so I carry a cane to make me feel that I am not working. My grindstone back home tends to close my mind. Here, with wide-open mind, I can walk along Fifth Avenue and Broadway and can pick up ideas which will help me when I discard my cane and become a manufacturer again."

Nothing could be more distracting than a stroll along the Atlantic City boardwalk on an Easter Sunday. And yet, a retailer friend of mine goes there every Easter, with no set aim as to what he is looking for, but with the confidence that if he keeps his mind open while there he will drink in ideas which will suggest other ideas. He regards that Sunday as one of his most valuable business days.

Alan Ward makes a date with himself to think up while washing dishes on Saturday mornings after breakfast. I have even dated myself to attack a creative task while driving. One morning I woke up to the fact that a certain problem needed immediate solution. I determined to brainstorm that problem during my hour's drive to work. On the way I saw a lad signaling for a hitchhike. I hesitated, but stopped; he got in and I said: "If you don't mind, please don't talk because I have to think." Since the road was straight and the traffic sparse, I could concentrate as well as if in my office. At about halfway, I suddenly got the wanted idea, pulled off the road, took out a pad and wrote an outline.

Starting off again, I said to my young passenger: "Now you can talk; but first, don't you think I'm kinda crazy?" "No," he replied. Our chat then revealed that he was just finishing high school at the top of his class and planned to become a newspaper reporter while, at the same time, studying law at night. That helped me understand why he had not thought me "nuts."

As a rule, offices are better for judicial functioning than for creative thinking. One man I know has found he can ponder creative problems far better by staying home in the morning. Once when I faced a hard creative task, I went to an inn over 100 miles away. Not only was I uninterrupted—not only did I get away from routine—but, because I had made such effort to go so far solely to engage in creative effort, my imagination seemed to work far better. The very taking of that trip tended to sharpen my creative wits.

5. *The "ivory tower" fallacy*

America's architecture is being enriched with more and more temples of research. These laboratories are the ivory towers of science. They provide not only equipment but also a climate ideal for concentrated contemplation. And yet, creative scientists would fall short if they created only while in their ivory towers. For example, Doctor Suits of General Electric has stated that he gets some of his best ideas in bed, while flying from plant to plant, or "while staring out of a Pullman window." A. J. Musselman claimed that he gave birth to his coaster-brake idea while speeding down a Rocky Mountain steep—not in a limousine, but on a runaway bicycle.

That tiled tower known as the bathroom is where creative minds seem to work best. A good long shower or a hot tub often induces ideas. One reason is that while we bathe we are shut off from distracting influences.

Beards are about the only advantage men have over women in the field of creativity. You often hear idea-workers confess: "That came to me while I was shaving." Doctor Suits recently told of one of his associates who had made two important discoveries. The basic idea for each of these came to the man while removing his morning beard. Shaving, like bathing, provides the same solitude, the same soothing sound of running water, and the same sense of well-being. Still another reason why shaving and creative thinking often go together is that the mind is usually more creative in the early hours. "The muses love the morning," said Erasmus.

Woodpiles likewise make good ivory towers. Elbert Hubbard was an advocate of chopping for the purpose of inducing ideas. Recently a creative researcher said that the best idea he ever had came to him while chopping ice from his front steps.

While at work on a creative quest, an atmosphere of reverie may intensify the creative flame. Many find that some of their best ideas come to them while in church. Others claim that attending concerts kindles their creativity. Some think the ideal ivory tower is the stern of a boat. There is something about sailing that lends itself to continuous contemplation. Doctor E. F. W. Alexanderson, the inventor, has testified that some of his best ideas have been plucked out of the blue while placidly sailing his sloop.

Jefferson lived 100 miles from Washington. At Monticello you can still see the buggy he drove back and forth between his plantation and the capital when he did not go on horseback. With a horse that needed no guidance, with a pace that made for tranquillity, with no stop signs to interrupt—what an ivory tower his one-man buggy must have been!

How seldom you see anybody really working on a plane or train! You occasionally catch someone reading a report, or studying figures. And a few of those who just sit and stare may also be working their minds for all we know. But it is unusual to see anybody active at creative work. And yet one of the classics of creative writing was perfected on a train—Lincoln's Gettysburg speech. And General George Marshall wrote his best spech in longhand, high above the Atlantic, while flying back from Moscow.

Even while waiting for a train or plane we can indulge in ideation. I am no mechanic, but one night when stuck on a railroad platform with an hour to kill, I gave myself a specific mechanical problem which had arisen that morning. Up and down the platform I strolled, playing with this puzzle. Aboard the train I made sketches of some of the ideas I had thought up, and at breakfast the next morning I made another sketch of another idea, and this turned out to be patentable.

Artists need ivory towers in the form of studios, and most writers isolate themselves in some kind of hide-out. And yet most artists and writers will admit that they think up their ideas here, there and everywhere. Edgar Lustgarten, the English author, works without timetable and without ivory tower. According to his publisher, "He never stops. He writes anywhere and everywhere—in pubs, on buses, even walking down the street."

Samuel Johnson may not have been entirely right when he said that any man could write anywhere, if he would only set himself to it "doggedly enough." But it is true that although artists and writers may require ivory towers, ideas can be created almost everywhere.

TOPICS

1. How does note-making help empower imagination? Discuss.
2. Why are check-lists helpful to ideation?
3. What is accomplished by giving ourselves a "deadline" on a creative job? Discuss.
4. What are the advantages of setting idea quotas? Discuss.
5. Why is walking favored as conducive to activity? Discuss.

EXERCISES

1. Make a check-list of the items and entertainment features you would include in a teen-age Fourth of July party.
2. With no advisor to lean upon, what steps would you take to de-

termine the vocations in which you would be most likely to succeed?

3. List six non-military uses to which you might put the coldbar insulated clothing developed by the Army for Korean winters.
4. Think of three devices you would employ to activate your imagination in writing a popular song.
5. What idea-starters could you list if you were to design a hat-rack for modern homes?

REFERENCES

CHORNESS, MAURY H., "Increasing Creativity in Problem-Solving Groups." *Journal of Communication.* 1958, pp. 16–23.

CRAWFORD, ROBERT P. *The Techniques of Creative Thinking.* New York. Hawthorn Books, Inc., 1954.

GABRIEL, H. W., *Techniques of Creative Thinking for Management.* Englewood Cliffs, N. J. Prentice-Hall, 1961.

GORDON, WILLIAM J. J., *Synectics.* New York. Harper & Brothers, 1961.

HEPNER, HARRY W., *Psychology Applied to Life and Work.* New York. Prentice-Hall, Inc., 1941.

"How to Use Idea Files; PI Questionnaire to 50 Advertising Managers." *Printers' Ink.* August 5, 1937, pp. 109–114.

MAUGHAM, W. SOMERSET, *A Writer's Notebook.* New York. Doubleday and Company, 1949.

MORRIS-JONES, D., "Ideal File—a First Aid Kit, not a Pulmotor." *Printers' Ink.* December 9, 1926.

MUSSELMAN, MORRIS MCNEIL, *Wheels in His Head.* New York. McGraw-Hill Book Company, Inc. 1945.

OSBORN, ALEX F., *Supplementary Guide* (Suggestions for the Use of Topics and Exercises Called for in Revised Edition of Textbook, *Applied Imagination*). Buffalo. Creative Education Foundation, 1957.

PAINE, ALBERT BIGELOW, *Mark Twain.* New York. Harper & Brothers, 1912.

STEVENSON, A. R., JR., "Development of New Products." *Mechanical Engineering*. September 1939, pp. 661–664.

TAYLOR, ROBERT LEWIS, *The Running Pianist*. New York. Doubleday and Company, 1950.

WALLAS, GRAHAM, *The Art of Thought*. New York. Harcourt, Brace and Company, 1926.

WHITING, CHARLES S., *Creative Thinking*. New York. Reinhold Publishing Corporation, 1958.

YOUNG, JAMES W., *A Technique for Producing Ideas*. Chicago. Advertising Publications, Inc., 1940.

Chapter XVI

Questions as spurs to ideation

THIS AND THREE succeeding chapters will outline about 75 idea-spurring questions. These are usable in individual ideation. And in group brainstorming they can be of value to the panel leader for use as hints—as directions toward which the panelists can point their imaginations.

Questions can also be used fruitfully in the pre-processing of a problem for brainstorming. Take the question of "How to make a better car?" That is too general for efficient attack. To narrow our target, we might ask questions like, "What to add to a car?" . . . "What to eliminate?" etc.

Under elimination we might ask more specifically, "What part of the electrical system could be dispensed with?" . . . "What part of the fuel system?" Or, even more specifically, "How could the carburetor be eliminated?" This very problem happens to be one which was taken on by the Rand research organization in Cleveland.

The *question* technique has long been recognized as a way to induce imagination. Professors who have sought to make their teaching more creative have often employed this device. For example, when Walter Dill Scott was at Carnegie Institute of Technology, he was known for the hypothetical questions he asked students—even weird questions like: "What if we had eyes both in the front and the back of our heads?" . . . "What if we could swim more easily than we could walk?"

In practical problem-solving we can give *conscious guidance* to our thinking by asking ourselves questions. The U. S. Army has successfully applied this method to both judicial and creative cogitation. During the last war, the question technique brought about far better thinking in the operations of all arsenals, motor-maintenance shops and many other war-production installations. "In only 50 installations which I happen to know about," said Bayard Pope, "that technique resulted in the saving of 6,000,000 man-hours per year."

This is the way that technique works: First you isolate the subject or problem you want to think about. Then you ask a series of questions about each step in that subject or problem. Here are the queries which the officers had to ask themselves: (1) *Why* is it necessary? (2) *Where* should it be done? (3) *When* should it be done? (4) *Who* should do it? (5) *What* should be done? (6) *How* should it be done?

A creative problem usually calls for far more questions, and necessarily looser questions, than the Army manualized. Imagination has to be guided by stabs such as "What *about* . . . ?" and "What *if* . . . ?" And always it must be prodded with "What *else?*" and again "What *else?*" By bombarding our imaginations with such queries we can pile up a quantity of ore in the form of all kinds of ideas—good, bad and indifferent. Out of that ore, our own judgment, or the judgment of others, can refine gold in the form of good ideas.

Even in preparation for, and analysis of, a creative problem, self-questioning can often bring us nearer to solution. In those earlier phases of procedure, we should think up the queries which could put our imagination on the right track. And even in evaluation, we can best assay our tentative solutions by thinking up the right questions to apply to our findings—questions such as: "Can this be tested?" . . . "What kind of tests would be best?"

A research project based on the application of questions to problem-solving was conducted at Leland Stanford University by Dr. Donald W. Taylor and Dr. William L. Faust and reported in the *Journal of Experimental Psychology*. The technique used was essentially that of the "Twenty Questions" game.

As Doctor Frank Kingdon has said, "Questions are the creative acts of intelligence."

2. *What other uses?*

When it comes to piling up hypotheses, one basic question has to do with other uses. This is so important that in his book entitled *Psychology of Invention in the Mathematical Field*, Jacques Hadamard referred to "two kinds of invention" and commented as follows:

"One consists, a goal being given, in finding the means to reach it, so that the mind goes from the goal to the means, from the question to the solution. The other consists, on the contrary, in discovering a fact, then imagining what it could be useful for, so that, this time, mind goes from the means to the goal; the answer appears to us before the question. Now, paradoxical as it seems, that second kind of invention is the more general one and becomes more and more so as science advances."

Under the heading of "other uses," there are many questions with which we can prime our imaginations—questions such as: "In what *new* ways could we use this as *is*?" . . . "How could this be *modified* to fit a new use?" . . . "What else could be made from this?"

"In what other ways could this be used?" Sometimes this trail leads to re-designing a product so as to give it extra functions. Edward Barcalo had long made conventional pillows. He thought up a new one called the "6-Way," a triangular cushion for reading in bed, for sitting up in bed, and for four other purposes.

"In what other products could my material be used?" This is an obvious question to ask ourselves when we have a certain material and want to widen its market. Doctor George Washington Carver thought up over 300 useful articles in which peanuts could be used. For the home alone, he worked up 105 different ways to prepare peanuts for the table.

Every manufacturer is constantly on the hunt for other things to make out of his own basic material. This has been particularly true of rubber. Out of thousands of ideas considered, here are a few that have been turned down by one big company: rubber bed-blankets, rubber bathtubs, rubber bathtub covers, rubber curbstones, rubber clothespins, rubber birdhouses, rubber doorknobs, rubber coffins, and rubber gravestones.

The success of most synthetic materials is based on thinking up new ways in which other people can use the product. Du Pont's neoprene has been built up into great volume through thousands of new applications, some of which could come only from shooting wild. For example, a toy-maker makes a chocolate-flavored bone out of neoprene for dogs to chew upon. A doll-maker has covered some of his creations with a magic skin of neoprene, and in a color so natural that a child thinks of it as a real baby. The list is endless

—a lamb with a coat like wool; a dog named Poochy; baby chicks; a whale that spouts water; a whale-like submarine; a ship with three smokestacks.

Likewise with cellophane and nylon. The latter, for example, has already displaced catgut on most tennis rackets. Fishing-lines of nylon have become more and more popular. Every woman knows about nylon clothesline. Huge hawsers and mammoth grommets are made of nylon, too.

Along about 1935 I happened to be in on the start on Fiberglas. Our big creative problem was, "To what uses could glass thread be put?" We dreamed up hundreds of applications; but hundreds more have since been thought up. And through these other-use ideas, that tiny thread of spun glass has been developed into a great industry. One use none of us foresaw was for fishing rods, which a manufacturer later developed by imbedding glass threads in a plastic binder. Nor did any of us pile up enough alternatives to hit upon by far the largest ultimate use of Fiberglas, which came when Hitler forced us to build a two-ocean Navy, and Fiberglas was adopted as a new and better insulation for our warships.

"To what use can waste be put?" Along this trail, the piling up of alternatives is particularly important. America's packing industry has been built on ingenuity in finding new uses for almost every by-product except the "pig's squeal."

Likewise in the steel industry. Slag used to be a costly waste. Now it is salvaged for ballast in railroad beds, for making cement, and for processing into building blocks. The slag from the Tennessee plant near Birmingham is so rich in phosphorus content that it is now packaged and sold throughout the South as a soil conditioner.

"What use could be made of those gases?" was the question some steel man must have asked himself long ago as he stared at the ugly fumes arising from his stacks. What a development that started! Today, through the use of by-product coke ovens, those gases are saved and are the source of literally thousands of products in the chemical and drug field. While most people think in terms of 50,000 end products from such salvaging, a friend of mine in the steel business believes that as many as 500,000 more uses may be developed in the future.

What to do with rejects is another creative challenge. Often it is easy to sell them as seconds. Ingenuity can sometimes provide a more profitable answer. And what to do with scrap likewise calls for imagination. L. A. Conley of B. F. Goodrich saw pieces of surgical tubing being thrown into the waste barrel. "Why not cut them into rubber bands of the size and width used by the millions to hold small items together?" he asked. Conley got $150 for his new-use suggestion. The profit his company made from that idea was velvet—velvet scraped from stuff which otherwise was worthless.

And then, too, there are cases where a new use may turn a dud into a triumph. George Westinghouse thought up about 400 inventions, of which the only dud was a rotary engine. But he refused to throw it away. Instead, he added a new invention and started another business—simply by turning his useless engine into a new and better water-meter.

3. *Other uses as* is?

"To what other uses could this be put?" is a good question to ask of our imagination in regard to a thing, a thought or a talent. For by adding uses we can often add value. Then, too, by piling up alternatives by way of other uses, a still *better* use is likely to come to light.

Thinking up additional uses can often widen markets for old products. A well-known scouring pad got its start in the kitchen sink. A new tire-cleaning use then opened up another market—a big one, too, consisting of 20,000,000 white-walled tires.

New uses for telephones have likewise opened up gold mines. A transcribed record now announces the correct time and the latest weather report. For this additional use, the New York Telephone Company charged a nickel per call and added $2,000,000 per year to its revenue.

The newest use of telephones is for inspirational messages. This was started in 1955 by the Y.M.C.A. of Baltimore. You dial Mulberry 5-3510 and you receive a 28-second message based on the Bible, secular writings, or both. In the first 90 days, 500,000 such messages were transmitted. This "other-use" for the telephone has since spread from coast to coast.

Sometimes the very life of a new product depends on thinking up many new uses. Helicopters might have turned out to be museum pieces, unless someone had thought up enough new jobs for them to do—jobs which they can do best, such as the new use of patrolling high-tension lines over the mountains.

Scotch Tape has grown from a little speciality into a great industry. Its manufacturer created a list of 325 unduplicated uses. Tom, Dick and Harry thought up a lot more. I happened to be the beneficiary of one of these ideas. The side of my face became partially paralyzed as the result of an icy draft. A nerve specialist in Canada told me that only time could cure my ailment, but that I could help myself meanwhile with Scotch Tape. He showed me how, before retiring, to push my face into proper shape and then strap it there.

Some great advances in science have come from finding

a new use for an old thing. In London, along about 1620, a woman was having a hard time delivering a baby. A doctor named Chamberlain appeared with something under his coat. He covered it with a sheet and quickly brought forth the baby. For nearly a century, the doctor's "iron hands" were kept a secret within the Chamberlain family—and yet similar tongs were on almost every hearthside. According to an obstetrician friend of mine, "Forceps have done more to shorten labor-pains and to preserve life than any other surgical gadget ever thought up."

4. *Scientific progress through new uses*

Lord Lister suspected Louis Pasteur as more or less guilty of boondoggling in trying to find a way to make wine stay sweet. But this work of Pasteur's led Lister to wonder whether a more important use could be found for Pasteur's findings. Specifically, he asked himself: "If germs ruin flavor, could germs be the cause of so many unexplained fatalities in surgery?" This *other* use of Pasteur's new theory led to proof that germs did invade wounds; and this truth became the key to the antiseptic surgery which immortalized Lister's name.

Roentgen was indulging in pure science when he hit upon the X ray. He had no way of knowing what the ray was and that's why he called it "X." He had no *use* in view. It is said that he himself was surprised when he found how widely his discovery could be used—not only as a therapy in itself—but as eyes to enable the surgeon to look deep into the body before applying the knife.

In modern science, the alert researcher is ever on the lookout for ways to apply old principles and new principles to new uses. Management no longer looks at pure research as a waste of money. Many a "worthless" theory has been turned into a profitable improvement by asking and answering the question, "To what use could this be put?"

New uses sometimes lead to progressive changes in engineering a product. When the Corning Glass Works developed a stronger globe for railroad lanterns, a Corning researcher sought new uses for this new glass, and hit upon the idea of battery jars. One day in 1913 he cut the bottom off one of these jars, took it home to his wife and asked her to bake a cake. It was thus that glass began to be used for baking. This led to the question of still other uses. "How would it do for top-of-stove cooking?" was one of the questions asked. Doctor Eugene Sullivan, chief chemist at the time, decided that the ovenware glass was not strong enough to stand the heat of direct flame. Four years of experimentation followed. This included thousands of actual kitchen tests in which 18,000 pounds of potatoes were boiled and fried in experimental saucepans and skillets. Out of this came Flameware, with a brand new use for glass.

Most of us think of Koroseal as one kind of product that is always the same. The fact is, however, that in multiplying the uses for Koroseal there has been a vast progression in kinds of Koroseal. Doctor Waldo Semon, who had most to do with creating Koroseal, estimates that since 1926 over 10,000 rubberlike materials have been created in order to adapt the original product to new uses. The raw materials of the process are still limestone, coke and salt. The basic characteristics of the product are still the shedding of water, and insulation against electricity. But variation of product has had to go along hand-in-hand with multiplication of use.

Similar progression has marked the multiplication of uses for electric lamps. For many years, bulbs were solely for illumination. Then came the change in wave-length that led to duplicating the ultra-violet rays of the sun. Also came another change which gave us infra-red heat rays. But the creative researchers at Nela Park, headquarters of General Electric lamps, kept on the hunt for still other uses. One of them asked: "I wonder if we could find a wave-length that would kill germs without harming people?" This led to a new Germicidal Lamp, which successfully killed airborne bacteria. When the product was modified for this purpose there came the question, "*Where* could these lamps best be used?" Out of the alternatives thus piled up, came new uses for this same lamp in hospitals, schools, military barracks, doctors' waiting rooms, meat-coolers, hotel-kitchens and homes. Yes, even in hen-houses. On the Casler Poultry Farm in Ohio, within six weeks, 240 baby chicks grew 14 per cent heavier than 240 others in a control-pen without benefit of G-E Germicidal Lamps. Three times as many chicks died in the lampless house.

5. *Other uses for "other-use" questions*

The application of "other-use" questions has been explained in terms of things. But the same technique can be applied to thoughts, themes, principles—in fact to almost any subject.

For example, in a vocational problem, the key can be: "For what other uses would these aptitudes be best fitted?" Along this trail, imagination can help a lot in vocational guidance. Parents can well send their creative minds in this direction. For instance, a little girl in the house behind ours loves to make things with her hands. Every Thanksgiving the windows in her room are alive with turkeys she has cut out and crayoned. At Halloween the windows are plastered with pumpkins, and at Christmas they are gay with stars and bells. Her mother showed me a list she had worked out of the vocations in which her daughter could best use this talent, and toward which she might steer her.

In some cases, new uses for a talent just happen. Daniel M. Eisenberg set out to find two rich great-uncles with whom his family had lost touch. Although he searched for months he never located them. But what he did find was that he had a talent for turning up missing relatives of others. He asked himself, "How to use this talent?" That led to the idea of operating a "missing-persons" business. More than 65,000 wives have since paid him to find their husbands.

Having failed as a rancher, John Gast knew he had an artistic touch and drove himself to think up a way to use it. Among his musings came this thought: "Even a weed can be quite pretty when you look at it the right way. Dressed up, it might even become a thing of beauty." As an experiment, he silvered some eucalyptus and smoke-tree branches, and a Los Angeles department store snapped them up for window decorations. That started a lucrative career for Mr. Gast. It is said that he now makes $50,000 a year out of weeds which others find a nuisance. Although many of his materials come from California, his staff goes to Kansas for lotus-pads, to Florida for sea-oats, and to other distant points for many special items.

Mrs. Joseph Watson was a fair photographer. She saw a newspaper picture of three rats sprawled on a cat. She decided that the photo was faked. "Why can't I make just as interesting animal pictures that are *not* faked?" she asked herself. From that idea, Mrs. Watson built a hobby which has paid her well. Her first picture was a Shetland pony modeling a straw hat. She has successfully combined as many as 13 animals in one shot.

Ray Giles tells the tale of four young artists who found

their landscapes not quite good enough to sell. They decided to think up all the different ways in which they could use their skills. One became a well-paid painter of pictures on drums used in bands. Another specializes in clay models for museums. The third does well by painting faces on "character" dolls. The fourth now names his own price for portraits of dogs, cats and horses owned by people who love pets more than money.

"What *new* use?" . . . "What *other* use?" All of us have enough creative power to pile up alternatives galore by sending our imagination along this highway and into its many by-ways.

TOPICS

1. What are the six key words in the questions used by the Army to stimulate cogitation?
2. When thinking up new uses, what specific questions might help activate imagination in the right direction?
3. What if we had eyes both in front and in back of our heads? What advantages would this give us? Can you think of ways in which this result might be approximated?
4. With what product is the name of George Washington Carver associated, and in what directions did he apply creative thinking to increase its usefulness?
5. If a plane could fly backward as well as forward, what advantages would it have over conventional aircraft?

EXERCISES

1. What changes can you suggest in the dial of a timepiece to increase its usefulness either in general or for a specific purpose?
2. Suppose you were a manufacturer over-stocked with tooth brushes. For what uses (other than brushing teeth) might you try to market your surplus inventory?

3. What new and additional functions can you think of for a helicopter?
4. To what uses might the shells of cocoa beans be put?
5. For Scotch Tape, think up 10 uses you have never even heard of.

REFERENCES

BEVERIDGE, W. I. B., *The Art of Scientific Investigation.* New York. W. W. Norton and Company, 1950.

BORAAS, JULIUS, *Teaching to Think.* New York. Macmillan Company, 1922.

CANNON, W. B., *The Way of an Investigator.* New York. W. W. Norton and Company, 1945.

GREGORY, R., "Discovery and Invention." *Journal of the Royal Society of the Arts.* May 16, 1941, pp. 394–407.

HUMPHREY, GEORGE, "The Problem of the Direction of Thought." *British Journal of Psychology.* January 1940, pp. 183–195.

HUTCHINSON, E. D., *How to Think Creatively.* Nashville. Abingdon-Cokesbury Press, 1949.

INDUSTRIAL RELATIONS NEWS, *Creativity* (a bibliography). New York. 1958.

KINGSLEY, H. L., "Search: a Function Intermediate between Perception and Thinking." *Psychological Monograph, 163,* 1926.

OSBORN, ALEX F., "How to Hunt Ideas." *Society of Automotive Engineers Journal.* December, 1951, p. 19.

PORTERFIELD, AUSTIN L., *Creative Factors in Scientific Research.* Durham. Duke University Press, 1941.

TAYLOR, DONALD W. and FAUST, WILLIAM L., "Twenty Questions: Efficiency in Problem-Solving as a Function of Size of Group." *Journal of Experimental Psychology.* November 1952, pp. 360–368.

WYMAN, W. I., "The Classification of Inventive Ideas." *Scientific Monthly.* September 1938, pp. 211–219.

Chapter XVII

Adaptation, modification, and substitution

In any search for ideas it pays to pursue all possible parallels, thus abiding by Aristotle's first law of associationism—similarity. To direct one's imagination along those lines, self-queries like these can be helpful: "What is like this?" . . . "What ideas does it suggest?" . . . "Does past offer parallel?" . . . "What else could be adapted?" . . . "Is there something similar I could copy?"

That last question may sound like an approval of plagiarism and infringement. Not so. Unquestionably it is wrong, both legally and morally, to steal another's creation to the damage of the creator; but it is legitimate to take a lead from what someone else has thought up. The sanction of this is good public policy; for without such adaptation, there would be far fewer ideas of benefit to the people. It is a common and inescapable practice. As Wendell Phillips pointed out: "In every matter that relates to invention, to use, or beauty, or form, we are borrowers." This is evidenced by the fact that the patent office is full of overlapping inventions.

Thomas A. Edison could not be accused of idea piracy. And yet, he advised as follows: "Make it a habit to keep on the lookout for novel and interesting ideas that others have used successfully. Your idea needs to be original only in its adaptation to the problem you are working on."

There are many cases where ideas are almost bodily transplanted. The "Book-of-the-Month" became the "Fruit-of-the-Month" and the "Candy-of-the-Month." Then came the "Hobby-of-the-Month," in which the first selection offered was an assortment of sharks' teeth for jewelry-making hobbyists.

More often the adaptation is but partial. Baseball, for instance, was adapted from the English sport of "rounders." Football came form rugby. Basketball is about the only game originated in America. Doctor James Naismith deliberately set out to devise a brand-new sport that could be played in a gym. The basket, however, was not a product of his imagination, but was an accident. The janitor, when asked to get some boxes, couldn't find any; so he came back with peachbaskets instead. Hence the name and the goals for the game.

It is well-nigh impossible for writers not to adapt. A novelist is forced to use a well-used basic plot, James N. Young counted 101 of these. Goethe claimed there were only 36. Willa Cather said, "There are only two or three human stories, and they go on repeating themselves as fiercely as if they had never happened before." Don Marquis held that there is only one basic plot. "The world hath just one tale to tell," wrote he, "and it is very old—a little tale, a simple tale, a tale that's easy told: 'There was a youth in Babylon who greatly loved a maid!' "

Shakespeare picked up a Danish legend and shaped it into *Hamlet*. He did not merely copy. He thought up enough ideas to make a brilliant drama out of a relatively dull legend.

As to humor, George Lewis of the Gag Writers Institute claimed that in every "new" joke he could detect the skeleton of one of six basic gags. That's all there are, according to him—every new joke is merely a new version of an old one.

"Whose style can I emulate?" is a question some writers ask of themselves. Robert L. May contemplated the perennial success of *The Night Before Christmas* and in the same style and meter wrote *Rudolph, the Red-Nosed Reindeer.* In 1939, Montgomery Ward put out 2,365,000 copies of this. Seven years later, a reprint of 3,776,000 copies was hardly enough. Then came a song as an adaptation of that adaptation.

Composing music is largely based on borrowing. Sometimes it is a bodily transplantation of an old melody into new words. At other times the adaptation is so different that the public—yes, even the composer—may fail to recognize its parallel. Of many hits which have been rebirths of classics, one example is *Till the End of Time.* This was taken bodily from a Chopin *Polonaise. The Star-Spangled Banner* —which was "created" to defy England—was substantially the same as a tune then popular in the pubs of London. Sigmund Spaeth has detected many such musical borrowings. Entirely new tunes are the exceptions.

2. *By way of adaptation*

"What can I make this look like?" . . . "What idea can I incorporate?" These are legitimate and helpful questions when it comes to fashions. Plucking ideas from parallels is a conscious part of creativity among stylists. A recent swimsuit was unblushingly based on diapers. Winston Churchill's overcoat inspired a box-shaped six-button creation. General Eisenhower's battle jacket was feminized into a dressy coat tied at the waist and garnished with military cuffs, lapels and a shoulder medal.

New York's Metropolitan Museum of Art offers a special service to creators of fashions. From its treasury of ancient art, New York designers take many ideas. The shape of an angel's wings in a fifteenth-century painting was the basis of some of Marcel Vertes' creations. Designer Lina Harttman found inspiration in the warriors pictured on a Greek vase of around 800 B.C. And in Hollywood, one of Adrian's great hits was a design taken from the helmet and eye of a warrior of around 500 B.C.

Sometimes an adaptation is a frank copy, but in far cheaper form. Mrs. Edith Holmes of Conley, Georgia, heard of an expensive doll supposedly owned by a child in a czar's family long before the Russian Revolution. The doll was a princess in royal raiment until you turned it upside down. Then it became a peasant in rags. Mrs. Holmes told me, "We just took that idea for our Topsy-Eva doll and cut the costs down to where we could sell it far and wide at $1.00."

Richard Moot was Landing Signal Officer on one of the big airplane-carriers. His responsibility was to control and direct the fliers in landing on the ship after each combat flight. In the black of the night, they could not see the signals on the deck; if enough light were used, the ship's location would be disclosed to the enemy.

Richard Moot remembered "Black Magic" at the New York World's Fair and recommended an adaptation of that idea. The result was that landing signal officers were equipped with uniforms and signal paddles of a material which became luminous and visible to the pilots—but not to the enemy—when invisible black light was used.

Not only new styles but epoch-making new products are arrived at via the adaptation highway. Rudolf Diesel wanted to burn fuel directly in the cylinders of his engine but did not know how to ignite the fuel. In piling up parallels he thought of a cigar-lighter. He analyzed one which had these essential features: (1) Both air and fuel were in its cylinder. (2) A piston suddenly compressed the air in the cylinder. (3) This caused the fuel to ignite. From this parallel he thought his way through to the invention of the first Diesel engine in 1892.

"What other *process* could be adapted to this job?" . . . "Could we make this better and cheaper with an assembly line?" Questions like these have led to ideas that have raised America's standard of living. In the same way, tools meant for one purpose have been successfully adapted for something else. An extreme example of this took place in an aircraft factory. The war was raging and the armed forces were crying for planes. But each plane had to be perfect right down to the last bolt. Girls had to string steel nuts on wire, spray them with graphite, and pass them through an induction coil in order to reveal faults in the metal. A supervisor, trying to think up a quicker method, thought of a corkscrew. He took a long wire, and curved it into corkscrew turns. This device, when swiftly rotated in a box of nuts, could pick up over a hundred per minute. The production of planes was thus speeded up by adapting something similar in order to provide a better tool.

"Out of whose book can I take a leaf?" This is a question which can send our imagination down the adaptation trail to the end of brightening our lives. For, in personal problems, too, it often pays to look for parallels.

An Italian-American had a son with a high IQ. The boy went to war as a private and came out as a top sergeant. Then he went to medical college. One day I asked old Joe how his son was. "He breaks my heart," was his reply. "He won't talk with me any more. Before he went to war, he and I used to talk sports all the time. We used to discuss batting averages, football scores, Joe Louis, and even the wrestlers. But now he won't talk. He studies hard to be a doctor. He wants to be a doctor in the Army. He doesn't care about sports any more and he keeps his thoughts to himself."

That bothered me, so I tried to figure how I could help Joe with his son. In thinking of parallels, I thought of their mutual interest in sports, and by way of natural sequence, that led me to ask, "Why not develop a mutual interest in the Army?" Joe thought this was a good idea, so he started to learn a new subject. He diligently read up on military affairs. Then he started to ask his son questions, to which the boy sparked. Now when the boy comes back from medical college, instead of giving his father the cold shoulder, the two of them discuss military affairs with almost as much gusto as when they used to discuss sports.

3. *By way of modification*

Having piled up alternatives through adaptation, as well as through other uses, let's now deal with modification. Let's ask ourselves: "What if this were somewhat changed?" "How can this be altered for the better?" "How about a new twist?"

Even a tiny change can often add much to a thing or to a thought. The jokesters make much of the new-twist method of modification. The ones who write the gags for the big network shows are paid around $100,000 a year, and yet hardly ever do they think up anything really new—mainly they think up new twists to old tales.

No matter what our creative problem, it is well to ask ourselves, "How could this be changed for the better?" Even when we have to make a speech, we might well challenge every feature of our talk with that question. For example, should we start out with a bang, or should we begin hesitantly—as some of the best speakers deliberately do?

"What change can we make in the process?" This is a good question when it comes to technology or even to cooking. A very slight change by way of toasting has added much to some products. Many process-improvements have come from mere changes in temperature. For the fermentation of wine, Pasteur found just the right heat to kill microbes without spoiling the flavor. When this slight change in process was later applied to milk, it became a momentous idea. How many lives have been saved by pasteurization, nobody will ever know.

Sponge rubber was unsuitable for cushioning. Then someone thought of cooking latex like bread; so now we have rubber seats and mattresses that are thermally comfortable.

"How about changing the *shape*?" . . . "In what *way*?" . . . "In what *other* ways?" Along such lines, we can profitably pile up alternatives when pondering a product.

Roller bearings go back to about 1500 and Leonardo da Vinci. For four centuries they were straight-sided cylinders, of less use than ball bearings. The revolutionary improvement came in 1898 when Henry Timkin first patented his *tapered* roller bearing. This entailed but a slight modification of shape in the cylinder type. But the new design took care of both radial and thrust loads, and thus surpassed all other forms of bearings.

"What if this were *curved*?" An appliance maker asked that to good effect and designed a bacon-grill with a curved center. The cover keeps the bacon from curling, while the curve serves to drain off the grease into the base of the grill.

Curving, or coiling, did much to give us the high-efficiency electric lamp. Doctor Langmuir of General Electric had to find a way to use a thin filament which would work as well as a thick one. By shaping it in coils—and with a new gas instead of vacuum—he created a bulb nearly 15 times as efficient as the first carbon lamps.

"In what other form could this be?" This is another byway which our imagination should explore. Sugar was first granulated, then powdered, then put into square lumps. Someone in the American Sugar Company then asked a shape question, "Wouldn't these dice-like lumps look more attractive if made into oblongs like dominoes?" "Domino" has been a successful brand ever since.

"What other *package?*" is a question that should go with "What other form?" Beyond that, we might even ask, "Could the package be *combined* with the form to provide a new twist?" Eskimo Pie was a triumphant idea along this line. It is one bit of our Americana which Russia has adopted inside her Iron Curtain. More and more edibles will be put in edible packages. Said Doctor Willard Dow, "We have learned to make synthetic sausage-coverings and ice-cream cones. Why stop there?"

4. *Senses as sources of ideas*

"What changes can we make to provide more *sense*-appeals?" Let's explore what to do to attract the eye and the ear, to tickle the taste, to please the sense of touch and the sense of smell.

Let's ask ourselves questions about eye-appeal and start with color. Along that line a scientist solved the problem of how to light up the outside of a home without attracting bugs. He merely changed the color of an ordinary Mazda lamp from white to yellow.

Three industries were basically affected by color in 1955. The extra appeal of variety of color helped raise that year's sales of automobiles to new heights. In 1955, the new pink lamp changed the pattern of the electric bulb market. In 1955, colored instruments became an important factor in the telephone industry.

More and more manufacturers of industrial machines are asking, "What color would be better?" Nearly all machines used to be black, but the newer ones are in bright colors which soak up far less light. Many a plant has increased production, reduced its rejects, and heightened morale by such changes.

Blasting-caps are now fired by wires colorfully coated with nylon plastic. The bright colors—red, yellow and blue—show plainly against the rocky walls of a mine tunnel. For coal mines, which are black, the nylon plastic is gleaming white. For salt mines, which are white, the nylon is black.

To achieve more eye-appeal, let's also ask, "How about *motion?*" We now have Christmas-tree lights which not only shine colorfully, but also bubble effervescently. Douglas Leigh has won a fortune by putting more movement into spectacular signs. Smoke-rings as big as street-circles come puffing out of the mouth of his cigarette-smoker; but it isn't smoke, it's steam.

"How about more *ear* appeal?" . . . "What can we do with sound?" Elmer Wheeler has won fame by sending his imagination down this trail. "Sizzling" steaks were his idea. He has delivered over 4,000 addresses on "Sell the Sizzle." For promotional purposes, many new twists have come from adding sound. A number of diaper laundries, for example, have installed on their trucks a new type of musical horn that plays *Rock-a-Bye, Baby*. An electric clothes-dryer automatically shuts off with the tune *How Dry I Am.*

We might also ask, "How can we appeal to the sense of smell?" Too little has been thought up along this line. Take bread, for example. We who have walked through bakeries know what a delicious aroma has filled our nostrils. Someday, someone will devise a bread-wrapper with that same fragrance. Even the question of touch-appeal might be worth exploring. And taste-appeal is obviously important.

The new twists to be thought up along those lines are limitless. Modification in terms of greater sense-appeal can be a major outlet for the creative imagination of anyone seeking to create or to improve a product.

5. *The technique of this-for-that*

Akin to modification and adaptation is the question of substitution. An obvious way to pile up what-else ideas is to think up what might be done by way of changing *that* for *this*, and *this* for *that*. So let's ask ourselves questions like: "What can I *substitute?*" . . . "What else *instead?*"

Searching for substitutes is a trial-and-error method which all of us can use in our everyday creativity; and yet the same technique is the key to scientific experimentation. Paul Ehrlich sought the right dye to color the veins of his laboratory mice. In this one phase of his long hunt for something that would kill trypanosomes, he used one dye after another —over 500 different colors all-told.

The change of this for that is not limited to things. Places, persons and even emotions can be transferred. Even ideas can be transferred. The classic example of this is the story about Archimedes. He had to find out whether a crown was all gold. How to figure the cubic area of the crown was too much for him. So he did that which often helps in creative thinking—he took a hot bath.

"My body makes the water rise. It displaces exactly the same cubic area. I will immerse the crown in water, measure how much it displaces, and thus find its cubic area. Multiplying that by the known weight of gold, I can then prove whether the crown is a counterfeit. *Eureka!*" Thus he interchanged ideas by substituting water displacement for metal measurement.

Many worthwhile new ideas have come from seeking a substitute component. So let's inquire, "What other *part* instead of this?" Driving-gears illustrate this avenue to creative achievement. Transmission was improved on trucks by substituting metal worms for conventional cogs. Why not use a fluid instead of metal gears on motorcars? That may have sounded far-fetched; and yet that was what was done to make our newest automobiles easier to drive.

Substitution has even gone so far as to replace something with nothing, and then to replace nothing with something. This dramatic feat of changing components helped to give us our improved electric lamp. Doctor Irving Langmuir started his search for better bulbs by first finding out why the original Edison lamps tended to blacken on the inside. Theoretically there was nothing there except the filament—not even air. Langmuir worked out a better vacuum, but still the lamps tended to blacken. Then he tried one gas after another, and finally hit on argon as the one best gas. The substitution of that gas for a vacuum—plus Langmuir's discovery of just the right coiling in the filament—resulted in a gas-filled lamp twice as efficient as the ordinary vacuum tungsten lamp.

Let's also ask ourselves, "What *other ingredient?*" For many centuries, soap was soap. Then one improved soap after another was developed by substitution of ingredients.

Who would ever think of putting glue into a cleaning compound? You might expect a great research laboratory to think that up. But, no, it was thought up by two Milwaukee men who were out of work and at their wits' end. They and their wives produced "Spic and Span." The women packaged it, the husbands peddled it. Housewives tried it and bought more. Procter and Gamble noted its meteoric success in the Midwest and paid the amateur chemists a fortune for their product.

The price of chicken and eggs would be even higher if poultrymen could not get vitamin D in the form of Du Pont's Delsterol. The material from which this food element had usually been extracted was liver-oil from tuna and halibut. But Du Pont substituted mussels—an abundant, cheap and hitherto unused source. It was lucky that this change was thought of in time, because the supply of tuna and halibut was shut off by the war.

"What other *process?*" is another idea-finding question. Should it be processed in vacuum or under pressure? Should it be cast, or should it be stamped? These are but a few of countless ways in which we can challenge a process in order to find a better idea.

"What other *power* might work better?" Although the foot-driven sewing machine called for but little exertion, the substitution of electric power for leg-power was a worthwhile achievement. And on new automobiles the air-powered devices for raising and lowering windows stem from a little idea hunted and caught by John Oishei, about 40 years ago. Spurred by an accident while driving his 1912 model through the rain, he thought up a hand-powered windshield-wiper which became standard equipment on all motorcars. Despite this success, he kept asking himself, "Why does this have to be worked by hand?" Search for a simpler and surer source of power led to a discovery which he likened to "finding a gas well in the front yard." By tapping the intake-manifold he pulled air through a tiny hose, and this air operated a motor on the windshield top.

John Oishei then adapted his engine-vacuum-power to auto horns and to fans for defrosting windshields. This same source of power was then used to squirt water on the windshield and thus wash and wipe the glass while driving in dry weather. His newest adaptation is the air device which provides instant touch-button control for raising and lowering car windows.

"*Who else?*" In piling up alternatives through substitution, we might ask ourselves questions along that line. "*Who* else could do this better?" can be a good question to ask. I had to write a circular to raise money for a war memorial. The more I thought of it, the more I realized that this called for more spiritual power than I could command. I made a list of those who might write a better letter and chose a man whose son had been in the Air Corps and whose heart was in the cause for which we were to seek funds. His letter was twice as good as any I could have written.

It is also well to ask, "*Where* else?" A change of place may change the emotional setting. For nearly 30 days the nation had been crippled by the 1948 coal strike. John L. Lewis of the miners and Ezra Van Horn of the mine-owners were irreconcilable. House Speaker Joe Martin arranged a new and unconventional place for them to meet—his own office. In 13 minutes, the two gladiators agreed on the point that led to the end of a strike that could have paralyzed the nation.

Substitution of one interest for another is often a key to personal betterment. A mother I know had a little son who loved to play with matches. She turned her mind to "what instead?" and hit on drinking straws as substitutes for flamemakers. The idea worked. In most cases of juvenile delinquency, the best answer might be to change the child's parents. The practical, though only partial answer, is to change environment—to substitute innocent pleasures for dangerous influences.

The trails of adaptation, modification and substitution are endless avenues to an infinite number of ideas. No matter what our problem, it is well to survey with our imaginations the many fields into which those roads lead.

TOPICS

1. Why is it in the public interest that the ideas of others should be subject to our adaptation? Discuss.
2. How many "of-the-month clubs" can you name? Think up three others that might succeed.
3. What modification created a new success in the bearing industry? What similar achievements can you name?
4. Name three ways in which the five senses have served as leads to ideas.
5. Name five ways by which products have been improved through thinking up substitutes.

EXERCISES

1. What features in a home might be improved if they were curved instead of straight?
2. Your guests romp with your children after supper and get them too excited to sleep. How would you solve this problem?
3. "Flip-over" booklets are composed of pictures in sequence which, when riffled with the thumb, gave the visual impression of a movie. To what new uses could this old idea be adapted?
4. Fathers notoriously find it difficult to converse with their teen-age daughters. Suggest six topics of conversation in which *both* would be interested.
5. List three songs that would be as appropriate to other household operations as "How Dry I Am" is to the completion of an electric dryer's job.

REFERENCES

BILLINGS, M. L., "Problem Solving in Different Fields of Endeavor." *American Journal of Psychology.* April 1934, pp. 259–272.

EASTON, WILLIAM H., *Creative Thinking and How to Develop It.* New York. American Society of Mechanical Engineers, 1946.

GUILFORD, J. P., GREEN, R. F., and CHRISTENSEN, P. R., "A Factor-Analytic Study of Navy Reasoning Tests." Reports from the Psychological Laboratory, The University of Southern California, No. 3, 1951.

HALL, S. R., "Adapting vs. Adopting Ideas." *Printers' Ink.* April 7, 1927, pp. 109–110.

OSBORN, ALEX F., *Wake Up Your Mind.* New York. Charles Scribner's Sons, 1952.

PATRICK, CATHERINE, "Whole and Part Relationship in Creative Thought." *American Journal of Psychology.* January 1941, pp. 128–131.

Scientific American, Vol. 199, No. 3, September 1958.

SPEARMAN, C. and JONES, WYNN, *Human Ability.* London. Macmillan, 1950.

THORNDIKE, E. L., "The Psychology of Invention in a Very Simple Case." *Psychological Review,* July 1949, pp. 192–199.

WEIL, RICHARD, JR., *The Art of Practical Thinking.* New York. Simon and Schuster, 1940.

Chapter XVIII

Addition, multiplication, subtraction, division

A SEARCH for "more-so" and "less-so" correlates is a major phase of the self-questioning technique which can spur imagination toward more and more ideas. The magnification category includes endless possibilities by way of addition and multiplication. The minification category calls for piling up alternatives through subtraction and division.

To help us explore the field of magnification, we might well ask ourselves the questions: "What to add?" . . . "Should it be *stronger?*" . . . "Should it be *bigger?*" . . . "What extra value?" . . . "What plus ingredient?"

Size is the simplest key to ideas through magnification. For example, tires used to be much smaller. Their narrowness made ruts a menace, and their cushion-effect was meager. About 35 years ago, a tire-maker asked, "Why not make 'em *fatter?*" This led to the balloon tire. Sensational at first, it won its way so fast that by 1928 the balloon tire became the conventional type. "Why not make it *still fatter?*" led to the super-balloon for which buyers of replacement tires are now gladly paying a premium.

"How about a *bigger package?*" may often be asked with profit. Chain stores have made great gains along this road. Rubber factories use quantities of rubber cement. Customarily this came in one-gallon cans, used once and then discarded. A workman suggested that the cement be put in

50-gallon drums with removable heads, and that each operator should use a refillable can. This saved waste and saved tin. The employee who suggested this was awarded $500 for his big-package idea.

In piling up alternatives through addition, we should also think beyond questions of size. "How about *more time?*" This might well be one of our queries. Many a process has been improved through longer aging. And in human affairs more time can often be a helpful factor. We do better when we count three before we talk back. Cooling-off periods have proved to be wise measures in labor disputes.

Greater frequency may also be worth exploring. "What if this were done *more often?*" Some wise doctor must have asked that question when up against the problem of treating stomach ulcers—with the result that eating light but frequent meals became an approved prescription.

"How can we *add strength?*" is still another key. More specifically we might ask, "How could this be *reinforced?*" Interwoven Hosiery shot ahead by reinforcing heels and toes of hosiery. Oneida Community added a new sales appeal by reinforcing the points of wear on teaspoons. By heat-treating the rims of table glasses, Libby made a success of no-nick tumblers.

"What can we *add* to make this stronger?" This query has often led to lamination. We must admit, however, that the adaptation of lamination to shatter-proof glass was largely an accident. The accepted story is that a chemist tipped over a bottle of collodion, tried to pick up the pieces of glass, and found that they stuck together. This led to shatter-proof glass, which is simply a sandwich of plastic material between layers of glass.

Along the more-so trail it is well to think in terms of "How can I add *more value?*" A sub-question under this head might be: "How about more in a package?" Stockings were always sold in pairs. A food-chain operator decided to add hosiery to his supermarket merchandise. He wanted to do it differently—to offer more value. So he thought up the idea of selling *three* stockings to a package instead of two—"You buy a pair and get a spare." He coined the name "Triplons" for this pair-and-one package of nylon hosiery.

The usual way to add value is to give more of the same for less. But adding something *else* may sometimes pull even better. Added value in the form of premiums is a big part of American business. In a normal year the amount of money which sellers invest in premiums exceeds $500,000,000.

Another question to ask is: "What *ingredient* could I add?" Many a woman instinctively asks this of herself while cooking. Many a hostess has made herself a reputation for salads by adding a touch of garlic or Burgundy. And when it comes to manufactured products, the plus of a new ingredient is often worth-while. Thanks to the University of Illinois, dentifrice manufacturers were able to add an ammoniated ingredient. Later they added chlorophyll. Then came fluoride.

"What can be added by way of an *extra feature?*" Westclox successfully followed that trail 30 years ago by endowing Big Ben with two alarms—one a shout, the other a whisper. Now Westclox has added a blinking *light* which calls the sleeper *silently;* but if that kindly light is ignored, a commanding bell comes into action.

What to add by way of pleasant environment is a key question in employee relations. In many cases, more light and more paint have done much to make workers like their jobs better. In other cases, cosier rest rooms, some with free coffee, have helped. Music throughout the plant, to offset the ugly clatter of machines, also adds to employee contentment.

2. *By way of maximizing*

Almost every figure of speech can provide a lead for new ideas; and *hyperbole,* the rhetorical term for *exaggeration,* is no exception. So let's ask ourselves, "What if this were blown up to the *nth* degree?" . . . "What if this were preposterously *overstated?*"

"How about a *jumbo?*" This is a key to much of Russia's propaganda. Outdoor portraits of Soviet leaders are usually as big as a house. The Statue of Liberty was a forerunner of this jumbo technique. England almost got a colossus of Churchill. A Yankee engineer offered to raise $100,000 here to start a fund for the erection of a 300-foot-high statue of Churchill on the white cliffs of Dover—with a cigar in his hand and an electric beacon at its lighted end. Churchill scotched the idea.

The carrying of "more-so" to the point of absurdity is a basic technique of cartoonists. Stan Hunt admits that exaggeration is his best stock in trade. "In a course of abnormal psychology," Hunt said, "I once learned that the characteristics of the insane were merely exaggerations of normal characteristics. Cartoon characters develop in much the same way."

Disney's art has been partly based on exaggerated multiplication. In his movie-short of an orchestra playing *William Tell* he showed one violinst playing five violins at once, and then five violinists playing one violin.

Most people want to be like everybody else and not stand out in personality. But those who have sought the limelight have often used sartorial exaggeration. Fiorello LaGuardia did this so successfully with his headwear that he won the nickname of "The Big Hat." Diamond Jim Brady did it by wearing an oversize sparkler on his shirt-front. Alexander Woollcott did it by wearing a huge and billowy cape.

In personal problems a wanted idea may sometimes be found in the realm of exaggeration. When coping with a serious fault in a child, we might ask, "How could I carry this to a dramatic extreme?" In this way a mother gave her daughter a telling lesson. The little girl had received from her aunt a box of candy as an Easter present. That night her father asked her for a chocolate. The daughter snapped back, "They are not for the family. They are all mine!" The next day, the mother brought home two big boxes of chocolates, one for herself and one for her husband. The little girl got the point and was the better for it.

Even in business, exaggeration can be a powerful club in driving home a point. Charles Brower found that one of his writers of radio commercials had fallen too much in love with the notion that sales messages had to be disliked by listeners in order to be effective. So Brower thought up this parable: "A man went to town to do the week-end shopping for his wife. He entered a grocery store where the clerks had been taught the psychology of selling through dislike. The first clerk stamped on his foot as he mentioned a popular brand of soap. Another clerk pulled the customer's hat down over his eyes because there was a special on canned soup that day. A third kicked him right in the shins in an attempt to sell him a new brand of shortening."

3. *By way of multiplying*

Along the "more-so" trail we might also look into multiplication and ask questions like: "How about doubling it?" For example, John Oishei originally conceived only one windshield wiper to a car. Later he doubled the use—two wipers became standard equipment on each windshield. Then came a third wiper installed on rear windows.

John Cornelius was confronted with the problem of introducing a new grocery product. He sought a different and harder-hitting appeal. Wisely, his first approach was to mull over the obvious. He toyed with the tried-and-true idea of a money-back guarantee, and then tried to think how to make something excitingly new out of so threadbare a device. By multiplication he came to the idea of "*Double* Your Money Back." This worked so well that at least 16 advertisers have since copied the device.

Multiplication has been the source of many new products, the latest of which is a boon to those who paint. They no longer have to scrape the pigments off their palettes. John Anthony now supplies a pallette made up of 50 sheets of impervious paper. Just by peeling off the smeared surface, a fresh, clean palette is at hand.

And, of course, multiplication is the basis of America's wizardry in production. Gang drills are only one of the many manufacturing setups based on multiplication. Here are two little instances of how this principle works. In a rubber plant, a four-hanger rack was used to dip small metal pieces in acid, preparatory to plating. "Why not six hangers instead of four?" suggested a workman. Production was thus increased 50 per cent. Similarly, an employee asked, "Why can't we use a *double* die instead of a single die to cut out this piece?" That *doubled* production.

In addition to asking, "How can I kill two birds with one stone?—a good question to ask is, "What if this were duplicated on a large scale?" The Soap Box Derby is a noteworthy example of how the "snowballing process" can turn one little idea into a nation-wide event. Myron Scott got the inspiration for this while watching youngsters race home-made cars in his home town of Dayton. At first the Derby attracted only local interest. But, godfathered by Chevrolet, it moved to Akron in 1935 and took over a new concrete track of its own.

4. *By way of minifying*

We can sometimes magnify our creative power by thinking up ways to minify. That's why, after having beaten the bushes for "more-sos," we should shift our hunt to "less-sos." In seeking ideas along this trail, we ask ourselves questions such as: "What if this were *smaller?*" . . . "What could I *omit?*" . . . "How about dividing?"

In pondering a product, here's a specific question to explore: "How could we make this more *compact?*" Thinner pocket watches and tiny wrist watches came from such thinking. Radios furnish another example.

In the early days of broadcasting, A. Atwater Kent made and sold over 1,000,000 sets in one year. He did almost everything himself, including his designing. At the height of his success, he announced: "Next year I am going to make my leading model one-*half* the size." His associates doubted the wisdom of this move. But Mr. Kent went ahead. His smaller model, called "The Compact," was an even greater success than its predecessor.

"What if they were smaller?" can even be asked concerning holes. Walter Irving, who created ready-made landing fields for our air forces in Africa, got his start by making big iron gates for banks, public buildings and country estates. Then he developed sidewalk gratings for subways. He found that women's heels were getting caught in these, and that baby carriages were being upset. So he thought up our newer and better kind of grating, with openings too small to catch the high heels. And that led to his idea for ready-made landing fields.

Under "more-so" we asked, "How about a *jumbo?*" Here we should ask, "How about *miniatures?*" Makers of chocolates have successfully followed that trail. A fountain-pen maker made a hit with a miniature version called "demi-size" for women to carry upright in their handbags.

Let's also ask: "How about *condensing?*" One example of good ideas along this trail is the full-size umbrella which can be folded up to fit a woman's purse. Another is the vest-pocket book of filmy sheets of soap, with pellets which expand into washclothes when dropped in water. An outstanding example along this line is a concentrate—frozen orange juice—which has revolutionized the citrus industry.

Just as on the "more-so" trail we looked into questions of height and length, we should also ask ourselves, "What if this were *lower?*" In designing new cars, a constant challenge to engineers is how to cut down the height. To make a car even a quarter-inch lower, a manufacturer will go to the expense of almost re-designing a new model.

Another good question is: "How about *less length?*" The ultimate in this has to do with sound waves and light waves. One of Nela Park's creative achievements has been the shortening of wave lengths to make lamps perform functions which formerly only the sun could perform.

The sun's radiant energy comes in three broad groups: (1) Long-wave energy, such as heat. (2) Visible energy which produces light and color. (3) Short-wave energy such as invisible ultraviolet. In dealing with wave-shortening, the scientific unit of measurement is an angstrom—1/250,000,-000th of an inch!

G. E. engineers produced the sun lamp by shortening wave-lengths and using a special glass. Still shorter rays of the sun can kill germs. About 95 per cent of this germicidal energy is in wave lengths so infinitesimally short that they measure only 2,537 angstroms. With the help of special glass, the new G.E. Germicidal Lamps reproduce the waves which so effectively kill germs. But these shortening triumphs stemmed from the original idea of isolating the different bands of the sun's wave lengths. This suggests that we might also ask ourselves, "How about *separating* this from that?"

"How about making it *lighter?*" An Italian inventor applied that question to passenger trains and created a new type of car which is only 20 feet long and as light as an auto trailer. Instead of eight wheels, each car has only two wheels—located at the rear end.

Part of Kettering's genius was to ask, "Why does this have to be so heavy?" It was an accepted belief that Diesels had to weigh too much ever to be used on automobiles. Kettering ignored this tradition, and with the help of his researchers at Dayton, he found the main answer was a new injector so infinitely precise that it would blow into the engine just the right amount of vaporized fuel, at high pressure and at just the right intervals. Diesel engines can now weigh 10 times *less* in relation to their power than before Kettering asked his unorthodox question.

There's big business in fire hose and competition is keen. A creative engineer asked, "Why can't we make our hose lighter?" Starting from this question, his company developed a new fire hose which is 18 per cent lighter than ever before and can be put into action in far less time.

Such time-saving is important, and suggests another question along the less-so trail, "Could this be done *faster?*" That's what led Birdseye to his triumph. The freezing of food was not new. Birdseye's discovery was a way to freeze so much faster that the freezing would penetrate the *inside* of the tiniest cell. He then brainstormed the question of how to adapt this technique to the *drying* of food, and after years of effort found a way to reduce the time of dehydration by over 16 hours.

America's efficiency in producing low-priced goods despite high hourly labor-cost has partly come from questions like, "How could this be *speeded up?*" . . . "What waste motions could be *cut out?*" Without creative thinking and time studies along this line, prices would be higher and purchases would be fewer. Similar attacks on the time element have likewise improved retailing. The success of cafeterias has been due to saving time and thus cutting labor costs. The growth of supermarkets is based on time-saving as well as other elements.

Even in home problems, the time question may be worth exploring. The child who does badly at school may be spending too much time listening to radio or television or some other time-consumer. It's a wise mother who, in her attack on such a problem, includes a query as to how to shorten periods of distraction.

5. *By way of omitting and dividing*

The "less-so" highway now leads us into the *omission* byway. Here we ask ourselves, "What can we *eliminate?*"

. . . "Suppose we leave this out?" . . . "Why not *fewer parts?*" This latter trail led to safer goggles during the war when a manufacturer worked his mind something like this: "Goggles have two lenses. Why *two?* Why not *one* lens, straight across both eyes?" The result was the Monogoggle.

Instead of eliminating parts, even whole units can sometimes be omitted. An example of this is the tubeless tire which virtually eliminates punctures and sudden blowouts.

Martin Pearson, a war worker in the Yellow Truck plant at Pontiac, made two suggestions which saved 76,000 feet of lumber in 60 days. One was an improved method of boxing Army trucks for shipment. The other idea was to stencil information directly on trucks and thus do away with separate boards. This saved 242 work-hours each month.

Elimination of the objectionable is an obvious creative challenge. Doctor Alex Schwarcman did this when he decided that castor oil didn't have to taste that way, and developed a tasteless type. C. N. Keeney noticed that string beans were hard to prepare, and unpleasant to eat if not stripped of their coarse strings. He had also noticed that some beans which came into his canning plant were stringless. He decided to seek these freaks. So in the growing season, he donned overalls and went through field after field on his hands and knees, examining every plant. He found a good many stringless beans, which he saved and replanted; and then he repeated the process until he had what he was after—a string bean without a string.

In seeking ideas through elimination, another question to ask is, "How can this be *streamlined?*" Thinking in this direction can lead to increased eye appeal and lessened cost, as in the automobile industry. Another instance has to do with jet planes. When they travel as fast as sound, air is unable to get out of the way—is compressed and piled up around the leading edges of the wing. Behind this "shock" wave, the air can be rough enough to tear a ship to pieces. Wright Field worked out a new type of wing construction to reduce skin friction to a minimum. The outside is finished and polished like a mirror—free from rivets, overlapping joints and other projections. The wing surfaces are made from several layers of glass-cloth cemented together.

Part of the genius of American industry is simplification; and nearly always this means thinking up what to cut out. Streamlining of design is good, but streamlining the steps in production is even more important.

"Leave-it-out" ideas need not be limited to making things. The factor of omission is often important in human relations. It is well to ask ourselves. "What could be left *unsaid?*" Such silence is often golden in diplomacy, and can play a big part in the everyday tact that helps people to get along better with each other.

In addition to thinking along lines of deletion, let's look for alternatives by way of *division.* Let's ask ourselves, "What if this were *divided?*" . . . "Suppose we *split this up?*"

My daughter's baby would not go to sleep unless covered with a certain crib blanket. This had to be washed; but how could it be washed when in use almost all the time? Little Barbie knew instinctively whenever a substitute was tried, and she rebelled. My daughter hit upon the idea of cutting the blanket in two and washing one half at a time. Her idea worked like a charm.

Let's also think of separating into *assortments.* This idea seems to work well in the chicken business. Many shops now specialize in splitting up fowl and selling legs to those who want legs, and breasts to those who want breasts.

"Divide and conquer!" was Hitler's master strategy. "How can we go at it *piecemeal?*" is a good question to ask even in everyday problems of human relations.

Another "less-so" trail worthy of exploration is that of *understatement.* This trail can lead to better writing, as when Shakespeare made Caesar say, "Et tu, Brute!" The Count of Turenne, after destroying the Spanish army, sent this message to His Majesty, Louis XIV, "The enemy came, was beaten. I am tired. Good night!"

In dramatic criticism, stings are sharpened through understatement. Brooks Atkinson once wrote this, "When Mr. Wilber calls his play *Halfway to Hell,* he underestimates the distance." And when Robert Benchley was covering plays on Broadway, he often used understatement to combine a barb with a smile. For instance, he described a certain drama as "one of those plays in which all of the actors unfortunately enunciated very clearly."

In caricature, the "less-so" technique often takes the form of understatement. The artist leaves out all possible details and creates the picture with the fewest possible strokes. Advertising craftsmen are thinking more and more in terms of understatement to achieve forcefulness. But this trend is still so new that New York City was startled when *McCall's* ran a full-page newspaper advertisement under this headline: "*McCall's Magazine* has been sort of dumb for four or five years."

A so-called joke of my high-school days asked the question, "Why is a mouse when it twirls?" The answer was, "The higher, the fewer." In an inane way, the "more" was thus joined with the "less." And it is true that the "less-so" trail and the "more-so" trail often cross each other.

TOPICS

1. What questions might you ask yourself when searching for alternative ideas by way of magnification?
2. Give three examples of new ideas arrived at through multiplication.
3. What questions might you ask yourself when searching for alternative ideas by way of minification?
4. Give three examples of new ideas arrived at through streamlining.
5. What would be the advantages to the housewife if soup were sold in cans half the usual size? Five times the usual size?

EXERCISES

1. Suggest a feature that could be added to the *Reader's Digest* to increase readership.
2. Suggest at least six ideas which might make the average classroom a more pleasant and efficient place to work.
3. Suggest at least six things to which chlorophyll might be added to give them extra sales value.
4. Think up at least three appropriate premiums to be given with the purchase of each of the following: (a) Men's shoes. (b) A washing machine. (c) A living-room suite. (d) An outboard motor.
5. If an aspiring politician wanted to stand out sartorially, what three ideas might you suggest along the line of Al Smith's brown derby or Chamberlain's umbrella?

REFERENCES

BROWNELL, W. A., "Problem Solving." *Yearbook National Society for the Study of Education.* Bloomington. Public School Publishing Company, Part 2, 1942, pp. 415–443.

CRAWFORD, ROBERT P., *Think for Yourself.* New York. McGraw-Hill Book Company, Inc., 1937.

DIMNET, ERNEST, *The Art of Thinking*. New York. Simon and Schuster, 1929.

MARKEY, F. V., "Imagination." *Psychological Bulletin*. March 1935, pp. 212–236.

O'CONNOR, JOHNSON, *Ideaphoria*. Boston. Human Engineering Laboratory, 1945.

OSBORN, ALEX F., *Your Creative Power*. New York Charles Scribner's Sons, 1949.

PARNES, SIDNEY J., *Creative Retailing*. Harrisburg. Department of Public Instruction, 1957.

REISS, OTTO F., *How to Develop Profitable Ideas*. New York. Prentice-Hall, Inc., 1945.

SCHNACKEL, H. G., *The Art of Business Thinking*. New York. John Wiley and Sons, Inc., 1930.

SMITH, PAUL, ed., *Creativity*. New York. Hastings House, 1959.

WERTHEIMER, M., *Productive Thinking*. New York. Harper & Brothers, 1945.

WOOLF, JAMES D. and ROTH, CHARLES B., *How to Use Your Imagination to Make Money*. New York. Whittlesey House, 1948.

Chapter XIX

Rearrangement, reversal, and combination

SELF-QUESTIONING CAN help us project our own imaginations into still other correlative fields. Countless ideas are to be found in the realm of *rearrangement*. The second law of association, contrast, opens up numerous new paths by way of *reversal*. And, of course, *combination* has always been known to be a major function of creative imagination.

Rearrangement usually offers an unbelievable quantity of alternatives. For instance, a baseball manager can shuffle his team's batting order 362,880 times—362,880 ways of rearranging the same nine players! Yes, there are countless alternatives—countless leads to ideas—to be had through questions like: "How *else* can this be *arranged?*" . . . "What if the *order were changed?*"

Luckily, the urge to rearrange is an inborn trait. Children pile up the same blocks in endlessly different patterns. Mothers continually shift the living-room furniture and this, plus a new lamp shade or doily, creates an entirely new room each time. Modern girls even rearrange their looks. Using the same elements with which they were born, they do things to their lips, eyebrows and hair to create one new face after another.

"What other *layout* might be better?" . . . "Where should this part be *placed* in relation to that?" Such questions will help us pile up alternatives via rearrangement of constituent elements.

"Should the cart be put before the horse?" used to be an academic query. "Should the motor be in the front or in the rear?" is a live and practical question. As to pleasure cars this idea has been agitated and re-agitated. On buses, however, rear engines have become common.

Likewise, in the early days of airplanes, a heated controversy developed over the question of whether the pusher type was better, with the propeller in the rear—or whether the tractor type was better, with the propeller out ahead. The latter type won out. In the new jet planes, however, the power comes from behind; whereas helicopters have their propellers on top. All of which points up the fact that there is always some *other* alternative, especially in the field of rearrangement.

"What other *floor plan* would work better?" This question is at the core of all architecture. And in merchandising, tried-and-true floor plans are being challenged by questions of rearrangement. When stores ran their counters lengthwise and parallel, customers would travel between two counters and "go down the slot," with too little chance of being tempted by other merchandise. The new idea is to run counters *across* the store, with narrow ends on main aisles.

Even banks have shown enviable ingenuity by way of rearrangement. The Bayside National Bank made national news when it announced its new "Pram Teller," which enables mothers to do their banking without parking their baby carriages. And many banks have erected new buildings for drive-in service. The tellers even have trays which they can extend right out into the customer's car.

"What method of *pay* would provide the most *incentive?*"

A trivial but significant case was that of a neighbor of mine. He loved to practice short golf shots when he got home in the evening. He would take 30 balls and hit them over the fence into a vacant lot next door. His five-year-old son liked to watch him and one day spoke up with: "Dad, how much will you give me for getting those balls for you?" The father was about to offer 10¢ but, instead, said: "I'll give you one penny for each three you find."

The boy went at this enterprise avidly, but time after time would bring back only 27 or 28 balls; he seldom stuck at it long enough to find the last two or three. The father feared this might induce a slipshod habit, so he rearranged the compensation. He told his son: "I will pay you 15¢ instead of 10¢ for finding all my balls. You'll get nothing for the first 28 balls that you pick up. You'll get 5¢ for the twenty-ninth and you'll get 10¢ for the thirtieth." The result was that all the 30 balls were retrieved each time and the little fellow enjoyed the hunt far more.

That father-and-son scheme is meant merely to illustrate how rearrangement of compensation can accomplish more top production, with more satisfaction to the toiler. New incentive plans of industry follow this same principle. Some of them are working well from the standpoint of the employer, the worker and the national economy. Rearrangement of compensation is still, and always will be, a creative challenge to all.

"What about *timing?*" . . . "How about a change of pace?" . . . "What if the *tempo* were different?" Such rearrangement is part of the genius of the stars among pitchers, speakers, preachers, and actors. Change of pace plays a big part in the skill of comedians like Jack Benny.

How about *schedules?* Business might well brainstorm the

question, "What working hours would be best?" Especially when it comes to office work, there are opportunities to rearrange work schedules for the better. For example, a lawyer had a summer cottage near mine about 40 minutes from his office. During the hot weather, he always drove to work at 5:30 A.M. so as to spend the afternoon at the lake shore. In the same way, many stores have rearranged shopping hours to the better convenience of the public and with less pressure on transportation facilities.

In family problems, it is often well to ask, "Should this be done earlier or later?" . . . "What other time would be best for that?" Even the timing of irritations can be profitably rearranged, as was proved by a woman writer who married a lawyer. Although resolved that she would allow no mundane details of housekeeping to mar their comradeship, she soon found herself greeting him on his home-arrival with anti-romantic subjects, such as a new pane for a broken window, a new washer for the kitchen faucet, and even a needed repair of the toilet. She went on the hunt for an idea to put a stop to all that. One evening she greeted her husband with nothing but pleasant topics. He wondered at this change, but said nothing about it. The explanation came the next morning. As he was leaving for his office she handed him a list of chores for him to see to during his working day. The couple has abided by this system ever since.

2. *What other sequence?*

"What about sequence?" . . . "What should come after what?" Authors and playwrights always have to think hard on such questions. Chronological order is the simplest and often the best; but a plot can sometimes be enlivened by jumping the hands of the clock backward and forward.

Rearrangement of sequences is a frequent problem in radio, especially as to just where to place commercials. The sponsor, of course, wants a maximum audience for his advertising messages, but not at the cost of causing listeners to tune out. For 20 years, broadcasting had to rely solely on personal opinion in this dilemma. Then, Arthur Nielsen worked out a system of scientific guidance. Through recording devices attached to home radios, he now reveals just how many people listen to a program *at each minute,* and how many tune out at each minute. With this factual help, sponsors can now rearrange sequence and place their commercials so as to insure maximum listening and minimum tuning-out.

Many a home problem can be solved by asking ourselves questions such as, "Should this come before that?" For instance, one of my daughters was frail in her early years, and the doctor insisted that she eat more vegetables. Notwithstanding all our scolding and coaxing, she would invariably eat her meat first and let her vegetables go uneaten. This impasse was solved by the question: "Why not give her the vegetables *first?*" From then on, while the rest of us ate both our meat and vegetables, she had vegetables only. And she ate them in order to get her meat. Strangely enough, when she became a mother, her little daughter presented the same problem; and this was recently solved through the very same strategy of rearrangement.

Changes of sequence in placement of foods have proved profitable for cafeterias. They have found that desserts sell better when shown near the *start* of the line instead of at the *end* where they used to be, and where logically they would seem to belong.

"What about *cause and effect?*" . . . "What if they were

transposed?" Even such questions of sequence can be sources of ideas. One reason for this is that we do not always know what is cause and what is effect; we still are not sure which comes first, the chicken or the egg.

There is the same confusion about sequence even in matters that should be scientific. Take medicine, for example. A person is toxic and runs a fever. Diagnosis traces the cause to an inflammation of the urinary system. In one case I know of, that "cause" was ultimately found to be the effect. The real cause was sluggish elimination, which put too big a load on the kidneys and resulted in inflammation of the bladder. By speeding elimination, the bladder was cleared up, and the toxicity and the fever were stopped.

That true history illustrates why it is well to think in terms of transposing cause and effect—of asking of an apparent effect, "Is this perhaps the cause?"—of asking of an alleged cause, "Is this perhaps the effect?" Carried into personal relations, such a creative challenge is often worthwhile. Many a person has given way to the alibi, "People don't like me—that is why I am morose and sensitive." Again, this may be a confusion of cause and effect. If that person should try hard enough to be cheerful and objective, instead of glum and subjective, the effect would probably be that people *would* like him.

By challenging sequence, we can break vicious circles. For example, a man comes home from his work all tired out. His fatigue causes him to quarrel with his family. The effect of this becomes a cause—it upsets him so that when he goes to bed, he cannot sleep well enough. This effect then becomes a cause. He is tired when he goes to work the next morning. This, in turn, causes him to go home even more tired and more crotchety than ever.

Obviously, he can change all that by simply changing the first effect. Even though tired, he could make himself act pleasantly when he reaches home. He could then sleep better; he would go to work the next day more refreshed. Therefor, he would be less tired at the end of the day; therefore, he would be less touchy.

Since cause and effect are not always immutable, it is always well for us creatively to think up changes in this relationship. And, of course, in addition to such a transposition, it is always well to send our imaginations in search of all other possible causes.

3. *The vice versa technique*

Not only cause and effect, but almost anything can be reversed. That is why contrast can be a source of ideative fluency. Among the many questions which can spur our minds alongs this line, here are some samples: "*Transpose* positive and negative?" . . . "What are the *opposites?*" . . . "What are the *negatives?*" . . . "How about *up-ending?*" . . . "Should we turn it *around?*" . . . "Why not *up* instead of *down?*" . . . "Or why not *down* instead of *up?*"

Through reverse twists we can carry rearrangement to the extreme—even to the point of absurdity, as comedians often do. Chase Taylor, for one, rose to fame, under the name of Colonel Stoopnagel, with his wacky reversals.

"Switcheroo" is Hollywood's name for topsy-turvy creativity. Many a movie plot has been thought up, or sparked up, by having the man bite the dog instead of *vice versa.* Rub two movie-writers together in a story conference, and you ignite thinking like this: "I've got it," one will cry. "Instead of having *him* fall in love with his stenographer, we'll have him be the steno, and make his boss a *girl* who gets crazy about *him.* When *he* sits on *her* lap to take dictation, it will kill 'em!"

Such creative thinking is based on a search for the opposite of the conventional, and Leo Nejelski has stressed the need of this even in business. "Many men," he said, "have found that they get original ideas when they systematically challenge the obvious." Thomas S. Olsen uses a slightly different version of reverse thinking. "When hunting for an idea," he has said, "I always go from the positive to the negative, and vice versa." By trying first to think of the obvious, and then of opposites of the obvious, he uses an alternating current to step up his creative power.

"How about *reversing* the *roles?*" Let's also ask that question. Carl Rose does this often, as instanced by his cartoon of a father reading a newspaper *inside* a play-pen while four brats are rough-housing *outside* the pen. As to serious use of reversal of roles, E. M. Statler explained: "I try never to look upon myself as a hotel proprietor, but always to put myself in the shoes of my guests. By thinking in terms of *their* wants, I have arrived at some of my best ideas." In competitive thinking, we might also do well to put the shoe on the other foot by asking ourselves: "What can my competitor do to go me one better?"

We might also ask ourselves: "How about *saying* it in *reverse?*" This is one of the humorists' bag of tricks. When used seriously, it comes under the head of *irony*—the figure which drives home a point by stating one thing and meaning the opposite. Unlike sarcasm or satire, irony can be kindly. We can often use it to add power to what we say.

Irony can also take the form of object lessons. For example, the Albright Art Gallery encouraged good taste with a chamber of horrors. It was called "*This Is Bad Design,* being an exhibition to end exhibitions." The event attracted crowds for three afternoons and evenings. The horrible examples consisted of household pieces so outlandish that only their unique appeal had saved them from the scrap-heap. A critic described the collection as "the most incredible gingerbread that a preceding generation ever cooked up."

"How about doing the *unexpected?*" . . . "What can be done by way of *surprise?*" Years ago a Hollywood press agent was asked to pinch-hit as commentator on a newsreel. One shot showed a baseball player coming to a sudden stop. "Put screeching brakes under it," he called to the sound man. When the reel was exhibited, movie patrons rolled in the aisles. From this idea, ex-press-agent Pete Smith went on to develop his successful series of comedy shorts.

John Wanamaker likewise believed in reversing the obvious. His right-hand man said of him: "Wanamaker deliberately planned to do the unexpected thing in a different way. So much was this true that some of his associates used to figure on the very opposite of what he was expected to do, and this opposite would be the best guess."

When it comes to brainstorming a product, we might well ask: "What if this were *up-ended?*" "Why not *turn it around?*" A furrier challenged his label in that way and now sews it into his coats upside down. This makes for distinction; but, more than that, when the fur coat is draped over the back of a chair, the merchant's name is right side up and easy to read.

"Why not try it on the *other end?*" The nub of Howe's invention of the sewing machine was that instead of putting the eye of the needle at the end opposite the point, he put the eye at the point.

"How about *building it upside down?*" Through such reverse thinking, Henry Kaiser spectacularly sped up the construction of ships during the last war. His idea was to build whole sections such as deckhouses *upside down,* so that the welders could work downhand instead of overhead.

Gene Commery of General Electric Lamp Works, in search of new ways to illuminate, asked himself, "Why not have the light go *upward* instead of *downward?*" The result was a brand-new idea for lighting dining-room tables. No lamp is in sight. The light is on the floor. The beam rises through a hole in the table up to a mirror on the ceiling. The mirror reflects a soft light which covers only the top of the table.

Life magazine reported an imaginative, amusing, but important example of switcheroo on the part of Dale Carson, an FBI agent who resigned to accept a Florida appointment as sheriff of Duval County:

"He noticed something that other sheriffs, over the ages, had failed to see: the bread and water treatment usually doesn't work. He discovered that young toughs gloried in being so punished because it proved how tough they were and they could brag about the bread and water treatment when they got out.

"So, ingeniously, Sheriff Carson substituted baby food for bread and water. Now the glory-seekers get strained beef, carrots, beef liver, spinach and applesauce. They eat it because they're hungry but they don't brag about it.

" 'It's no fun,' says Carson, 'to tell your buddies you were so tough they had to put you on baby food. One day usually gets them on their best behavior.' "

4. *Combination ad infinitum*

Most ideas are by way of combinations—so much so that *synthesis* is generally regarded as the essence of creativity.

To project imagination into this field, we can ask ourselves questions like these: "What *ideas* can be combined?" . . . "How about an *alloy?*" . . . "What about a *blend?*" . . . "Combine *units?*" . . . "Combine *purposes?*" . . . "What about an *ensemble?*" . . . "How about an *assortment?*"

"What *materials* could I *combine?*" is an idea-starter which can lead to endless alternatives. According to Albert W. Atwood, the last war "was largely a war of alloy metals." For instance, after Pearl Harbor we needed lots of cannons in a hurry. The old method was to cast and bore each barrel; but this took too long. Luckily, a new alloyed tubing had been developed which was so strong that the tube itself could be quickly turned into barrels.

Alloys have played a big part in industrial progress, especially in the automotive field. On a score or more places in Chrysler-made cars there are bearings which combine metals *and oil.* We think of tires as rubber, but the best crude rubber would fall far short unless combined with chemicals such as the accelerators and de-agers. And, of course, the carcass is mostly fiber. At first this was cotton, later converted into cord. Then rayon was substituted for cotton in certain tires; and in some others, nylon has now been subsituted for rayon.

We should also ask ourselves, "What other *article* could advantageously be *merged* with this?" . . . "What goes with this which might better be *combined into a single unit?*" An example of the latter is the modern shirt for men. We don't have to be too old to remember what a chore it was to put on a separate collar and separate cuffs.

Another such combination is now seen in train yards for washing car windows. It's a big brush with a built-in water hose which thus combines two operations in one. The newest adaptation of that idea is a self-feeding paintbrush. In this, the liquid is fed to the bristles much as it is fed to a nozzle in a paint-sprayer.

Such combinations bring together uses as well as products, and therefore suggest this question: "What can I combine to multiply the *purpose?*" Many oldsters might still be switching back and forth from distance glasses to reading glasses had it not been for Benjamin Franklin. He tired of changing from one set of specs to another; so he cut his lenses in two and stuck them together, with the reading halves below. Thus he originated bifocals.

"What could be done with combination in *packaging?*" is a question that can lead our imagination to still more alternatives. A brush-top on a bottle of spot-remover was a natural; and so was the idea of packaging cheese in tumblers.

Let's also ask: "What could we do by way of putting things together in *ensembles?*" One simple example is what Cluett Peabody did in offering Arrow shirts, neckties, and handkerchiefs, in combinations of matching colors. Another handkerchief maker combined his product with a book, *The Night Before Christmas.* Tucked into each large colorful illustration is an appropriate hanky.

"How about an *assortment* of *assortments?*" This was the basis of a new business. With most employees being paid by check, the cashing of these had become a headache costly to banks. B. F. Studebaker brainstormed this problem. As a result, many banks are now collating paper money into assortments of $10, $20, $25, $50, $60, and so on. This assortment is slipped into a paper band with the total prominently printed. These packages are then pigeonholed in special racks on tellers' counters. Thus during busy hours, instead of counting money, the tellers can simply hand out the exact bundle of bills plus the change.

Science creates largely through combination. We find it hard to realize that nylon is made from air, coal and water, petroleum, natural gas, and agricultural by-products, such as corn cobs and oat hulls. Admittedly, to put it thus is to oversimplify; but the fact is that the elements are as stated.

The importance of thinking up combinations in the field of scientific research was brought out by Lewis E. Walkup of the Battelle Memorial Institute: "Then comes a period of playing around with the problem and with the various jigsaw pieces of data and relationships that might fit to give a final answer. During this most exciting period, many false combinations spring into consciousness, with the appearance of being the sought-for solution. Most of these combinations drop stillborn because of some obvious defect. A few survive briefly only to die after a short calculation or other consideration shows a serious fallacy in their makeup. To survive, ideas must be plausible and useful; novelty is not enough, neither are expressions of wishful thinking. However, all of these false starts serve a valuable purpose: they show where the solution does *not* lie. Hence, they narrow the fields that are important to the roaming imagination of the thinker."

Over 40 years ago, in *Mind in the Making,* James Harvey Robinson pointed out: "Up to date the chemist has been able to produce artfully over 200,000 compounds, for some of which mankind formerly depended on the alchemy of animals and plants." Incidentally, in that same book—written 20 years before Pearl Harbor—Robinson made this prophecy: "The day may not be far distant when, should the chemist learn to control the incredible interatomic energy, the steam engine will seem as complete an anachronism as the treadmill."

Probably the most fruitful combinations are combinations

of ideas. So when we pile up lists of alternatives by self-questioning, we should regard the resultant ideas as possible elements that could be combined into still better ideas. As Ernest Dimnet observed, "An idea grows by annexing its neighbors."

5. *Summary of self-questioning*

The last three chapters have suggested many guides to help us make the most of our imaginations. It all boils down to piling up alternatives in one way or another to the end that we have *plenty*—so many that among them there is a mathematical likelihood of our finding the ideas we seek. Quantity may thus insure quality, as was brought out by Doctor J. P. Guilford, President of the American Psychological Association: "The person who is capable of producing a large number of ideas per unit of time, other things being equal, has a greater chance of having significant ideas."

Here is a summary of some of the kinds of self-interrogation that can lead to ideas:

Put to other uses? New ways to use as is? Other uses if modified?

Adapt? What else is like this? What other idea does this suggest? Does past offer parallel? What could I copy? Whom could I emulate?

Modify? New twist? Change meaning, color, motion, sound, odor, form, shape? Other changes?

Magnify? What to add? More time? Greater frequency? Stronger? Higher? Longer? Thicker? Extra value? Plus ingredient? Duplicate? Multiply? Exaggerate?

Minify? What to subtract? Smaller? Condensed? Miniature? Lower? Shorter? Lighter? Omit? Streamline? Split up? Understate?

Substitute? Who else instead? What else instead? Other ingredient? Other material? Other process? Other power? Other place? Other approach? Other tone of voice?

Rearrange? Interchange components? Other pattern? Other layout? Other sequence? Transpose cause and effect? Change pace? Change schedule?

Reverse? Transpose positive and negative? How about opposites? Turn it backward? Turn it upside down? Reverse roles? Change shoes? Turn tables? Turn other cheek?

Combine? How about a blend, an alloy, an assortment, an ensemble? Combine units? Combine purposes? Combine appeals? Combine ideas?

That list was adapted by M.I.T. personnel and published in an illustrated booklet, copies of which are available on request to the Creative Education Foundation, State University College, Buffalo, New York 14222.

An example of how these self-queries have been used came from Mrs. Bonnie Driscoll. She reported: "About to produce a fashion show at the Waldorf Astoria, I tried in vain for nearly a month to line up the needed ideas. Then I started to ask myself that list of questions. Within two hours I had 28 ideas—28 in two hours after three weeks of no ideas at all."

There are, of course, no clear-cut boundaries between those different hunting fields. For instance, through *addition* we may arrive at an idea, only to find that its value depends upon thinking up a *new use*. Such was the case when Pittsburgh Plate sought a bigger volume in mirror glass. The first idea was to sell *larger* mirrors. Fine, but where? A relatively new use was thought up and tried out—large mirrors to cover *doors*—and this turned out to be the answer.

A Rochester manufacturer thought up an adaptation of scissors so as to make a better kind of tweezers; and he called his new product "Twissors," thus combining two common names into a name that he could own.

The *Reader's Digest* is another example of cross-ruffing. Just after the first World War, De Witt Wallace thought up the idea of condensing the best of articles into a little magazine, a magazine which grew until its circulation now covers nearly 12 million homes in America alone. Mr. Wallace then asked himself, "How about *multiplying* this success?" So now there are 28 foreign editions. Although none as yet covers Russia, the others are carrying America's torch into almost every other corner of the globe.

* * *

When all is said and done, it is combination which overshadows any of the other categories outlined above as a means to the generation of good ideas. And, in this regard, let's hark back to the fact that nine ball-players can be rearranged into 362,880 batting orders. This formula indicates the mathematical soundness of the principle that, in dealing with ideas, quantity can help insure quality of ideas. This is especially true when it comes to the geometrical progression of *combinations* of ideas.

TOPICS

1. What questions might you ask yourself when searching for alternative ideas by way of rearrangement?
2. In considering alternatives by way of sequence, why should we ask: "Should cause and effect be transposed?" Discuss.
3. What questions might you ask yourself when searching for alternative ideas by way of vice versa?

4. Name six examples of ideas that could have been arrived at through the reversal technique.
5. What questions might you ask yourself when searching for alternative ideas by way of combination?

EXERCISES

1. Name three ways in which television sets might be improved.
2. What could a needy woman with a family do to locate part-time jobs?
3. What ideas could you suggest to help a mother persuade a child to pick up his room?
4. Suggest at least three devices to wake people up in the morning, gently but firmly.
5. Which of the following would best lend itself to starting a fire: (a) Fountain pen. (b) Onion. (c) Pocket watch. (d) Light bulb. (e) Bowling ball. (This exercise suggested by Dr. J. P. Guilford.)

REFERENCES

BAINBRIDGE, JOHN, *Biography of an Idea: the Story of Mutual Fire and Casualty Insurance*. New York. Doubleday and Company, 1952.

BENTON, MILDRED, *Creativity in Research and Invention in the Physical Sciences*. U. S. Naval Research Laboratory, Washington 25, D. C., June 1961.

CHASSELL, LAURA M., "Tests for Originality." *Journal of Educational Psychology*. June 1916, pp. 317–328.

DUNCKER, KARL, "On Problem Solving." *Psychological Monograph, 270*, 1945.

FEDERICO, P. J., "The Invention and Introduction of the Zipper." *Journal of the Patent Office Society*. December 1946, pp. 855–876.

FISICHELLI, V. R. and WELCH, L., "The Ability of Art Majors to Recombine Ideas in Creative Thinking." *Journal of Applied Psychology*. June 1947, pp. 278–282.

GILFILLAN, S. C., "Inventions and Discoveries." *American Journal of Sociology*. May 1932, pp. 868–875.

GUILFORD, J. P., WILSON, R. C., CHRISTENSEN, P. R. and LEWIS, D. J., "A Factor-Analytic Study of Creative Thinking." Reports from the Psychological Laboratory, The University of Southern California, No. 4, 1951.

KEYES, KENNETH S., JR., *How to Develop Your Thinking Ability*. New York. McGraw-Hill Book Co., Inc., 1950.

LUCHINS, A. S. and LUCHINS, EDITH H., "New Experimental Attempts at Preventing Mechanization in Problem-Solving." *Journal of General Psychology, 42,* 1950, pp. 279–297.

MARCOSSAN, ISAAC F., *Wherever Men Trade, the Romance of the Cash Register*. New York. Dodd, Mead and Company, 1945.

Printers' Ink, Vol. 276, No. 11, September 15, 1961.

ROSSMAN, J., *The Psychology of the Inventor*. Washington. Inventors Publishing Company, 1931.

SYMONDS, P. M., *Education and the Psychology of Thinking*. New York. McGraw-Hill Book Company, Inc., 1936.

TAYLOR, DONALD W. and MCNEMAR, OLGA W., "Problem Solving and Thinking." *Annual Review of Psychology,* 1955, Vol. 6, pp. 455–482.

WELCH, L., "Recombination of Ideas in Creative Thinking." *Journal of Applied Psychology*. December 1946, pp. 638–643.

Chapter XX

The effect of emotional drives on ideation

ROUGHLY SPEAKING there are two sources of motivation: 1. Internal. 2. External.

The external type includes all kinds of effort-spurring incentives such as the awards offered in suggestions systems. Other incentives are less specific and less immediate. These include prospects of promotion, prestige, publicity, and other forms of recognition.

The incentive for monetary gain stands out as the most potent of all spurs. Without this incentive, the United States would probably be trailing in inventions instead of being so far ahead of the rest of the world.

Encouragement is a widely applicable incentive, as was pointed out in the fourth chapter of this book. The power of this kind of motivation helps explain why a creative climate within an organization can do so much to cultivate creative effort at all levels.

The "reinforcement" technique in programmed instruction encourages the student to think harder. Encouragement is likewise an essential feature of group brainstorming. Incidentally, this procedure also helps remove the blocks discussed in earlier chapters and also automatically brings into play most of the idea-spurring devices covered in preceding chapters.

Acquisitiveness and vanity are two facets of the type of

motivation we refer to as *internal.* The intensity of these inner urges largely determines the spurring potency of external incentives. The more acquisitive we are, the more we are spurred by the lure of dollars. The vainer we are, the harder we strive for kudos.

Just as necessity often mothers inventiveness, austere environment makes for acquisitiveness. The pinch of poverty and the fear of the poorhouse no longer goad the average American. Necessity has ceased to be a spur, and acquisitiveness has lost its edge. Consequently, there is a slump in our creative effort—a slump that threatens the future progress of our nation unless some way is found to make up for the loss of this source of motivation.

The traits that determine our inner drives are inherited or are acquired so early in life that they become fairly well fixed. These behavioral tendencies develop into instincts, and these instincts manifest themselves as habits of thought and habits of action.

Attitude is a habit of thought that can hurt or help creative efficacy. But attitudes can be improved by better understanding, by deliberate effort and systematic procedure.

Maslow's theory of human motivation lists five basic needs: (1) Physiological welfare (2) Safety (3) Love (4) Esteem (5) Self-actualization. The last is rated by Maslow as the healthy man's primary motivation. By self-actualizing Maslow means realizing one's potential—becoming everything one is capable of becoming. "What a man *can* be, he *must* be," said Maslow. The yearning for self-actualization should motivate our effort to remove the blocks which mar creativity, and also to do those things which can develop maximum creativity. For instance, an understanding of these blocks and of the ways in which creative talent can be implemented should help strengthen the internal source of motivation which Maslow rates as primary.

* * *

The emotional character of inner drives would seem worthy of further discussion, especially in regard to their effects on the workings of imagination. Therefore the balance of this chapter will cover some major aspects of this type of internal motivation.

2. *Fear can spur and can spoil*

According to Doctor William Easton, our feelings are the stronger and more common source of creative energy. Doctor Easton said: "Even scientists must be motivated by enthusiasm, devotions, passions; for creative thinking is not a purely intellectual process. On the contrary, the thinker is dominated by his emotions from the start to the finish of his work."

Brain surgeons are now linking emotions with imagination. Their knives are proving that every brain has a section that can create ideas. It is called the "silent area" since it controls no body movement and has naught to do with what we see or hear or physically feel. Back of this area is a lump of tissue called the thalamus. In this lobe, our basic emotions are centered.

We have always known that ideas flow faster under emotional stress. Now we know that our emotional lobe is wired by nerves to the frontal area in such a way as to affect creative thinking. In modern surgery for insanity, the nerves are severed between the emotional lobe and the "silent area."

This development in psychosurgery apparently provides physiological evidence that the creative part of the human brain is hooked up to, and can be driven by, emotions.

A chronic dread can drive a person to attack a problem with feverish energy, as was illustrated in the case of Louis Pasteur. The sight of a dog always terrified him. Even a distant bark would agonize his mind with memories of neighbors driven crazy and poisoned to death by bites of a mad wolf which raged through his boyhood village.

Pasteur had just startled the world with his man-guarding vaccines. Dozens of deadly diseases were crying for his genius. But suddenly he gave up everything else and started on a mad hunt for the secret of rabies. Thus did a childhood memory push Pasteur into a new field, a field in which relatively few human lives had ever been lost. That was in 1882, when he was past 60.

For three long years he risked his life living with mad dogs. At last he came through with a vaccine to cure the victims of rabies. On a July night in 1885 he tried the first injection on a little boy whose life seemed doomed. The boy lived. That was Pasteur's last work, and probably the triumph which gave him his greatest thrill—so closely was it linked to those heart-rending cries which had haunted him for over 50 years.

When fear takes the form of sudden fright our imaginations often soar. But this does not mean that crises make our creative *talent* any greater; it merely means that exigencies can throw our emotional drive into high gear. Napoleon laid great stress on this human trait. He held that mental excitement fuses acquired knowledge with imagination and thus produces, right then and there, the winning strategies and tactics.

That may have been true of Napoleon; but far safer and better is the steadier kind of creative planning as exemplified by the Eisenhowers. Normally, it is good creative policy to make our imagination shoot wild as long as we still have time to choose our good ideas from our bad. But when extreme passion takes possession of the mind, imagination is too prone to go berserk.

That fact has been demonstrated in many ways, and especially in fires. When the Winecoff Hotel in Atlanta burst into flames, desperate ideas led to death. To save her small son, a woman on the seventh floor threw him out of the window. A girl made a rope out of her sheet and tried to let herself down to an aerial ladder which was just about to reach her. She lost her grip and met her death on the marquee.

Fright is too treacherous a drive because it is an animal urge which throws us back to where we were before our intellects developed. As Doctor Harry Fosdick has said, "It works without benefit of brain." More specifically, the ideas we thus generate are put into action without recourse to evaluation.

Fear of punishment may force people to work harder physically; but coercion tends to cramp imagination, according to Doctor Howard E. Fritz, research head of the B. F. Goodrich Company. "To induce creative thinking," he said, "we cannot dominate or threaten. Such methods will not and cannot inspire."

"Inspiration is and can be the product only of free men," added Doctor Fritz. If this is so, then democracy provides the healthiest climate for creativity. Fortunately in America, creative minds are not paralyzed by fear of what their political beliefs might bring down upon their houses. Totalitarian rulers have helped overcome this handicap by providing special security and extraordinary incentive for scientists.

After the last war, our government sent to Germany Doctor Max E. Bretschger, one of America's most creative chemists. His mission was to determine how far German scientists might have gone ahead of us in devising new chemicals for advanced warfare. The creativity of German chemists had been proverbial. It might be expected that, under the Nazi whip, they would have been driven far beyond what our chemists had achieved.

"No," said Doctor Bretschger. "To our surprise we found that we had out-thought them." *Because* they were so concerned about their personal lives in the hands of Hitler, they could not fully focus their minds on their work.

Psychological experiments have confirmed the principle that most people can think better when not unduly pressed. For example, the F. E. McKinney tests on 157 students at the University of Chicago demonstrated the extent to which time pressure and blame can be detrimental to optimal motivation and therefore detrimental to efficiency in thinking. Experiments on animals by H. G. Birch similarly pointed to the conclusion that moderate motivation is a most desirable factor in problem-solving efficiency.

3. *Effects of love and hate*

Love can be a steady driving power. Love of country inspired hundreds of thousands of our people to think up ideas that helped win the last war. Their spur of patriotism was intensified by love of sons, husbands, brothers and sweethearts far away on the fighting fronts. An outstanding wartime creator was Mrs. Frances Herman, mother and grandmother. She thought up a way to speed up production of war instruments by over 33 per cent. She accounted for what she did on the grounds that her own son was in uniform, and also that her extra efforts made her feel "as though we were a second front right here."

Love makes the average woman unceasingly think up things for her family. The overpowering drive of maternal instinct has been scientifically proved beyond doubt. Among others, a group of Columbia scientists has demonstrated that, even with animals, the *maternal* drive generates far more effort than thirst or hunger or sex.

Love turned to grief can sometimes intensify creative drive. This was true of the young Toronto girl who, in her first attempt at song-writing, composed a smash hit. Her husband, a handsome young pianist, had died shortly after they were married. She was left to face the future alone, with a piano that remained closed—until one night when she decided to sublimate her heart-sickness by trying to compose a song. She succeeded; she wrote *I'll Never Smile Again.*

Love turned to hate can likewise lift a person to creative heights, as in the case of the man who devised a camera gun to wreak revenge on a woman. According to Bellevue Hospital, he was a man of "average intelligence." He had been a good-for-nothing floater. His wife threw him out. His hatred led him to invent a machine to kill her.

Time magazine described this device as "a package-camera ingeniously devised of cream-cheese boxes, wire, and an empty tin can with an innocent baked bean label. This casing concealed a 12-gauge single-shot, sawed-off shotgun." With fiendish ingenuity, the man picked up a girl and led her to hunt his first wife so as to "snap a picture of her" with that lethal camera. He gave her the story that he was a detective and the quarry was a jewel thief. The empty-headed girl innocently shot off the wife's leg with that "camera."

What imagination! To what heights that man may have risen if his talent had been steadily empowered with decent emotions and reasonable will power!

4. *Ambition, greed, adversity*

"I address myself only to those among you who have ambition to become millionaires." Andrew Carnegie thus greeted a student body. Greed for gold does provide an emotional drive in all pursuits including the creative. "But," said W. B. Wiegand, "the motive power which stokes the fires of creative thought is far more subtle, and indeed far more potent, than the lure of gold. It is ofttimes a spirit of intellectual adventure which will supply this magic touch of motivation." Yes, adventure—and let's own up to it—vanity, too, in the guise of self-realization.

The dread of poverty is an even stronger urge than the hope of riches, and this fact makes adversity an ally of creative effort. Many of our most creative people came from immigrant forebears who had long faced starvation or persecution, or both. From them, their Americanized children acquired urges akin to those bred by adversity.

Even a generation ago, the shadow of the poorhouse made native Americans strive so hard as to induce the habit of effort on which imagination feeds. I know that in my own case, my chronic drive goes back to a childhood of insecurity. My sharpest memory of early years is the night I was awakened from my sleep by voices in the next room. I was only about six, but I can almost recall the very words my father said to my mother, in their double bed:

"I can't help it, Kitty. I am going to lose my job and we are going to have to scratch to make ends meet. We haven't enough saved to live on for more than a few months, and I am worried about you and the kids."

Eventually they went to sleep, but I stayed awake. An hour later, about four o'clock in the morning, I went in and woke them up. "I heard you and Mama talking," said I, "and I couldn't get back to sleep. Don't worry about money. Remember that box of pencils you gave me last Christmas? I still have them and I'll go down on the corner and sell them for five cents apiece—so we will be all right." Undoubtedly I over-dramatized this crisis at the time; but it did serve to spur me into an incurable habit of effort.

It is often true, as George Moore remarked, that "the muse was with us when we were poor, but when we were rich she deserted us." When economic pressure is lifted, a man has to pump back into himself some of that feeling of *must*. Gerald Carson, a successful idea-man in New York, replied when asked how he forces his imagination: "I just make myself think of Baby needing new shoes." His baby has had no cause for any such worry, but prosperous Carson prods his imagination by using it to re-create the motivation of his struggling days.

The drive we need to make the most of our imagination is usually a mixture of inner urges and self-imposed spurs. And even these may change from time to time. In Michael Sadleir's analysis of Anthony Trollope's mother he said: "Her novels were first written from stark necessity—later from congenial and profitable habit." Thus it is that a person may first be forced by economic compulsion or some other strong emotion, and then be driven by habit. Even habit may wane, and public acclaim may then become the main urge.

But the habit of effort is the surest standby, according to Edna Ferber, who wrote as follows in her autobiography: "With millions of others I have been a work worshipper. Work and more work. Work was a sedative, a stimulant, an escape, an exercise, a diversion, a passion. When friends failed or fun palled or spirits flagged, there was my typewriter and there was the world, my oyster. I've worked daily for over a quarter of a century, and loved it. I've worked while ill in bed, while traveling in Europe, riding on trains. I've written in wood sheds, bathrooms, cabins, compartments, bedrooms, living rooms, gardens, porches, decks, hotels, newspapers offices, theatres, kitchens. Nothing in my world was so satisfactory, so lasting and sustaining as work."

Very few will admit it, but just plain fun ultimately becomes one of the urges, after a habit of creative effort has been formed. Many of those who have to sweat out ideas on their jobs prefer to play with ideas for diversion. The editor of a great magazine, with two hours to spend on a train, amused himself by imagining himself to be a struggling publisher of a one-man weekly newspaper. Before he reached his destination, he had thought up about 50 things he would do if his circulation were in the hundreds instead of in the millions.

In the long run our creativity will be more dependably empowered by unemotional drives such as habit and curiosity, than by emotional drives such as fear, anger, love, grief, hate, or lust. Occasionally one of these stimuli may prove all powerful; but such forces are too unsteady to rely upon, and they may tend to vitiate the reasoning power which imagination needs for worthwhile creativity. Anyway, as human beings, we cannot control our feelings as readily as we can control our thinking. Therefore, to increase our creativity, our best hope is to harness our wills.

TOPICS

1. In what ways can emotional drive help make us more creative? Discuss.
2. In what ways does emotional drive tend to mar the production of good ideas? Discuss.
3. Is love a dependable motivation for ideation? Cite evidence.
4. Which is the more helpful emotion—the hope for wealth or the fear of poverty? Discuss.
5. Can you think more creatively about someone else's problem than you can about your own? Discuss.

EXERCISES

1. Imagine you are acting in a crowded theater. From backstage comes a scream and a shout of "Fire!" What would you do?
2. If you were caught out in the open sea in a powerboat and lost your rudder, how would you steer to port?
3. What would you do with a 6-year-old child who goes into tantrums when he doesn't get his way?
4. What if you were asked to give the sermon at your church next week? What subject would you select?
5. What would you say if suddenly called on to offer a prayer for peace?

REFERENCES

BAEKELAND, L. H., "Dreams and Realities." *Journal of Chemical Education.* June 1932, pp. 1000–1009.

BIRCH, H. G., "The Role of Emotional Factors in Insightful Problem-Solving." *Journal of Experimental Psychology,* 38, 1945, pp. 295–317.

BURGESS, C. F., "Research for Pleasure or for Gold." *Industrial and Engineering Chemistry*. February 1932, pp. 249–252.

JACKSON, JOSEPHINE A. and SALISBURY, HELEN M., *Outwitting Our Nerves*. Garden City. Garden City Press, 1944.

KINDLEBERGER, J., "We Use a Club to Keep People Thinking; Kalamazoo Vegetable Parchment Company." *Factory Management*. June 1933, p. 221.

LEFFORD, A., "The Influence of Emotional Subject Matter on Logical Reasoning." *Journal of General Psychology*. April 1946, pp. 127–151.

MAIER, N. R. F., "The Behavior Mechanisms Concerned with Problem Solving." *Psychological Review*. January 1940, pp. 43–58.

MCKINNEY, F. E., "Certain Emotional Factors and Efficiency." *Journal of Genetic Psychology*, 9, 1933, pp. 101–116.

MEARNS, HUGHES, "Creative Education." *Child Welfare*. December 1931, pp. 196–199.

MORGAN, J. J. B., "Effects of Non-Rational Factors on Inductive Reasoning." *Journal of Experimental Psychology*. April 1944.

MORGAN, J. J. B., "Weight Given to Untenable Factors in Thinking." *Journal of Educational Psychology*. October 1945, pp. 396–410.

PARNES, SIDNEY J., ed., *Compendium of Research on Creative Imagination*. Buffalo. Creative Education Foundation, 1958.

PEALE, NORMAN VINCENT, *A Guide to Confident Living*. New York. Prentice-Hall, Inc., 1948.

SPOONER, THOMAS, "Father of Invention: Scientific Curiosity." *Electrical Journal*. March 1939, pp. 92–94.

TRUNDLE, G. T., JR., "Insulated from Ideas." *Dun's Review*. November 1952, p. 31.

UPDEGRAFF, ROBERT R., *The Subconscious Mind in Business*. Chicago. A. W. Shaw Company, 1929.

Chapter XXI

The effect of effort on creativity

MANY FIND it easy to exert themselves physically; and yet few ever even try to exert themselves mentally. This paradox helps explain why so many of us are much less creative than we could be.

We can easily make our minds work in non-creative ways, such as reciting the Lord's Prayer either aloud or to ourselves. We could do that quite effortlessly even while standing in Times Square on a New Year's Eve—despite all the noises and sights. Yes, we "can tyrannize over the mind every hour of the day and in no matter what place," as Arnold Bennett said. But not without real effort can we drive our imaginations. When Emerson called thinking "the hardest task in the world," he must have meant *creative* thinking.

A few still believe that geniuses gush ideas without effort. The geniuses themselves say otherwise. Doctor Willard Henry Dow, who helped win the last war by wringing magnesium out of the ocean, has openly resented his being hailed as a wizard of science. According to him his "genius" is nothing but hard work. Ideas have not come easy even to men like E. M. Statler. His personal secretary, Bert Stanbro, told me: "Although the hotel world thought of E. M. as a genius, I know that every one of his great ideas came from sweating and sweating hard."

The electrical industry is a monument to man's imagination, and the General Electric Company has had many so-called geniuses. If you look closely into their beliefs, you will find agreement with a remark made by Charles E. Wilson when he was General Electric's president: "There just ain't no gold chariot that will take you there."

That is true even in the arts. Most writers recognize as "rhythms of creativity" the up and downs of their power to produce. Since each person's talent is the same from day to day, those cycles must be solely cycles of energy—a fact which helps prove how largely our creative productivity depends on conscious effort.

Relatively few people deliberately try to think, and most people are not even conscious of ever indulging in cogitation. An extreme example was that of the Swiss gentleman who meticulously recorded his 80 years, and calculated that he had spent 26 years in bed, and 21 years at labor. Eating took him six years. He was angry nearly six years. He wasted more than five years waiting for tardy people. Shaving occupied 228 days, scolding his children took 26 days, tying his neckties 18 days, blowing his nose 18 days, lighting his pipe 12 days. He laughed for only 46 hours in all his life. He recorded no time spent on *thinking* in all those 80 years.

Battista Grassi divided mankind into three classes: (1) Those who work their minds. (2) Those who pretend to do so. (3) Those who do neither. "Unless you are in the first class," said Grassi, "you will probably fail to summon up the energy to make yourself do the things that you have to do to get the most out of your imagination."

2. *Concentration as a creative key*

The German psychologists made much of what they called *Aufgabe.* In its simplest term, this means all-out concentration. To help insure this type of attention, we can sometimes intensify our interest.

Intent is stronger when we have a goal, such as making money. We can make it even stronger by making our goal more graphic—like working for the wherewithal to buy a new home. And we can intensify intent by making a start. "This snaps a trap," said Doctor William Easton. "It arouses interest which immediately attracts the imagination; and, from then on, one's mental energy is likely to devote itself to finishing the affair. A writer, for example, may intensify his interest by setting down various titles for a proposed composition; and a scientist may do the same by working out a diagram of apparatus to be used in an experiment; and so on."

Self-priming is not so needed by those who engage only in tasks which interest them and which can be dropped when interest lags. But, industrial researchers, illustrators, advertising men and others in commercial lines are often assigned tasks which almost bore them; they, therefore, have to force themselves into enough intent to start creating. Whether self-generated or not, an intense interest is needed fully to command the services of our imaginations.

Purposeful musing is often productive. But such spells are apt to be misunderstood by those around us. The wife of a lawyer friend of mine was prone to criticize him for just sitting and thinking during the evening. After he had won his most lucrative case, he gently chided her: "I hope you can understand now that when I am sitting here of an evening, and seem to be daydreaming, I am really doing my hardest and most profitable work. I am thinking up my strategies."

According to Justice Felix Frankfurter, we don't devote

ourselves sufficiently to that kind of brown study. He once chided his friend, General Lauris Norstad, rated by many as the creative brain of our Air Force: "You are just another executive. If you were a success, you would devote only three or four hours a day to being an executive and the rest of the time to *thinking*."

To concentrate while thus musing is not easy, as an authoress observed: "I once tried to keep track of the things my mind touched upon when left to its own devices while I ironed one shirt. I lost count. My mind roamed like a drunkard and got nowhere. I have to lasso, hog-tie, and sit on my thought processes to get anything out of my mental meandering. I believe that exercise in imagination should include exercises in concentration itself."

Arnold Bennett strongly believed in putting one's mind through its paces, and he believed in the efficacy of continual practice to that end. "When you leave your house," said he, "concentrate your mind on a subject—no matter what, to begin with. You will not have gone ten yards before your mind has skipped away from under your very eyes and is lurking around the corner with another subject. Bring it back by the scruff of the neck."

If we concentrate hard enough and persistently enough, the problem in hand can be cogitated regardless of distractions. My best idea was born on a subway. For months I had tried to think up a plan to mutualize the ownership of our company. One night, on the way to the subway, I was about to buy a newspaper when it occurred to me that I might use those 20 minutes on the train to get nearer to the idea I had been seeking. I found a seat and began to make notes. Pretty soon the car was crowded. The chatter was babel, and the noise was bedlam. In the midst of all that I hit on *the* idea for which I had strained for so long.

I would not then have solved that problem if I had bought that newspaper. And I doubt if the solution would have come if I had not courted concentration in that subway by rubbing a pencil against paper. For pads and pencils can do much to help us make ourselves think—with or without an ivory tower, while sitting still or on the move, in quiet or amid noise. And such concentration is in turn a key to creativity.

Lack of confidence often leads to inferior effort. Dr. Sidney Parnes demonstrates this in his courses in creative problem-solving by asking his students if they could recognize and name ten varieties of birds. Most of them usually say they could not. Then he asks how many could recognize the following 12: canary, parakeet, chicken, turkey, owl, pigeon, sparrow, robin, duck, pheasant, crow, eagle.

"The moral of this," says Dr. Parnes, "is that you probably know more about almost anything than you *think* you know. But it is easier for you to say "No" to a question than to try to think out the answer. Likewise you probably have more creative talent than you *think* you have. Your main need is to apply enough effort to utilize your potential more fully."

3. *Concentration intensifies awareness*

All-out intent begets an all-around *awareness* which also helps us creatively. I have often admired the alertness of those in charge of the Abercrombie and Fitch windows in New York. There is almost always something in them that makes us stop and gaze. For instance, during wartime I noticed people packed three deep peering at one of the displays, so I wedged my way through. The magnet was nothing but a hunk of rag with a little card saying: "This piece of cloth came from the parachute of a bomb that devastated a large section of London."

In my newspaper days, such awareness was known as a "nose for news" and is still the distinguishing mark of star reporters. But even a chemist can set himself apart by developing the same power. Through awareness we can multiply our intake of materials for our minds to assort and to apply to specific creative problems.

When awareness goes beyond receptivity, it becomes active curiosity. Nobody should ever apologize for, or seek to discourage this trait. Even "idle" curiosity is to be looked up to rather than sneered at. Veblen's ridicule of idle curiosity caused James Harvey Robinson to strike back at him with this: "Curiosity is idle only to those who fail to realize that it may be a very rare and indispensable thing. Even occasionally and fitfully idle curiosity leads to creative thought."

Creativity also calls for *keeping going.* We too often give up too easily and too early, mainly because we tend to overrate the power of inspiration and wait for lightning to strike us. There is no truth stronger than the threadbare maxim of "try and try again." The renowned rowing coach Ten Eyck used to harangue his crews with this: "If you hang on two strokes longer than your opponents, you will lick 'em." That is good counsel for anyone who wants to pull ahead in the creative race.

Because a man named Lester Pfister kept going for five years straight, there is more likelihood that the world can eat well. For America's corn would be less plentiful if Pfister hadn't made it hardier. In a chance conversation, he got the idea of inbreeding stalks of corn in order to kill off weaker strains and build up a hardier species. He started with 50,000 stalks and tied a bag around each tassel. When this was full of pollen, he inverted it over the silk of an ear on the same stalk. Then the tassel was snapped off.

The whole process had to be done painstakingly by hand, season after season. Five years later, Pfister was left with four ears out of his original 50,000 stalks. By that time he was destitute, but had a fortune in hand. For those four ears, unmarred by disease after five generations, represented the source of a perfected seed for which farmers ever since have gladly paid a premium.

Few of us can hope to keep at it as hard as Lester Pfister, or others who have made history by creative doggedness. And yet all of us can keep our imaginations on the grindstone just a little longer and thus spark more and better ideas.

4. *Effect of effort on association*

Concentration naturally tends to make association of ideas more fruitful. And its pays to put effort into associating one idea with another, as was brought out by the statement which Dorothy Sayers put into the mouth of her resourceful hero, Lord Peter Wimsey:

"If ever you want to commit a murder, the thing you've got to do is prevent people from associatin' their ideas. Most people don't associate anythin'—their ideas just roll about like so many dry peas on a tray, makin' a lot of noise and goin' nowhere, but once you begin lettin' 'em string their peas into a necklace, it's goin' to be strong enough to hang you, what?"

That kind of stringing together is what Graham Wallas hailed as "correlation." This calls for scanning the little ideas which well up into our minds and scrutinizing them for likenesses. By such conscious thinking we can supplement the automatic power of our associationism. One of the deliberate ways to stimulate associative correlation is consciously to apply the idea-spurring questions listed in previous chapters.

Ancient Egypt and modern Arizona are much alike and both are lush with dates. But without man's toil, Arizona dates would be mostly stones. The date meat comes from a mating between the male palms and the female. In Africa, this fertilization is done by nature. In Arizona, human effort has to transfer the pollen from the male trees to the female trees every spring.

Thus it is with cross-fertilization of ideas. We should nudge nature with purposiveness, according to Aristotle, who recommended that we "hunt for the next in the series, starting our train of thought from what is now present or from something else, and from something similar or contrary or contiguous to it."

James Ward, English psychologist and philosopher, stressed how association can be enriched by *selective attention*. The more persistent our interest is, said he, the more we can profit from association. In other words, although association normally runs through our mental hose hither and yon, and willy-nilly—if we keep its nozzle trained on the creative task at hand, we can make our flow of association sprout more seeds for us.

While working on this book, my mind increasingly dwelt on the subject of imagination. One morning I went to the cellar and noticed an old kiddy car which reminded me of my son. I thought how glad I was that he was back at college, and had escaped the fate of so many of his mates while crossing the Rhine with the 17th Airborne. That reminded me of planes. And that reminded me of jet planes. "I wonder who thought up the first jet plane and how he came to do so." That was my next thought. And it came to me because my mind was focused on the subject of creative thinking.

But we cannot count too much on association. Anybody who aspires to be creative should consciously seek to be creative. The best way to become more creative is to practice creativity—actually to reach out for creative problems, rather than to deal only with those which are thrust upon us.

Many young men have applied to me for creative positions, and I have been amazed to find how few have ever called on their wills to work their imaginations. One of my test questions has been, "What did you ever try to think up on your own initiative?" In most cases the answer has been, "Nothing." Those who have never deliberately tackled a creative task seem to think that if they had a job which called for imaginative effort they could generate ideas because they then would be compelled to do so; but they seem dubious whether imagination can be energized without some such outside pressure.

There can be no question but that nearly all of us can captain our minds more than we do. To more or less degree we are all endowed with will power; and that is a key to creative effort. As Pasteur observed, "Work usually follows will." As William James wrote, "The *normal* opener of deeper and deeper levels of energy is the will." And as Brooks Atkinson attested: "*Every man* can achieve a great deal . . . according to the burning intensity of his will and the keenness of his imagination."

TOPICS

1. Do you agree that we can tyrannize over the mind every day and in no matter what place? Discuss.
2. What steps can anybody take deliberately to induce concentration?
3. Was Veblen right in deriding idle curiosity? Discuss.
4. In what ways can associative power be stepped up?
5. Does a person's creative power depend more on the "intensity of his will" than "the keenness of his imagination"? Discuss.

EXERCISES

1. What front-page news stories might be hidden in: (a) Two people meeting on a corner. (b) A cat fight. (c) A child's toy. (d) A glove.
2. Name six goals which would provide strong incentives to spur your own creative thinking.
3. Make up a parody of a Mother Goose rhyme.
4. If you were a cartoonist, what objects (other than human) would you depict to denote: (a) Autumn. (b) Greed. (c) Happiness. (d) Poverty.
5. A man living on the 22nd floor could take his automatic elevator all the way down, but not all the way up. Why?

REFERENCES

Barkan, Manuel and Mooney, Ross L., eds., *The Conference on Creativity.* (A Report to the Rockefeller Foundation), Ohio State University, 1953.

Bennett, Arnold, *How to Live on Twenty-four Hours a Day.* New York. Doubleday and Company, Inc., 1939.

Campbell, Murray and Hatton, Harrison, *Harbert M. Dow—Pioneer in Creative Chemistry.* New York. Appleton-Century-Crofts, Inc., 1951.

CRABB, A. RICHARD, *The Hybrid-Corn Makers.* New Brunswick. Rutgers University Press, 1947.

CURTIS, CHARLES J., JR. and GREENSLET, FERRIS, *Practical Cogitator.* Boston. Houghton Mifflin Company, 1945.

DELEEUW, ADELE and CATEAU, *Make Your Habits Work for You.* New York. Farrar, Straus, and Young, 1952.

FERBER, EDNA, *A Peculiar Treasure.* New York. Doubleday and Company, Inc., 1939.

FOSDICK, HARRY EMERSON, *On Being a Real Person.* New York. Harper & Brothers, 1943.

GORDON, K., "Imagination and the Will." *Journal of Psychology.* April 1935, pp. 291–313.

MAUGHAM, W. SOMERSET, *Strictly Personal.* New York. Doubleday and Company, Inc., 1941.

PARNES, SIDNEY J., "Effects of Extended Effort in Creative Problem-Solving." *Journal of Educational Psychology.* June 1961, pp. 117–122.

ROE, ANNE, "A Psychological Study of Physical Scientists. *Genetic Psychology Monograph.* May 1951, pp. 121–235.

SADLEIR, MICHAEL, *Trollope, A Commentary.* Boston. Houghton Mifflin Company, 1927.

SZEKELY, L., "The Dynamics of Thought Motivation." *American Journal of Psychology.* January 1943, pp. 100–104.

Chapter XXII

Periods of incubation invite illumination

THE PART of the creative process that calls for little or no conscious effort is known as incubation. The root of that noun is a verb meaning "to lie down"; thus it carries a connotation of purposive relaxation. In medical terminology, incubation denotes the development stage of infectious diseases. In its application to the workings of imagination, the term covers the phenomenon by which ideas spontaneously well up into our consciousness.

Incubation often results in "bright" ideas, and perhaps that's why it is said to invite *illumination.* And because its flashes are sometimes sudden, it has also been referred to as "the period of luminous surprise." Poetically, John Masefield has painted a picture of stray ideas as "butterflies" fluttering in through our mental windows.

Henry James made much of the "deep well of unconscious cerebration." Emerson took time out each day for "meditating quietly before brooks." Shakespeare called incubation "the spell in which imagination bodies forth the forms of things unknown." Somerset Maugham wrote, "Reverie is the groundwork of creative imagination."

Much of the literature on incubation consists of similar comments—subjective observations, usually based on personal experience. The paucity of scientific research on this phase of psychology is surprising.

One experiment by Adamson and Taylor is mentioned later in this chapter. The research most widely cited was done by Rokeach. The net of his findings was this: An increase in time between divulging the problem and subjecting it to creative attack resulted in a decrease in "rigidity" in the solution effort. Incidentally this is why the group brainstorming procedure (as set forth in Chapter XIII) calls for acquainting panelists with the problem on the day before their session.

Some textbooks on psychology practically ignore creative imagination. However, one of the most widely adopted devotes about 14 of its more than 500 pages to constructive thinking and stresses the function of incubation. This textbook is *Psychology: The Fundamentals of Human Adjustment* by Norman L. Munn. Its section on creativity is summed up in these words: "Analysis of creative thinking by the thinkers themselves, and by others, has led to the conclusion that four stages are more or less clearly evident. These are: preparation, the gathering of relevant information and attempts to organize it; incubation, a period of relative inactivity, perhaps with recurrence of ideas about the problem, but no evident progress; inspiration, the sudden illumination, or "aha" experience; and verification or revision, the testing-out and evaluation of the idea, inference, or hypothesis, either by implicit processes or by actual experiment."

This outline gives full credit to the importance of incubation, but omits the part of the problem-solving process which calls for idea-finding—especially the deliberate type of ideation which can produce leads which incubation can transform into valuable ideas.

2. *The inexplicability of illumination*

Modern science recognizes the productivity of illumination. Doctor Walter B. Cannon of Harvard, after 40 years in physiological research, wrote in his book entitled *The Role of Hunches:* "From the years of my youth, the unearned assistance of sudden and unpredicted insight has been common." His investigation of the creative habits of 232 highstanding chemists revealed that over a third of these scientists gave credit to hunches.

Many scientists of the past likewise stressed illumination. Said Darwin in his autobiography, "I can remember the very spot in the road, whilst in my carriage, when to my joy the solution occurred to me." Hamilton, describing his discovery of quaternions, reported that his basic solution came to him as he "was walking with Lady Hamilton to Dublin, and came up to Brougham Bridge." But Darwin and Hamilton had put in years of deliberate thinking to reach those points of illumination.

Poincaré, the pioneer in higher mathematics, likewise acknowledged his indebtedness to incubation. He had been developing the theory of Fuchsian functions but was frustrated in his effort to complete his clarification. At this point he had to go on a geologic excursion. "The changes of travel," he reported, "made me forget my mathematical work. Having reached Coutances, we entered an omnibus to go some place or other. At the moment when I put my foot on the step the idea came to me—without anything in my former thoughts seeming to have paved the way for it—that the transformations I had used to define the Fuchsian functions were identical with those of non-Euclidean geometry."

Another distinguished mathematician, John Von Newman, attested to his belief in what he called the "sub-conscious." He testified that he often went to bed at night with an unsolved problem on his mind and woke up the next morning able to scribble the answer on the scratch pad he kept at his bedside.

In literature, the same phenomenon has been marveled at by Goethe, Coleridge and countless others, and often referred to figuratively. Stevenson spoke of his "Brownies" as helpers who worked for him while he slept. Barrie gave much credit to "McConnachie"—whom he described as "the unruly half of me, the writing half." Milton dubbed as "droughts" his periods of illumination. He actually courted these spells by just brooding over a theme and deliberately writing nothing. Sometimes in the night he would awaken his daughters in order to dictate his poetry to them.

Modern authors have similarly attested. "A story must simmer in its own juice for months or even years before it is ready to serve," wrote Edna Ferber. A newer novelist, Constance Robertson, told me this: "I have found that it pays to hold a plot in suspension, and not to worry it or force it. At the right point, I go into a long lull. *Then,* I tackle my typewriter and write whatever comes. My story then seems to reel itself off in a most extraordinary way."

Illumination has been explained as "intellectual rhythm"; but that seems more poetic than expository. A clearer psychological explanation was put forth by Doctor Elliott Dunlap Smith: "If the knowledge of the inventor and the clues which will bring the invention into being have been brought nearly into position to provide the inventive insight, his inner tension will be strong. . . . As he nears his goal he will become increasingly excited. . . . It is no wonder that the sudden release of such inner tension is often described as a 'flash.'"

Unconscious effort in the form of *inner tension* appears to be a most likely theory. But there may be other ways to explain illumination, and one of these has to do with motivation. Creative thinking thrives on enthusiasm, and this tends to lag when we force our minds beyond a certain point. By letting up a while, we tend to regenerate our emotional urge.

Another explanation is that our power of association often works best when running freely on its own. During time-out, this untiring helper is more likely to scurry around in the hidden corners of our minds and pick up the mysterious ingredients which combine into ideas.

Physiological explanations have also been advanced, based mainly on the effect of fatigue. But no theory has as yet gained general acceptance. When all is said and done, it is likely that illumination, like life itself, will remain a mystery.

3. *Passive ways to induce illumination*

Even when idling, we sometimes need to use a bit of will power to set the right climate for illumination. For instance, when I sit down for a haircut, I usually say to my friend the barber: "If you don't mind, Joe, I'd like to do a little thinking." I don't really *try* to *think*, but rather to let myself meander. Usually, by the time the hot towel is pulled off my face, something by way of a sought-for idea will have mysteriously flown into my mind.

Such short snatches of illumination are like naps compared to a long sleep. After a sustained creative drive, we should coast far longer—long enough to brood, for brooding helps to woo an idea. Although Newton called this process "thinking of it all the time," he, too, believed in periods of star-gazing between his spells of conscious straining.

Sleep, above all else, helps court illumination, for it tends to step up our power of associataion as well as to recharge our mental energy. While William Deininger was turning the General Baking Company from failure to success, I had free access to his office, even though I was less than half his age. "My boy, do you know that I nap here now and then?" he asked me one day. I sheepishly confessed that I knew. "Well, my lad," he went on, "I want you to realize that those naps of mine are not wastes of time. I keep pondering a problem and don't get the answer. Then, if I feel like it, I doze off, and when I wake up, the solution is right there looking at me, more often than not."

While naps may help, a good night's sleep will do more. But if we rush at it too hard on first arising, we may lose some good ideas. It is better to breakfast leisurely, or even to loaf a bit, and thus prevent premature pressure from nipping the buds of our nocturnal illumination.

Burdette Wright had to turn out more and more war planes every day during the time when Hitler had our backs against the wall. I knew Mr. Wright and wondered how, with his mind so tortured by pressure, he could do the creative thinking his job demanded. So I asked one of his right-hand men, who told me this: "He would eat with us at noon, but very lightly, and then would lock himself in his office for an hour. During that time he would lie on a sofa and—as he later told me—would just dream with his eyes open. Almost every afternoon, after one of these siestas, Mr. Wright would bring into our conference at least one good idea he had thought of in his 'do-nothing' period."

Beardsley Ruml, the "national idea man," locks himself up for at least an hour a day and does nothing but muse. He describes this kind of brown study as "a state of dispersed attention." Incidentally, he ardently believes in man's ability to turn on his creative faucet at will. While a professor at Chicago University, he jokingly challenged President Robert Hutchins with: "If you can't give me a new idea in the next 15 minutes, you're fired."

To cultivate illumination Lowell Thomas recommends a prescription from Yoga which calls for "a deliberate, sustained period of silence—just an hour of silence, sitting still, neither reading nor looking upon anything in particular."

"Soak!" That's Don Herold's prescription for creative incubation. He claims that we can never think up as well in showers as in tubs. Joseph Conrad habitually took his bath for his spells of illumination. On the other hand, Shelley found that by floating paper boats in his tub he could best court his muse. And, of course, shaving is a proverbial inducer of ideas. Composer Brahms, however, claimed that his best musical flashes came to him while shining his shoes.

Mark Twain believed in inducing illumination by letting himself loose—even playfully so. In describing his periods of incubation he wrote: "I use the meridians of longitude and parallels of latitude for a seine, and drag the Atlantic Ocean for whales. I scratch my head with the lightning and purr myself to sleep with the thunder."

4. *Less passive ways to induce illumination*

One effective way to give maximum play to illumination is to allow more time for a creative project; and one way to do that is to start sooner. Monday is supposed to be my minister's day off, but he finds he can turn out a better sermon if he makes a good start on Monday instead of later. By spreading his creative work over a longer span, he gives illumination more chance to help. Henry Ward Beecher is said to have conceived every one of his sermons at least two weeks in advance of delivery.

One enemy of ideation is functional fixedness—the tendency to keep the wheels of imagination in ruts. The experiments conducted by psychologists Robert Adamson and Donald Taylor at Stanford University confirm the principle that, by taking more time, we can reduce functional fixedness and thus ideate more adequately.

We can sometimes induce illumination deliberately by turning our creative line of thought into another direction. For instance, in my travels I ran across a story that struck me as a possible article for the *Reader's Digest.* So I gathered the facts and went to work on my narrative. Failing to think up the right angle, I dashed off the tale in a letter to my son instead of forcing myself further, and thus deliberately brushed it off my mind. Two days later, the needed idea came to me and I quickly wrote my manuscript almost exactly as published.

Psychologist Ernest Dichter has recommended complete shifts in activity: "If you have difficulty in sticking to a certain goal, give in to your natural desire to change to something else. This is particularly important when you do creative work." Edison habitually switched from one project to another and worked on several simultaneously.

Doctor Suits, director of General Electric research, recommends switching to hobbies, saying: "Mine are skiing and playing the clarinet. I have friends in the laboratory who botanize, collect Indian relics, study the stars. One business executive I know has discovered that his mind is more likely to be full of fresh ideas at the morning conference if he spends the evening fiddling with his ship models instead of poring over reports."

For a year before Pearl Harbor, I worked from time to time with Admiral Nimitz. Even then, his problems were almost too much for any man's mind; what a mental strain he must have been under when later directing the strategy of our fleets against the Japs! One of his aides was an associate of mine, and he told me this: "The Admiral would work feverishly and for long hours, but he would take time out, morning, noon and night. Before breakfast he would take a hike, each morning he would practice for 15 minutes on our pistol range, once a week he would swim for at least a mile, and almost every day he would either play tennis or pitch horseshoes."

Whitney Williams made a study of what Hollywood writers do for inspiration. Script writer Herbert Baker turns to the piano and improvises while waiting for new ideas to come his way. Dorothy Kingsley meditates in a church across the street from her studio. Mildred Gordon, who coauthors with her husband, woos her muse by going out and buying a new hat.

A simple way to court illumination is to take a walk. Since the days of Thoreau, hiking has been accepted as an aid to ideation. I found this so in Syracuse one evening when I took a stroll in the rain. The community struck me as a cross section of America. Out of that thought came the idea of establishing a consumer-research panel of 1,000 families in that county—an insignificant inspiration which turned out to be a fruitful idea for my company.

Schopenhauer advised against diversionary reading during periods of incubation. Graham Wallas likewise has warned against passive perusing as "the most dangerous substitute for bodily and mental relaxation during the stage of incubation."

Since there is something mystic about illumination, we might well do things which can help kindle the spiritual in us. When William Congreve penned "Music hath charms to soothe the savage breast . . ." he might have added that music also helps to woo the muse of illumination. Concerts are recommended. A record-changing phonograph can be a helpful accessory.

Going to church tends to breed ideas, according to Robert G. LeTourneau. He climbed to the heights through his inventions of earth-moving apparatus. On receiving an urgent order from the Army for a device to pick up shattered war planes, he and his assistants went to work feverishly, but ran up against a stone wall. "I am going to prayer meeting tonight," he told them. "Perhaps the solution will come while I am there." Thus, as far as he could, he erased the problem from his conscious mind. Before the closing prayer, the picture of the wanted design suddenly flashed before him. He went home and made a working sketch of it that very night.

5. *Pinning down our stray ideas*

There is disagreement as to what to do, if anything, about ideas that come to us by way of illumination. Some believe that we should reach out and grasp them; others believe that we should sit back and do nothing.

At least one authority on creative thinking recommends inaction to the point of restraining oneself from making a notation; but the weight of testimony seems to be on the side of those who favor action, even to the point of quickly pinning down the idea with a pencil. As witnesses in behalf of this policy, here are five who could well qualify as experts:

Physiologist R. W. Gerard of the University of Chicago advocates making notes of ideas, whenever and however they come, and he cites this case: "Otto Loewi, recently awarded the Nobel Prize for proving that active chemicals are involved in the action of nerves, once told me the story of his discovery. His experiments on the control of a beating frog heart were giving puzzling results. He worried over these, slept fitfully and, lying wakeful one night, saw a wild possibility and the experiment which would test it. He scribbled some notes and slept peacefully till morning. The next day was agony—he could not read the scrawl nor recall the solution, though remembering that he had had it. That night was even worse until at three in the morning lightning flashed again. He took no chances this time, but went to the laboratory at once and started his experiment."

Doctor Harry Hepner, Professor of Psychology at Syracuse University, writing of illumination as "the appearance of a good idea seemingly from nowhere," expressed himself as strongly in favor of catching each gleam and caging it as it comes: "Failure to record the flash, or to follow it through, may entail a tragic inability to do so later," was his conclusion.

Brand Blanshard, Professor of Philosophy at Yale, urges: "Seize the intimations of the unconscious when they come. . . . One should keep a notebook always ready to record them."

Graham Wallas testified that many of his best ideas have come to him while in his bathtub, and that he felt there was need for new creative tools in the form of waterproofed pencils and waterproofed notebooks.

Ralph Waldo Emerson put the case just as strongly: "Look sharply after your thoughts. They come unlooked for, like a new bird seen on your trees, and, if you turn to your usual task, disappear."

An ingenious method of memo-making is used by a New York lawyer. He always carries a pack of government postal cards, addressed to himself. Whenever an idea hits him—whether on the subway or in the bathroom—he jots it down on one of the cards and sticks it in the mail.

As an author, Edward Streeter likewise believes that illumination calls for recording. He puts it this way: "The stream of ideas flows continuously during all our waking hours, and along this stream priceless ideas are passing. The thing to do is to try to catch them as they go by. We should make a rough note of every idea just as soon as it occurs to us, regardless of where we are. Somehow or other the very doing of this seems to stimulate kindred ideas."

TOPICS

1. Are flashes of illumination purely spontaneous, or are they the result of previous cogitation? Discuss.
2. Why do hard-working ideators deliberately plan on "do-nothing" periods?
3. What is the essential difference, if any, between creative incubation and adolescent daydreaming?
4. Describe three instances in your own experience where "sleeping on a problem" provided a possible solution in the morning, or at least got you off to a fresh start.
5. What, if anything, should we do about pinning down our "stray" ideas?

EXERCISES

1. Think over the word games you know, like crossword puzzles, Double Crostics, Ghost, Inky-Pinky, Authors, etc. Suggest a new variation of one of the old ones.
2. What to do with old razor blades is a standing joke. Suggest six ways they might be put to practical use.
3. You have discovered your 15-year-old nephew has started to smoke. What ideas could you think up to induce him to stop?
4. If a live bird were in the fireplace of your living room, what methods would you devise to get him back outdoors?
5. If students attending a neighborhood school too often parked their cars in front of your home driveway, what steps would you take?

REFERENCES

Adamson, R. E. and Taylor, D. W., "Functional Fixedness as Related to Elapsed Time and to Set." *Journal of Experimental Psychology, 47*, 1954, pp. 122–126.

Bulbrook, Mary E., "An Experimental Inquiry into the Existence and Nature of 'Insight.'" *American Journal of Psychology*. July 1932, pp. 409–453.

Duncker, Karl, "A Qualitative Study of Productive Thinking." *Journal of Genetic Psychology*. 1926, pp. 33, 642–708.

Hadamard, Jacques, *The Psychology of Invention in the Mathematical Field*. Princeton. Princeton University Press, 1945.

Hartmann, G. W., "Insight vs. Trial and Error in the Solution of Problems." *American Journal of Psychology*. October 1933, pp. 663–677.

Hartmann, G. W., "The Concept and Criteria of Insight." *Psychological Review*. May 1931, pp. 243–253.

Leigh, R., "How Do You Get Your Good Ideas?" *Printers' Ink*. October 6, 1927, pp. 49–50.

Maier, N. R. F., "Reasoning in Humans. The Solution of a Problem and Its Appearance in Consciousness." *Journal of Comparative and Physiological Psychology*. August 1931, pp. 181–194.

MUNN, NORMAN L., *Psychology: The Fundamentals of Human Adjustment.* Boston. Houghton Mifflin Company, 1951.

PARNES, SIDNEY J., ed., *Compendium No. 2 of Research on Creative Imagination.* Buffalo. Creative Education Foundation, 1960.

PLATT, W. and BAKER, R. A., "The Relation of the Scientific 'Hunch' to Research." *Journal of Chemical Education.* October 1931, pp. 1969–2002.

REIK, THEODOR, *Listening with the Third Ear.* New York. Farrar, Straus and Young, Inc., 1949.

THOMAS, LOWELL, *How to Keep Mentally Fit.* New York. Howell, Soskin, Inc., 1940.

Chapter XXIII

The element of luck in creative quests

"He was lucky—he just *stumbled* on that idea." Quite often there is some truth in such comment; but nearly always the whole truth is that the inspiration would not have come to him if he had not been on the hunt for ideas *at the time*. Several writers have referred to this kind of luck as "serendipity." Although not in the dictionaries commonly used, the word was coined by Horace Walpole nearly two centuries ago. He used it to describe the good fortune of three of his characters, the princes of Serendip.

The term *inspiration* is quite widely used to cover both illuminative and lucky sources of ideas; but in its strict sense, inspiration implies a more definitely fortuitous factor. The main distinction between illumination and inspiration, according to Doctor William Easton, is this: Illumination wells up from obscure sources, whereas *inspiration* usually comes from "an accidental stimulus" which can clearly be traced. Another difference is that illumination is associated with our idle periods of incubation, whereas the luck of inspiration may strike us even while we are striving most strenuously.

Let's first dispose of sheer accidents, as when Charles Dickens wanted to go on the stage but was turned down because of his husky voice due to a head cold—a happenstance that made him become an author instead of an actor.

The discovery of coal in America was likewise an out-and-out accident. A Pennsylvanian, hunting in the mountains, built his campfire on an outcropping ledge of black rocks and was amazed when they caught fire and burned.

The discovery of iron in Minnesota in 1892 was far less "accidental." The seven Merritt brothers had long tramped the Mesabi Range, convinced by the vagaries of their compasses that worlds of ore lay hidden there. When their wagon mired down in rusty red mud, they found the iron. How "accidental" could we call that? Let's remember that they had been working toward that goal for nearly 10 years.

Wagner was always thinking of new ideas for operas; and yet, if he hadn't gone to sea and ridden through a storm, he might never have thought of *The Flying Dutchman.* Mendelssohn stumbled on his theme for *Hebrides Overture* when he heard waves lapping into a cave he was exploring. If a young lawyer had not gone down the Mississippi in a river-boat, his patent for an attachment to speed up stern-wheelers would not be on file in Washington, D. C. The "lucky" inventor was Abraham Lincoln. But in each of those instances, the inspiration furnished only the lead to a creative triumph—it did not supply the answer.

As in the piling up of hypothetical alternatives, creative accidents follow the law of probabilities—the more we fish, the more likely we are to get a strike. As Matthew Thompson McClure has told us, the idea that comes "as a flash" usually comes to the man who is experimenting with the problem.

"Some people deliberately hunt for inspiration," said Doctor William Easton, "as one hunts for game. They go where they are likely to find it; they keep constantly on the alert for it. Although inspiration is uncontrollable, the chances that it will occur can be increased by enlarging the stock of ideas in the mind and by multiplying observations."

Here again quantity attracts quality. And it takes driving power to pile up our opportunities for helpful accidents. Therefore, in the main, luck is the by-product of effort. It is indeed a rare accident when inspiration comes without perspiration.

2. *Observation capitalizes inspiration*

Luck does most for those bent on a specific search; and the more alert they are, the more likely they are to take advantage of lucky breaks. Sometimes even a chance remark may provide not only the lead but the answer. For example, when telephone engineers were developing Permalloy—which ultimately sixfolded the speed of underocean cabling—they were stuck for a flux that would weld the ends together. "Let's try salt," said one of them in fun. A saltcellar happened to be handy, so he shook it; the cap flew off and soon a foam-like flux completely covered the weld. Salt turned out to be the answer.

Frank Clark, a General Electric engineer, could have been reading the comics on a certain evening; but his mind was on a certain hunt. So instead of loafing he leafed through a technical publication. A word leaped up and hit him in the eye. "That's it!" he exclaimed. It was "Diphenyl," which turned out to be the missing-link in his search for a way to prevent short circuits in power-line transformers. That was a stroke of luck plus awareness which now keeps communities from being thrown into darkness when transformers are struck by lightning.

Keen observation enabled two Frenchmen to convert an accident into the discovery of photography. Louis Dageurre and Nicephore Niepce had long been on their hunt and had found a way to sensitize glass plates so as to "catch" images; but how to *keep* those pictures on the plates had the Frenchmen baffled. Nothing seemed to stop the images from fading, until one day Daguerre accidentally left some exposed plates next to a flask of mercury. Something startling had happened to those plates. "That," said Hendrik van Loon, "was the beginning of a marvelous piece of chemical sleuthing which ended with the invention of the art of photography, 'the art of drawing by means of light.'"

When I was sales manager of a bed factory, we had a chance to bid on a large hospital order. But the legs of the beds had to be fitted with sliding glass casters, and the only ones we could buy were too high-priced. So I gave my mind the task of trying to think up a way to meet that specification at less cost. The next noon, at the desk of my boss, we were talking about other matters when my elbow touched his water bottle. I looked at it and saw its glass stopper. That started me on the idea of casting glass into plugs with spirally grooved stems. A nick in the bottom of the bedpost provided a bayonet catch. The result was a tight-fitting sliding glass caster at a cost of about $1.00 per bed less. Thus did observation plus luck show me how to turn a glass stopper into a bed caster.

If we keep aware enough while on a certain quest, luck may lead us toward an entirely different objective. Koroseal was discovered in 1926 by Doctor Waldo Semon of B. F. Goodrich while he was looking for something else. The far better lightbulbs which Doctor Langmuir gave us were filled with argon. This gas was found by Lord Rayleigh, back in 1894. But he was not on the hunt for argon at the time; he was determining the density of nitrogen and noticed some strange discrepancies in his measurements. "He was led by this accidental observation to the discovery of argon," according to Henri Le Châtelier.

In 1876, Robert Koch noticed that spots on a boiled potato were of different colors. This observation led to his discovery of how each species of germ multiplies and colonizes. A similar accident led to penicillin. Alexander Fleming didn't know exactly what he was looking for, but when a culture plate became contaminated with mold, he examined it carefully and saw colonies of bacteria that looked like islands—each surrounded by *clear* spaces. This suggested that the mold might be preventing the spread of the bacteria. Chance thus opened the door to penicillin. But let's not forget that many biologists had often handled just such molded plates; it was only Doctor Fleming who observed the possible significance of that contamination.

Mistakes sometimes turn into lucky accidents. One day when William H. Mason went to lunch, he forgot to turn off the heat and pressure on an experimental press in which he was trying to create a new form of porous insulation out of exploded wood fiber. He dawdled at lunch, and when he went back to his lab was chagrined to find that heat and pressure were still being applied on his experimental fiber. He assumed that the batch was ruined; but when he released the pressure, there he had a hard, dense, smooth board—the first piece of "hardboard" ever made. That new "Masonite Presdwood" of his was only one of his creative triumphs, and the only one in which accident played a part.

At this point in my original text I gave a version of the "accidental discovery" of Duco. I have since found this to have been erroneous. My report was based on an interview with a man who seemed to be in a position to know the facts. And he sincerely believed what he told me. His version is repeated here because it tends to reveal how an unintentionally fictional report may come to be regarded as factual. Here's the story as published in previous printings:

"After the first World War, Du Pont had a huge amount of left-over explosives on hand. To salvage this material, chemists thought they might make from it a new kind of paint. They conducted thousands of experiments, and came close to the answer; but no paint worthy of the Du Pont name came out of all their research.

"One of those chemists happened one day to visit another Du Pont chemist and on his way out of the latter's laboratory noticed a can of stuff which he picked up and smelled. Excitedly he asked, 'What is *this?*' The other chemist said it was just one of those mistakes. 'I got some of that material you fellows are working on, hoping it might do for something I am trying to make. I put the stuff in an oven, but forgot to take it out when I went home last evening.' The paint chemist dashed back to his own lab yelling, 'We've got it! We've nearly had it for a long time. We didn't know we had to heat it *all night.*' Thus Duco was discovered. Luck played a part; but that chemist's observation provided the magic."

Du Pont officials have since authorized the following as the authentic version of the origination of Duco:

In July 1920, a chemist in the Du Pont plant at Parlin, New Jersey, observed that the addition of a small amount of sodium acetate to a thick solution of nitrocellulose, followed by storage, caused the solution to become thin enough for spray application. Other methods were later devised to reduce the viscosity of nitrocellulose, but this discovery led to an intensive research program to develop lacquers based on this "low-viscosity" nitrocellulose. The formulation of such lacquers, having the durability, together with the toughness and flexibility needed for use on an automobile, involved a vast amount of experimentation with many different gums, resins, plasticizers, and pigments—with durability test panels exposed all the way from New Jersey to Florida. A clear (unpigmented) lacquer made from "low-viscosity" nitrocellulose was put on the market in 1921 as a furniture finish, followed by the introduction of pigmented "Duco" as an automobile finish in 1923.

That is the true history of the discovery of, or rather the development of, Duco. But an "accident" did play a vital part. When that chemist in 1920 hit upon a way of thinning a thick solution of nitrocellulose, he was not aiming at a better paint; he was trying to find a way to eliminate static electricity in *motion picture film* based on nitrocellulose; he was seeking a way to prevent static from streaking the film.

3. *Perseverance capitalizes inspiration*

"Time and time again throughout the history of science," wrote Doctor James Conant, "the consequences of following up or not following up accidental discoveries have been very great. There is a real analogy to a general's taking advantage of an enemy's error or a lucky break, like the capture of the Remagen bridge."

A Dutch naturalist named Swammerdam had observed the same frog-leg accident long before Galvani did; but Swammerdam never followed up his observation. On the other hand, that twitching electrified Galvani into action. "Whereupon," wrote Galvani, "I was inflamed with an incredible zeal and eagerness to test the same and to bring to light what was concealed in it."

Madame Curie and her husband have been said to have "stumbled upon" radium. What happened was that Madame Curie's thesis for a doctor's degree dealt with the problem of why uranium seemed to shed light rays. She tested countless chemical elements, compounds and minerals, but was frustrated at every turn. Her husband then joined her in the search and at long last they "accidentally" got on the trail of a new and mysterious material which they called "radium." After spending four years in a dilapidated shed, processing ton after ton of ore, they finally produced a batch of radium as big as a baby's tooth. Whatever luck the Curies had came from unswerving perseverance.

According to Colin Simkin, lithography was the "accidental" discovery of Alois Senefelder in 1796. As a young playwright, he found that he could sell a number of copies of his plays, but that the printing costs ate up his profits. So he set out to find a cheaper way to make copies.

He began by writing in reverse on copper plates from which he might print; but these proved too costly. So he resorted to the use of floor tiles.

Meanwhile he had created a writing ink made out of soap, wax and lamp black. One day he had to jot down some memos. And finding that his writing ink had caked, he picked up a piece of his concoction and made notes with it on a tile. When he later tried to wash these off, he found that the porous stone absorbed water everywhere except where he had inked. "Thus," records Colin Simkin, "was established the basic principle of lithography, which is that water and grease do not have affinity for each other."

Although luck played a part in Senefelder's discovery, nothing would have happened had he not deliberately set himself to the task of finding some way to print his plays at lower cost. If he had stopped with metal plates, he would have failed. In his search for other alternatives, he hit upon the use of stone. His luck consisted mainly in the fact that the stone he found at hand happened to be of a peculiar porosity. But without perseverance he would not have invented lithography.

The heart and soul of the so-called Edisonian philosophy of creativity is perseverance. Edison believed but little in luck, but he profited by it in several instances. Once he was working on telephone transmission and incandescent lamps at the same time. He was stumped on both. On his table was a mixture of tar and lamp-black which he had been testing for his telephone transmitter. Absent-mindedly he rolled some of this material between his thumb and forefinger and formed it into a string. There he had the lamp idea he was hunting for—a filament of just such a carbon element could solve the problem of his electric bulb. And it did—thanks to a bit of luck and a lot of perseverance.

Edison's search for a lamp filament further illustrates his belief in the value of quantitative ideation in problem-solving. Among the myriads of alternatives he thought up was bamboo fibre. He actually tested over 6,000 varieties of this material in his search for a filament.

4. *Luck supplies leads*

Good breaks count most in what they lead to—*if* we follow through. A fortuitous turn may merely speed our way toward the idea we seek and which we might have captured anyway, only later. Most creative experimentation is done in tiny steps, and a bit of luck may bring a long leap.

Luck may likewise switch us from one creative pursuit to another. According to Lorton Stoddard, Sir Walter Scott was looking in a drawer for fish-hooks when he fumbled upon a part of a novel he had written and thrown away. He was losing out as a poet, eclipsed by Lord Byron. "So," wrote Stoddard, "Walter Scott looked over the forgotten fragment with interest, went to work on it—and began a new and greater literary career. For this chance discovery led to the whole series of the Waverley novels."

Some fortunate leads occur when we are not on the hunt for anything special, but are creatively alert at the time. Robert Louis Stevenson tells in *Juvenalia* how he hit on the idea for one of his classics. He was entertaining a little boy by drawing a map of an island, serrated with capes and coves, under which Stevenson lettered "Treasure Island." "Immediately," said he, "the characters of the book began to appear in the imaginary trees."

Edna Ferber tells a similar story in her autobiography. After rehearsing an early play, a co-worker said to the cast, "Next time I'll tell you what we'll do—we'll all charter a showboat and we will just drift down the rivers."

"What's a showboat?" asked Miss Ferber, for she had never heard of such. "A showboat is a floating theatre. They used to play up and down the southern rivers, especially the Mississippi and the Missouri. They'd come downstream, calliope tooting, and stop at the town landing to give their show." Miss Ferber, always on the alert, immediately recognized that description as an exciting lead for her to go to work upon.

Accidental leads may embark amateurs upon creative undertakings. Wilbur and Orville Wright were wild about flying kites. They were in the bicycle business and had no thought of airplanes. One day they read about a German meeting his death in an attempt to glide off a mountain with giant wings fastened to his arms and a tail fastened to his back. That led the Wright brothers to construct a glider with nothing but sport in mind. The history made by the Wrights at Kitty Hawk was traceable to a news clipping; but, it was only a lead; it supplied but a puny part of the answer.

Physical accidents have been known to start new creative aims. It is said that Charles Kettering once broke his arm cranking a car, and it was that which set him in search of a self-starter. Gene McDonald's car got out of control on Lookout Mountain. He came out of the wreck with a fractured skull and a deaf ear. This started him thinking about a new hearing aid. About thirty years later, as head of Zenith Radio, he offered his brain-child to the hard-of-hearing at less than half the usual price.

Young George Westinghouse, riding on a railroad, was held up by a collision between two freight trains. Such smashups were then taken for granted, because the brakes on each car had to be set by hand and a long train took a long time to stop. It was that accident which inspired Westinghouse to seek the answer to the problem of how a whole train of cars could be stopped at once.

In this case, a flash of new information provided the key to an invention. Here's the story as it appeared in the *Reader's Digest:* "George Westinghouse worried for years over ways to bring a long string of railway cars to a simultaneous stop. The answer came in a flash the moment he read that compressed air was being piped to drillers in mountains miles away: he would pipe it along his line of cars and stop them with an air brake. But such inspirations come after long preparation and thought."

The son of Elmer Sperry put to him this question: "Daddy, why does a top stand up when it spins?" That chance remark led Sperry to undertake his invention of the gyrocompass, which revolutionized marine navigation and helped make modern aviation possible. But wasn't it lucky that Sperry was alert enough to recognize that lead and industrious enough to follow it up?

Music writers speak of accidental leads as "tips." A few hits, like *Shoo, Shoo, Baby,* have come largely from chance remarks. But according to Gertrude Samuels, *Shoo Shoos* are far from typical. In her judgment, talent, plus knowledge, plus effort—instead of accident or inspiration—account for nearly all of the 50,000 songs which publishers annually audition. Miss Samuels' contention was confirmed by George Gershwin, who attested as follows: "Out of my entire annual output of songs, perhaps two—at the most three—came as a result of inspiration."

Doctor L. L. Thurstone has summarized the part played by luck in creativity: "We do not ordinarily hear about how professional men get their useful ideas, but there is much anecdotal material on how discoveries have been made. Such stories often sound as if discoveries were quite accidental. It is more likely that the investigators had previously identified themselves with a problem, in terms of which they interpreted some accidental effect. Scientific discoveries at all levels are probably not so accidental as they look to the casual observer."

TOPICS

1. Distinguish between illumination and inspiration. Discuss.
2. It is football tradition that the better-coached team gets the "breaks." How does this likewise hold true in creative pursuits? Discuss.

3. What incident enabled two Frenchmen to invent photography? To what extent was it an "accident"?
4. Why does the Edisonian principle of ideation tend to court good luck? Discuss.
5. Famous show producers have almost as many flops as successes. Is it, therefore, fair to conclude that their "hits" are due to luck? Why or why not?

EXERCISES

1. Typewriters are available in a number of type faces and almost every foreign language. Think up three other types of keyboards which might be useful for specific purposes.
2. Devise three ways to adapt an old snare drum to other uses.
3. Think of six ways a bicycle might be used *inside* the home.
4. In what respects could your overshoes be improved?
5. Name three items of everyday use which seem capable of betterment. In each case suggest what specific improvements might be made.

REFERENCES

"A Romantic Achievement in Industrial Chemistry." *Scientific American*. July 1926, pp. 34–46.

"Accidental Discoveries." *Mechanical Engineering*. August 1926, pp. 865–866.

CANNON, WALTER B., "The Role of Chance in Discovery." *Scientific Monthly*. March 1940, pp. 204–209.

DALE, HENRY, "Accident and Opportunism in Medical Research." *British Medical Journal*. September 4, 1948, pp. 451–455.

EWING, A. M., "Turning Accidents into Profit Through Careful Observation; Simultaneous and Independent Discoveries." *Journal of Chemical Education*. November 1936, pp. 530–532.

GRISWOLD, F. H., *Creative Power; the Phenomena of Inspiration; an Inquiry into the Practical Methods Used by Men of Genius in De-*

veloping Original Ideas. Philadelphia. David McKay Company, 1939.

GUILFORD, J. P., CHRISTENSEN, PAUL R., and WILSON, ROBERT C., "A Bibliography of Thinking, Including Creative Thinking, Reasoning, Evaluation, and Planning." Department of Psychology, University of Southern California, July 1953.

HARDING, ROSAMOND E. M., *An Anatomy of Inspiration.* Cambridge. W. Heffer and Sons, Ltd., 1948.

MCLEAN, F. C., "The Happy Accident." *Scientific Monthly.* July 1941, pp. 61–70.

MONTMASSON, J. M., *Invention and the Unconscious.* New York. Harcourt, Brace and Company, 1932.

SARTON, GEORGE, "The Discovery of X-Rays." *Isis.* 1936–1937, pp. 26, 346–369.

Chapter XXIV

Evolution and obsolescence of "new" ideas

To a large extent it is true that "nothing is new under the sun." Most ideas are combinations of, or improvements upon, other ideas. That is why synthesis is so often claimed to be the most fruitful phase of creative procedure.

Synthesis is the opposite of analysis; and yet, the better we analyze at first, the better we can synthesize later—the more intelligently we have picked our problems to pieces, the more likely we are to find the pieces that can be combined into the ideas which can lead to solutions. Just as analysis is important in synthesis, so also is the power of association of ideas. As Doctor Easton has said, "A creative thinker evolves no new ideas. He actually evolves new combinations of ideas that are already in his mind." To the extent that this is true, associative thinking empowers synthesis. Then, too, most combinations are based on groupings of like things and thoughts; and similarity is the basic law of association.

2. *New ideas through evolution*

Akin to synthesis is the evolutionary character of most of the important developments by way of "new" ideas. Almost without exception, they have stemmed from other ideas, either by way of combination, or evolutionary improvement. This step-by-step characteristic is illustrated by the history of ice cream, covering a span of 1,800 years.

When I was a child, a Mrs. McCabe ran a candy store around the corner from our home. One day she bought herself a new gadget so that she could make "sundaes" by shaving ice into snow-like balls which she could then douse with flavor. Mrs. McCabe's flavored snowball was new to her, and yet the same concoction was served by Nero in 62 A.D. To celebrate a gladiatorial contest, he rushed runners from Rome to the mountain tops, whence they brought back snow which Nero's cooks flavored with honey.

History loses track of ice cream until about 12 centuries later, when Marco Polo brought a startling new recipe from Asia to Rome—a kind of dessert just like Nero's ices. Two centuries later, the Medicis made a hit by climaxing their feasts with what Catherine called "fruit ice." In the 17th century King Charles paid a French chef a small fortune to make ice cream for the royal table; but the chef kept his recipe a secret.

The idea of ice cream came out in the open about 1707 when the New York *Gazette* ran advertisements announcing our first ice-cream parlors. George Washington is said to have bought ice cream from a New York shop around the corner from where he lived when he was President.

Dolly Madison made ice cream in the White House entirely by hand. The new idea of a crankable ice-cream freezer was the brain-child of Nancy Johnson just about 110 years ago.

And so it went, improvement after improvement, one new idea on top of another—until came Eskimo Pie, and now a ready-prepared sundae in a paper box with the chocolate syrup frozen right over the ice cream! And newer ideas will keep coming.

The history of ice cream not only illustrates the step-by-step process and the long lapses between new ideas on a given subject, but also illustrates how often a person thinks up something "new" without knowing that someone, somewhere else in the world, had thought up almost the same idea.

Inventors legitimately set out to improve upon the ideas of others, but a composite brain like that of Nela Park almost continually improves upon its own ideas. Here's a high-spot record of what General Electric scientists did with lamps at that research center, over a span of only 20 years, starting 25 years after Edison created his first incandescent.

In 1905 a new filament, electrically treated, lifted the efficiency of lamps by 25 per cent. In 1911 a new rugged metal filament made possible more efficient sources. In 1912 new chemical "getters" reduced bulb-blackening and made smaller sizes adequate for any given wattage. In 1913 came the gas-filled lamp, with another big jump in efficiency. In 1915 the coiled filament was re-designed and made non-saggable. This meant still more light and longer life. In 1919 the bulb was made tipless. This reduced breakage and improved appearance. In 1925 the glass bulb was frosted on the inside instead of the outside. This gave us smooth bulbs which diffused light, with practically no loss in output. And since then the same improvement upon improvement has gone on with even greater success.

3. *The time factor in ideation*

Ideas come and go in cycles. A friend of mine recently invented a new plumbing gadget, only to find that it had been patented 40 years ago. Such is a frequent occurrence.

During the Truman administration, I visited Nela Park, where I asked General Electric vice-president M. L. Sloan,

"Have you heard about the fellow who has taken advantage of President Truman's popularization of bow ties and has thought up a new one with a light at each end?"

"Yes," said Mr. Sloan, "and it interests me a lot; because when I came to work here 30 years ago my first assignment was to work with a customer who wanted tiny lamps for stickpins."

Sometimes a man may have the seed of an idea but fails to make it grow. Near a southwest hamlet, I saw a group of people in a vacant lot, and, being curious, joined the crowd. The magnet was a photographer who, for 25¢, would take your picture while you sat on a 1,000-lb. steer. He pointed his black box at me, clicked a shutter, fumbled around in the box, and in about a minute handed me my finished photo. His name was Russell Chamberlain. He had been taking pictures all over the West for 22 years with that self-developing camera which he had made for himself out of an old lunch box. Although his product was a tin-type, I couldn't help but think: "What if Russell Chamberlain had not stopped with his creation of that one crude device, but had gone on in search of the similar, but far superior, all-in-one camera developed and perfected 16 years later by Polaroid scientists?"

Many patents are based on ideas which someone else thought up first but did nothing about. Many more patents are slight improvements on the ideas of others. Remember the story of the clerk who resigned from the U. S. Patent Office some 60 years ago because there was nothing left to invent? Over 1,500,000 new patents have been granted since then. According to my patent attorney, "About 50,000 patents are now issued every year, and about 40,000 of them are for nothing but *improvements* on ideas already patented."

Even a specific project of creation takes time and more time—a fact which we should realize lest discouragement stop us too soon. "Inventions become perfect by slow improvement," said Joseph Jastrow, "and each step is itself an invention."

In 1867, Christopher Sholes, a piano-tuner, invented the typewriter, and typed a letter to James Densmore on the machine he had just completed. Densmore agreed to finance the invention; but he found it so full of bugs that Sholes had to make one improvement after another during the next five years. It was not until 1874 that Remington and Sons, gunmakers, sold the first typewriter as designed by Sholes. (Parenthetically and paradoxically, the first *adding machine* was invented by Blaise Pascal 225 years *before* Sholes turned out the first typewriter.)

As fast a worker as was Thomas Edison, he early learned how long it took to develop an idea. "Many people think of inventions as coming on a man all in one piece," said Edison. "Things don't happen that way, much. The phonograph, for example, was a long time coming, and it came step by step. For my own part, it started way back in the days of the Civil War, when I was a young telegrapher in Indianapolis." That was in 1864. It took him till 1877 to work out his first crude model.

Then, too, an idea can be ahead of its time, like Leon Forcault's gyroscope. He worked this out in 1852 to demonstrate the rotation of the earth. Thus its only use at that time was to prove something already known. On the other hand, when Elmer Sperry worked out his gyrocompass, there was an urgent need for it on airplanes, as well as on modern ocean liners.

When Robert Thompson thought up pneumatic tires in 1845, there were no motor vehicles. But when, in 1888, John

Boyd Dunlop brought out an improvement on Thompson's creation, Dunlop's new air-filled tire fitted a need that was just starting to snowball—automobiles were on their way.

Ideas by way of improvement sometimes have to wait on other ideas before they count. For example, the medical profession had made great progress in diagnoses, but these new ideas largely depended on new ways to explore the human body. Diagnosis of tuberculosis took a long stride forward as soon as fluorescent X-ray screens were able to reveal the inside of chests in less than a second.

The fluoroscope made it possible for diagnosticians to watch the actual functioning of living organs. This internal camera was another example of improvement upon improvement. The basic idea originated with William Roentgen and was improved by Thomas Edison. It was an unknown man by the name of Carl Patterson who developed, in his home laboratory, the new material which finally led to fluorescent X-ray screens.

An inventor can sometimes overcome the factor of timeliness by thinking up other uses to which to apply his brainchild. Steam was used in Egypt in 120 B.C.—but only to spin a toy. The world might not have gone without benefit of steam for the next 16 centuries if that Alexandrian thinker-upper, instead of being content with its use as a child-entertainer, had asked himself: "To what *other uses* could this steam be put?" . . . "How about using it as a labor-saver?"

4. *Obsolescence of "new" ideas*

The biggest lesson we can learn from the step-by-step nature of ideas is that *we can never stop improving*. This fact hit me hard one day in 1922 while on the way to the General Motors Research Laboratory at Dayton, Ohio. Passing a group of abandoned buildings, I asked what they were.

"There," said my Dayton friend, "is where the great firm of Barney and Smith used to make most of the world's railroad cars. When steel cars started, they stood firm in their belief that wooden cars were better. That's why they went out of business."

The early development of the automobile was far from a continuous process of improvement by one man or one staff. Gottlieb Daimler, "the father of the automobile," turned out his gasoline motor in 1884. In 1891, Panhard and Levassor used Daimler's engine on the world's first commercially made motorcar.

Reference books give credit to Charles E. Duryea for the first automobile made and sold in the United States; but the fact is that J. *Frank* Duryea was the man who created and ran America's original gasoline motorcar. He developed his first model in 1892–1893. He won the first American automobile race in Chicago in 1895, the only rivals being Benz cars imported from Germany. In 1896 he made and sold 12 Duryeas, one to Barnum and Bailey.

Henry Ford, meanwhile, was busy perfecting his car; but he never sold one commercially until 1903. Incidentally, this was the year when the Wright brothers flew America's first airplane, which was substantially a new version of the automobile, with wings instead of wheels.

Back in 1879, George Selden of Rochester, N. Y., had applied for a fundamental patent on a road vehicle powered by a gasoline motor—12 years before any motorcar was ever offered anywhere in the world. Selden had the *idea;* but he let Henry Ford and others run away with it by their creation of improvement after improvement and by actually producing cars.

Henry Ford in his early years was almost a one-man creative staff. Throughout his active life, part of his wizardry was to pile one improvement on top of another. For instance, before he adopted the final design for his first tractor, he worked up 871 successive models.

Along about 1910, Pierce Arrow was the best-known car. At one time just those two words, "Pierce Arrow," could easily have sold for at least a million. But while competitors were innovating one idea after another to make cars better and cheaper, Pierce Arrow engineering stood still creatively. Just before the company's end, an effort was made to sell the Pierce Arrow name, but by that time, no other car manufacturer wanted those two words at any price.

At the age of 68, James F. Bell, head of General Mills, said this: "By resorting to the stimulus of imagination, we can look on daily tasks, machines, or any other thing with interest and a questioning mind. 'Yes, it is *good,*' we say, 'but how can it be made *better*?' . . . One of the greatest dangers that any man or corporation faces is coming to believe, after a period of well-being or success, in the infallibility of past methods applied to a new and changing future. If we are to enjoy continuing success—our ideas, methods, goods and services must always be 'better-than.'"

TOPICS

1. What is the difference between analysis and synthesis? Discuss.
2. Why is synthesis so often hailed as the key to creative achievement? Discuss.
3. Outline the development of ice cream, from its beginning to today. List important steps in its evolution.
4. A bad idea today may be a good idea tomorrow. Discuss.

EXERCISES

1. Think of five new ways to use the "electric eye."

2. Invent a new toy to amuse children under 10 years of age.
3. Describe a candy bar which you think might be popular but which is different from any now on the market.
4. Write a jingle around each of these words: resident, dawn, agile, Eisenhower.
5. If you thought that original paintings by free-lance artists could be successfully sold through supermarkets, what steps would you take to go about starting such a business of your own?

REFERENCES

Burton, W. H., "Problem-solving technique; its appearance and development in American texts on general method." *Educational Method.* January, pp. 189–195, February, pp. 248–253, March, pp. 338–342, 1935.

Deland, Lorin F., *Imagination in Business.* New York. Harper & Brothers, 1909.

Dickinson, H. W., *James Watt.* New York. The Macmillan Company, 1936.

Downing, E. R., "The Elements and Safeguards of Scientific Thinking." *Scientific Monthly.* March 1928, pp. 231–243.

Duncker, K. and Krechevsky, I., "On Solution-Achievement." *Psychological Review.* March 1939, pp. 176–185.

Killeffer, D. H., *The Genius of Industrial Research.* New York. Reinhold, 1948.

Kramer, Dale, *Ross and The New Yorker.* New York. Doubleday and Company, Inc., 1951.

Overstreet, Harry Allen, *Let Me Think.* New York. The Macmillan Company, 1940.

Stern, B. J., "Resistance to the Adoption of Technological Innovations." Section 4, pp. 39–66, *Technological Trends and Their Social Implications.* National Resources Committee, Washington. U. S. Government Printing Office, 1937.

Vaughan, Wayland, *General Psychology.* New York. Odyssey Press, 1936.

Chapter XXV

Indispensability of creativity in science

WHILE AT a college commencement, I met Doctor James B. Conant. After thanking him for having written *On Understanding Science,* I remarked: "What impressed me was the way you stressed the part played by creative imagination in science."

"It's the *whole* of it," he replied without hesitation. Of course he did not mean that literally. But he left no doubt that, in his judgment, creative power is indispensable to scientific achievement.

When I later quoted Doctor Conant to a young doctor of engineering, he stated: "I'm just beginning to realize how true that is. Throughout my undergraduate and postgraduate years only one professor ever talked to us about the creative side of science, and he did that outside our curriculum."

Science is usually defined as "classified knowledge." But where has this knowledge come from? Where else but from men's hunches—from their thinking up countless alternatives—from their dreaming up new ways and new devices by which to test their guesses? The basis of such testing is still trial and error; but this is now known as scientific experimentation, and rightly so, because of its orderliness and its controllability.

Doctor T. Percy Nunn has urged that the "*static* conception of science as a body of truths" be changed into a "*dy-*

namic conception of science as a definite pursuit." According to him, "science is a *creative* process." And Doctor Conant concurs: "Science is that portion of accumulative knowledge in which new concepts are continuously developing from experiment and observation and lead to further experimentation and observation."

Before the dawn of science, imagination in the form of superstition conceived and maintained many false beliefs. The exploding of such fallacies was the first triumph of Galileo and other early scientists. As science strode forward in the 17th, 18th, and 19th centuries, and even more swiftly in our century, its techniques were naturally glorified.

Only recently have scientists recognized the part played by creative power. Kettering of General Motors did much to stimulate this recognition, and so have Doctor Suits of General Electric and many of the younger leaders. The American Society of Mechanical Engineers has conducted seminars solely "to emphasize the importance of creative ability in engineering." The American Chemical Society's Committee on Professional Training recently reported: "It is lack of ability in *original thinking* that makes far too many men of doctoral training unsuitable for industrial research."

Starting in 1954, engineering schools have been giving more and more recognition to the need for creative training in their curricula. This trend was pioneered by M.I.T. and Rutgers.

To help make up for lack of undergraduate orientation in creativity, many companies have recently inaugurated intramural courses of their own. Chrysler, Ford and General Motors are but three of the organizations which have provided such training for engineers and research scientists.

The outstanding example of this type of education is found

in General Electric. Its Creative Engineering Program is a postgraduate course, well over a year in length. It covers engineering fundamentals, conception of new ideas and reduction to practice. It especially stresses problem approach, creative techniques and creative attitudes.

General Electric also conducts short courses in creative thinking for engineering executives. These "Creative Approach Seminars" comprise 16 sessions. Some 700 G.E. engineers take such a course each year.

"Many have insisted that the imaginative process is different in art and in science," said Doctor R. W. Gerard. "On the contrary, the creative act of the mind is alike in both cases. . . . Imagination enters into the devising of experiments or of apparatus or of mathematical manipulations and into the interpretation of the results so obtained. But these are likely to be minor miracles compared with the major insight achieved in the initial working hypothesis."

"It's generally a hunch that starts the inventor on his quest," said Doctor Suits of General Electric. . . . "Later on, perhaps after weeks of fruitless searching, another inspiration, arriving when he least expects it, drops the answer in his lap. I've seen this happen over and over. But I've yet to meet that 'coldly calculating man of science' whom the novelists extol. Candidly, I doubt that he exists; and if he did exist, I fear that he would never make a startling discovery or invention."

More often than not, it is the more imaginative scientist who rises to the post of research director. Of course, he must be of sound technical background but, to be the real spark plug of his group, he personally has to shoot wild at times, and must encourage those about him to do likewise.

A research head also must create co-operation. This is particularly stressed in the Du Pont organization, where teamwork is zealously sought "not only on the part of men in a particular laboratory, but also as regards interdepartmental co-operation." So said Doctor E. K. Bolton of Du Pont.

Doctor Ernest Benger, also of Du Pont, stressed the fact that Du Pont's directors of research actively seek ideas from *throughout* the organization. "I do not know what percentage of our ideas comes from other sources," remarked Doctor Benger, "but certainly a great many do. Some of our best thoughts have come from managers, from production people and from salespeople."

2. *The essence of organized research*

Although the 17th century shone with illustrious discoveries, it created almost nothing really useful to mankind, except by way of navigation. "It is not until the 19th century," said Doctor Conant, "that we begin to see anything like the *practical* influence of scientific progress to which the first scientists so confidently looked forward."

According to Alfred North Whitehead, "the greatest invention of the 19th century was the invention of the *method* of invention. *This* is the real novelty, which has broken up the foundations of the old civilization."

Organized research, as we know it today, began in this country in 1902 when Du Pont's first formal research laboratory was started. The great upsweep came from 1920 on. In 1920 there were about 300 industrial research laboratories in America. In 1950 there were 2,845 such laboratories, staffed with over 165,000 people, and costing over a billion dollars a year. And now there are over twice as many.

Substantially there are two kinds of scientific research: one the *specific,* and the other the *fundamental.* "The aim of *specific* research programs," said James Bell of General Mills, "is the continual improvement of existing goods and services, and the creation of new goods and services at constantly diminishing costs." Perhaps the outstanding record in research for creation of new products is that of Du Pont. Over half of this company's present products were not even thought of 25 years ago.

Du Pont is also doing more and more in *fundamental* research, which was started by Doctor Stine in 1927. Its purpose, according to Doctor Bolton, is "to establish or discover new scientific facts without regard to immediate commercial use." Specific or practical research calls for imagination; but scientists in fundamental research need even more creative power. To quote Alexis Carrel, their minds "must pursue the impossible and the unknowable."

The path to any research project must be paved with ideas. There must be an "imaginative, new approach," said Research Director W. B. Wiegand. Plenty of "tentative stabs" at the problem must be made at the start. Much of the most brilliant research has started from an idea that seemed wild at the time. Pasteur soared high in such thinking. His assistant learned to listen bright-eyed to his fantastic imaginings. "Another man might have thought his chief completely crazy," remarked Doctor Paul de Kruif.

In our country, our outstanding trail blazers have likewise been noted for their startling ideas for starting scientific quests. Doctor Kettering of General Motors sought a gasoline of unbelievable mileage. From that starting point, he and Dr. Midgeley finally arrived at an anti-knock fuel called Ethyl.

Doctor Edward Goodrich Acheson reached for the sky and started a great industry. His original idea was to hunt for "diamond" dust. He had a hunch that an abrasive material could be created which would be harder, sharper, faster-cutting than abrasives made by nature, such as emery, corundum, and garnet. He knew that carbon was used as the hardening agent in making steel, and that, in its crystalline form, it was the hardest known substance. He, therefore, started experimenting by impregnating clay with carbon under a high temperature.

In his first examination of the fused mass, Doctor Acheson was painfully disappointed. However, his trained eye detected a few tiny sparkling crystals—crystals that man had never seen before. He collected the crystals on the end of his pencil and drew them across the surface of a pane of glass. They scratched the glass as sharply as a diamond. The first few handfuls of the new substance were eagerly purchased by cutters of precious stones at the rate of $880 per pound. They found it worked as well as diamond dust which cost $1,500 per pound. Thus Carborundum was created.

Most scientific advances depend, not on one idea, but on many hypotheses from which to choose at the start. "Hundreds of new ideas will flow from preliminary conferences," said W. B. Wiegand. "From these, one, or perhaps two new approaches may emerge. Upon the soundness and fundamental originality of these new approaches much will depend." Thus *imagination* must supply the springboard for scientific *knowledge.*

3. *Imagination in experimentation*

From the imaginative approach, the aim is set. Then comes the shooting in the form of experimentation; and, here again, imagination is called for at every turn. For one thing, there are scores of different ways in which experiments might be made, and an unheard-of method often has to be thought up.

To stimulate the kind of creative thinking needed in experimentation, Doctor Paul Eaton, professor of mechanical engineering at Lafayette, has recommended that teachers of science "arrange the problems to be determined through test in the laboratory in such a manner that 'cut-and-dried' technique through mere formula substitution is eliminated. The student should be set free to pick and choose his path."

The early scientists had to think up not only methods, but also their own devices. After Galvani got the first inklings of electricity from the twitching of a dead frog, Volta, in 1790, invented a new instrument for better detection of small charges of electricity. With this he found that he could experiment with almost any moist material instead of with frogs' legs. Thus, solely for the purpose of conducting his experiments, Volta had to invent the electric battery.

Experimentation is far more scientific today because new devices have eliminated guesses—especially by way of *measurement*. "And," said Doctor James B. Conant, "new degrees of accuracy in measurement often, but not always, *bring to light unsuspected facts*." Mainly through these new devices, research can now carry on *controlled* experiments. "And this means in essence," said Doctor Conant, "the control of the relevant variables such as temperature, pressure, light, and presence of other materials, particularly small amounts of air and water."

With the creative researcher the power of association must come into play at every step. "This" suggests "that," and "that" leads to something else. "New concepts," said Doctor Conant, "arise from experiments and observations; and these new concepts in turn lead to further experiments and observations." It is along this winding trail that our scientists finally find the *new* for which they search.

Experimentation can never be a machine into which you slip a coin and get the answer on a neatly printed card. Any slavishness to a notion like that is a handicap to any scientist, according to Elliott Dunlap Smith. He carefully traced the steps that led to typical inventions and concluded: "The act of inventiveness which achieved the solution was not logical scientific thought at all. Unless the inventor is willing to relax the meticulous step-by-step procedure of logical science, he will get nowhere."

Optics is one of the most rigid of the sciences. In creating the 200-inch mirror for Mt. Palomar, the researchers of Corning could, through calculations, arrive unerringly at the composition of the glass needed for that unprecedented product. And yet the project met with failure, at first—the huge disc cracked while cooling. A simple idea solved the problem. They cast another mirror with deep indentations in its back, and thus reduced the thickness enough to permit the white-hot molten glass to solidify without cracking.

The solution of that problem was not as "scientific" as it was just plain ingenious. And years later, when the mirror was about ready to pry into the heavens, the scientists were stumped as to how to clean the disc. They successfully solved that problem by using a lanolinized hair tonic!

4. *Imagination in scientific testing*

Creative research is packed with questions like "How about?" . . . "What if?" . . . "What else?" At the end come the questions *"Will it work?"* . . . *"Can it be made commercially?"* Technology has created ways to answer this last question through pilot plants and similar techniques. For example, each and every step of the nylon process, together with the equipment for it, was worked out on a semi-works scale—so thoroughly that, except for size, the first commercial plant went into full blast as a large-scale duplicate of the pilot plant in all details.

Automobile companies have created vast proving grounds on which to verify the findings of their research laboratories. Chrysler goes beyond this and, by means of huge guinea-pig fleets, road tests the products of the minds of the Chrysler engineers.

"These cars," says the Chrysler Corporation, "cover high, cold mountains, big-city traffic and open highways, back-country dirt roads and winding tourist routes. And every day —by phone or wire or mail—detailed reports on the day's performance of each car go back to Detroit. Facts reported today may set designers and engineers to work tomorrow, and lead to another improvement on our cars. Thus we apply *creative imagination* even in such a practical thing as road testing."

B. F. Goodrich pioneered with a tubeless tire over 50 years ago. About 30 years later the company tried out a tubeless tire cured directly to the rims. The tubeless idea stayed on the shelf until World War II, when the Army asked for a tire which, even when deflated, could carry a load at least 75 miles. The combat tire developed by B. F. Goodrich to answer that call was the first successful tubeless tire. Improvements went on until, finally, scientific tests and scientifically controlled road tests had proved the tire worthy. But even that was not enough. Before offering the tire nationally, the new tubeless tires were put to actual *user* tests on many private cars, taxi fleets and police cars.

It takes creative imagination to think up the best ways to test. The scientists in charge of the proving have to do more than just answer the question "Will it work?" Of course, their judicial judgment does come into play, together with their power of analysis. But they cannot stop with "This won't do," even if they add, "Here's why." Their challenge is to help think up the "What if?" and the "How else?" and thus solve the problems which their tests have brought to light.

From start to finish, creative imagination plays an indispensable role in every project of scientific research.

5. *What about education?*

Dr. James Killian, Jr. of M.I.T. fame has urged "marked changes in engineering education" in order to instill more creativity into scientific endeavor. In stressing the need of this in America, he points out that our nation could lose its leadership in technological innovation because "the comparative scientific strength of countries can change." He cites what has happened in this country, as evidenced by the distribution of Nobel prizes in science.

In the first decade, the score of those countries that won the most prizes was as follows: Germany 33%, France 21%, United Kindom 4%, United States 4%, and the U.S.S.R. 4%.

In the 50's, the Nobel prizes in science were distributed as follows: United States 47%, United Kingdom 20%, U.S.S.R. 13%, and France 0%.

Between 1910 and 1950, no Nobel prizes in science went to Russia. Therefore the figures for the last decade are foreboding. As to whether our nation will excel in the 60's, 70's, and 80's will largely depend on what education does to develop creative ability in its science students.

Our supremacy in scientific innovation also depends on whom we choose for the preferential education which is to be provided for our most "gifted" young men and women. Up until recently, this selection was based mainly on IQ and teacher-preference, without regard to creative potential. The fallacy of these criteria has been exploded by scientific research—especially by the investigations by Dr. E. Paul Torrance at the University of Minnesota and by Dr. J. W. Getzels and Dr. P. W. Jackson at the University of Chicago. Their research has brought to light this frightening conclusion: If selection is based only on IQ and teacher-preference, our nation is likely to be deprived of the majority of those best fitted to become our scientific leaders.

One of the nation's leading psychologists in this field of research is Dr. Calvin Taylor of the University of Utah. *The New York Times* reported him in general agreement with the above findings and quoted him as pointing out that many academic programs stress *non*-creative activities to the point that the work habits being developed are valuable only in accomplishing non-creative things.

Much of the $100,000,000 available annually for college scholarships has been going to the wrong students—"good-grade-getters" who often lack creative talent. So says Dr. John L. Holland, research director of the National Merit Scholarship Corporation, the country's largest single dispenser of scholarship funds. These criteria, Holland asserts, place heavy emphasis on good high-school grades. "Generally," said Dr. Holland, "such measures are moderately accurate for predicting college grades, but have little relation to *post*-college achievement."

Time magazine later reported that the 1961 winners of National Merit Scholarships included 85 boys and girls who were chosen mainly on the basis of "exceptional creative performance."

Since our environment no longer develops the ingenuity of our people to the extent that it formerly did, the only way to offset this loss is for education to do more to develop creative ability. In doing so, our colleges and universities will be heeding this conclusion of a conference sponsored by the National Science Foundation: "Develop educational programs which require the student to exercise a high degree of originality."

TOPICS

1. How does Dr. James B. Conant rate the importance of imagination in scientific research? Why?
2. Distinguish between specific and fundamental research. Give examples.
3. From a creative standpoint, in what major respects did the 19th century differ from the 17th century?
4. What, according to Alfred North Whitehead, was the "greatest invention of the 19th century"? Do you concur? If not, why not?
5. Do you believe the imaginative process in art is the same as in science? Why or why not?

EXERCISES

1. Look at a simple screw driver (metal blade—wooden handle). Jot down all the ways screw drivers have been improved to make them more effective instruments. Suggest three further improvements.
2. You have just invented a new breakfast food. List six ways in which you might test it before offering it to the public.
3. Everybody has "pet peeves." Write down three of yours—along with creative suggestions as to how they might be alleviated.
4. As the symbol of the U.S.A., the eagle is criticized for its connota-

tion of predatoriness. What three other birds or beasts would you suggest, and why?

5. Imagine and list the three improvements in motor cars most likely to be announced two or three years from now.

REFERENCES

BUHL, HAROLD R., *Creative Engineering Design*. The Iowa State University Press, 1960.

BUSH, VANNEVAR, *Science—the Endless Frontier*. Washington. U. S. Government Printing Office, 1945.

CONANT, JAMES B., *On Understanding Science*. New Haven. Yale University Press, 1937.

CONANT, JAMES B., *Science and Common Sense*. New Haven. Yale University Press, 1951.

DE KRUIF, PAUL H., *Hunger Fighters*. New York. Harcourt, Brace and Company, 1928.

GILFILLAN, S. C., "Invention as a Factor in Economic History." *Journal of the Patent Office Society*. April 1947, pp. 262–288.

GRAS, N. S. B., *Industrial Evolution*. Cambridge. Harvard University Press, 1930.

HAYNES, WILLIAM, *This Chemical Age, the Miracle of Man-Made Materials*. New York. A. A. Knopf, 1942.

KAEMPFFERT, WALDEMAR B., *Science Today and Tomorrow*. New York. Viking Press, 1945.

KETTERING, C. F., "The Role of Invention in Industry." *Journal of the Patent Office Society*. June 1932, pp. 500–511.

MAGOUN, F. A., "Selection of Men with Creative Ability." *Mechanical Engineering*. September 1940, pp. 670–672.

MANCHESTER, H. F., *New World of Machines; Research, Discovery, Invention*. New York. Random House, 1945.

MOONEY, ROSS L., "Groundwork for Creative Research." *American Psychologist*. September, 1954, pp. 544–548.

STEVENSON, A. R. and MCEACHRON, K. B., JR., "Education of an Engineer." *Journal of Engineering Education*, 1944–1945, pp. 275–284.

Taylor, Calvin W., ed., *Research Conference on the Identification of Creative Scientific Talent.* (Three Separate detailed reports of the first, second and third biennial conferences, with complete papers by a variety of researchers). Salt Lake City. University of Utah Press, 1955, 1957, 1959.

Torrance, E. P., ed., *Creativity* (Proceedings of the Second Minnesota Conference on Gifted Children). Minneapolis. University of Minnesota, 1959.

Torrance, E. P., *Status of Knowledge Concerning Education and Creative Scientific Talent.* Minneapolis. University of Minnesota, 1961.

Wyman, W. I., "The Scientific Genesis of Basic Inventions." *Journal of the Patent Office Society.* January 1936, pp. 22–32.

Chapter XXVI

Careers depend largely upon creativity

WHETHER YOU are looking for a job, or tying to get ahead in a business, imagination is a key to achievement.

Job hunting should call for strenuous idea hunting. And yet a famous employer reports: "In my experience, not one applicant in 500 uses any imagination in applying for a position. Anyone who suggested ideas of possible use to his prospective employer would stand out and be almost sure to get preference—even though his suggestions were unusable."

For 15 years, Sidney Edlund, former head of Lifesavers, Incorporated, has made it his hobby to teach people how to go after new jobs. His basic principles are these:

1. Offer a service instead of asking for a position.
2. Appeal to the self-interest of your prospective employer.
3. Be specific as to the job you want, and as to your qualifications.
4. Be different, and still be sincere.

All these principles call for thinking ahead, or thinking creatively, or both. Even in the matter of our personal appearance, we might well look into the mirror of imagination before looking for a job. And to be "different"—to lift ourselves above the other applicants—we need to generate ideas before we knock on employers' doors.

We also need imagination to help us set our job-seeking sights. Our first question might well be: "In what vocations would I be most likely to succeed?" Let's jot down all lines that seem at all likely. Having done that, let's use some check-lists. Let's run through the classified section of the telephone directory and scan the 200 or so different lines listed there. Then let's go to the library and look over some of the "career" books. Let's talk to some experienced friend and seek his guidance. But let's not make him do our creative thinking for us—let's show him our list of likely lines and ask only for his judgment.

Walter Hoving, of department store fame, estimates that of the 500,000 college graduates looking for jobs each year, only a few think creatively about what to try to do and where to find the right job. "I am constantly staggered," said he, "by this passive waiting for someone else to do the thinking that they should do for themselves."

Nowadays our aptitudes can be revealed to us through scientific testing. But such knowledge should be but a prelude to our own creative thinking about our future career.

2. *Resourcefulness in seeking openings*

Knowing which vocations we might best explore, we next need to seek openings. Imagination can help a lot in such quests, as it did in the case of the young Clevelander who read a "blind" advertisement of just the newspaper job he wanted. The ad stated only that the opening was in Ohio. He realized that there would be hordes of applicants, and he determined to stand out from the mass. So he secured the names of the managing editors of all the dailies in the state, and wrote letters to each of them. He hit the right man at the right time and landed the job. Two other editors also made him offers.

In writing letters of application we should see ourselves through the eyes of the person addressed. Since nobody wants a slovenly employee, even our spelling is important. A member of the Procter and Gamble personnel department analyzed 500 letters from applicants and found that 82 per cent of them were marred by misspellings.

Instead of individual letters, a job-seeking broadside may be indicated. Robert A. Canyock, about to graduate from Syracuse University, sought a career near his home town. To a list of 170 possible employers, he mailed a folder which was so persuasive that it brought him 32 invitations for interviews. Likewise, Leon Turner, while still a student at Saint Louis University, created a photo-offset brochure which he mailed to 58 companies. A dozen of them replied that they had openings of the kind he was seeking.

A job-seeking interview calls for creative thinking in advance. In planning our strategy we should ask ourselves all kinds of questions, including plenty of "What-ifs?" For the better we foresee contingencies, the better we can meet them. Thus prepared we can more readily answer questions which otherwise might cause us to say the wrong things, or make us seem slow-minded.

It often pays to go idea hunting in advance of an interview. One young friend of mine came back from war eager to get into a different line. He knew almost nothing about the field he wanted to enter, but he did know what firm he wanted to join. He feared that his first interview would spell success or failure. So, instead of applying in the routine way, he spent a week calling on customers of his prospective employer. Within a week he acquired nearly 50 ideas. Then he secured his interview, during which he modestly brought up his 10 best ideas in the form of tentative questions.

His new boss later told me that my veteran friend was getting along famously. "I am mighty glad he didn't just ask for a job in the usual way," said his employer. "I had already made up my mind not to take on any more men. So I would have turned him down if he hadn't shown in our first meeting that he was a man who knew how to get ideas. And I'm glad to say that the same ingenuity he used in getting the job is showing up in his work."

Some employers send representatives to colleges in search of promising young men. An undergraduate friend of mine wanted to work for one of these firms. So he spent four weekends interviewing the company's dealers and competitive dealers. The visiting representative was amazed to find out how much this young man knew about that business. These two are now at work in the same department.

The higher you aim, the more creative your preparation must be. A man who was making over $15,000 a year decided to go after a better job. He picked the company he wanted to join. He subscribed to all the trade papers in that line of business, and bought all the books that bore on that company's problems. On Saturdays he called on its dealers. After four months of such preparation, he wrote a short note to the head of the company, enclosed an idea for overcoming dealer indifference, and asked for an interview. His plan was turned down; but the officials were so impressed with his grasp of their problems that they offered him the post he was seeking.

3. *Creativity in presentation*

The United States Navy has proved that people absorb up to 35 per cent more when an appeal is made to the eye as well as to the ear, and that they retain what they thus learn 55 per cent longer. Our job-seeking presentation should therefore be as graphic as possible. A Harvard Business School graduate, after 14 years of successful experience, was applying for a still bigger job. Instead of a conventional summary, he submitted a pictorial chart which visualized his impressive experience. This not only intensified the employer's attention, but made him covet the applicant's creative power.

A graphic portfolio scores even better when tailor-made to fit the prospect. For example, just after World War II our firm was taking back 160 of our own people from the armed services; we were therefore seeking no new employees. At that very time a young man came to see me, and I hired him on the spot. Why? Because he had completed so many missions over Germany and had been decorated so much? No. It was because he had taken three months to study our business and its needs, had thought up just how he could be of most use to us, and had prepared a portfolio especially for that one interview with us—a job of work which proved to me that he was highly creative and in no way allergic to effort.

The planning of a follow-up campaign entails still more creative thinking. The ideal follow-up is a crop of new ideas. When we go back to the employer with more suggestions for the good of his business, we will probably find him eager for our creative capacity, and may find him desirous of our services.

A friend of mine, in search of his first job, applied at Macy's. He was flatly told that there were too many applicants ahead of him. Unbeaten, he walked through the store; then he telephoned the personnel director.

"I want a job," he said, "and I've just spent several hours in the store looking for places where I could help. I have listed 10 spots where I think I could be useful right this minute. May I come up and tell you where they are?" He thus secured the interview and was soon a Macy trainee.

George R. Keith was a lawyer who retired at 40. As a creative hobby he conducted a system of finding openings for unemployed people at no expense to them. Over a span of 30 years he contrived ways to help over 80,000 job-seekers. By developing ingenious methods of smoking out opportunities, he was able to find more jobs than people to fill them —even during depressions. He thus proved in a big way that creative imagination can secure the kind of employment sought—in slumps as well as in booms.

4. *Imagination wins promotion*

Doctor F. L. Wells reported to the American Association of Applied and Professional Psychologists the results of his study of a high-salaried group of people in comparison with a group of average salary. In four intelligence tests, these two groups rated about equal in all respects except one—creativity. Those who had climbed higher were the ones who could think up more things to do and more ways of doing them. As Montaigne wrote: "A strong imagination begetteth opportunity."

That seems obvious enough, but "lamentably enough," said Victor Wagner, "every day, several million young men resign themselves to sterile drudgery by thoughtlessly ignoring, or blandly defaulting, the marvelous faculty of imagination."

In any phase of business, many a promotion is based on demonstrated creativeness. The head of a big firm was about to retire. He had seven able assistants. When I asked him how he had picked his successor, he replied: "Year after year, one of my aides had sent me frequent memos which usually began, 'This may sound screwy but . . !' or 'Maybe you've thought of this, but . . !' Even though many of his ideas were trivial, I finally decided that he was the man to succeed me, because this business would dry up without a leader who *believes* in ideas, and has the gumption to spout plenty of his *own*."

George Morrison, president of the General Baking Company, had to select an executive vice-president. He picked 60-year-old Thomas Olsen, an accountant. I asked Mr. Morrison why. "Because he *thinks* young. He always has an idea," replied Mr. Morrison.

In days of old many an employee was pushed ahead by relatives who owned the business or by bankers who financed it; but that royal road is a rarity nowadays. In nearly every case the man who now rises toward the top is propelled by two forces: (1) His superiors want to pull him up to work with them because they need his help. (2) His immediate associates want to shove him up because they believe in him *and like him*. If he lacks creative energy his superiors won't covet him. If he lacks vicarious imagination, his associates won't cotton to him.

It's a rare employee who can envision his firm's need for economy. A company president who is personally openhanded recently complained to me: "During the course of the year I have hundreds of requests from our people for this or that expenditure, but hardly anyone ever comes to me with a suggestion as to how we could save money." Just think how favorably one of his young men could make himself stand out by thinking up some money-saving ideas!

It strains imagination but little to think up ways to find things out; and yet the failure to do just that has held back many an employee. A Sears, Roebuck executive recently remarked to me: "We take on the brightest minds we can find, but too often our new employees are helpless when called upon for something beyond their routine. They seem to have no inkling as to how to go about looking up this or that." Thus many a boss hungers for more ingenuity on the part of his people.

Carl E. Holmes, business consultant, believes that most employees stand still because of their creative shortcomings. "God gave us imagination," says Mr. Holmes, "and imagination can be the most potent force in our lives, yet few use it constructively. . . . Knowledge is a good thing, industry is a good thing, but imagination is a miracle worker."

5. *The key to salesmanship*

Creative power can promote an employee's progress in any phase of business, especially in salesmanship. A salesman has to use his imagination, deliberately and consciously, to think up just what little thing he can do to be helpful to each customer. Every case calls for different tactics. That fact helps explain why aptitude testers maintain that the two traits most needed for success in selling are an objective personality and creative imagination.

After a long drive I reached my hotel in Rochester one night at about nine. I had previously made a date with myself to devote an hour before retirement to thinking up how to persuade my prospect the next day. During the evening I piled up and jotted down ideas. My next morning's interview succeeded, largely because of the creative thinking I had done the night before. That victory happened to be a turning point in my career.

A vice-president in charge of purchases told me about a salesman who had long called on him without landing a single order. "He never got discouraged. Each time I turned him down, he'd just smile and say he'd try it again. Eventually I found myself giving him over $100,000 worth of business a year. What won me over? It was his habit of giving me an idea each time he called."

While working on the revision of this chapter, I received a letter from Whitworth Ferguson, head of an electric construction company. He enclosed a list of 93 suggestions, thought up in a one-hour brainstorm session, with his associate executives as panelists. The problem was: "What could be built into a bank to make it more efficient and more attractive to customers?" He explained that his company was soliciting the contract for the electrical work in a large new bank building and that the best of the suggestions would be used as extra sales ammunition.

Sales-training directors have recognized the need for a creative orientation of new salesmen by including this subject in their educational programs. The Reynolds Metals Company and Crown Zellerbach pioneered this trend. The Christmas Clubs of America pioneered the practice of providing creative training for the entire sales force.

As to the value of ideas in retail selling, Stephen W. Barker offers this hypothetical computation with particular regard to food stores: "If one little idea leads to one extra purchase of a 29 cent article, once a month, by just one in

100 families, this would be an extra sales volume of $1,750,-000 a year on a nation-wide basis."

If a man on the road keeps his imagination awake, he can capture ideas that can help his home office. For example, G. Cullen Thomas, General Mills Vice-President and Director of Product Control, reported this case:

"One of our salesmen sent us some partially-baked dinner rolls that he had picked up at a small bakeshop in Florida. They were blond, almost white in color, anything but appetizing. But when we reheated them to complete their bake, we had delicious, hot rolls with a delightful home-made flavor. We immediately secured the rights to this simple process and turned it over to our research and technical personnel for further experimental study. About eight weeks later, we were able to present to the baking industry the revolutionary 'Brown 'n' Serve' bakery products that have since won their way into millions of American homes."

Thus an imaginatively alert salesman can be a long arm of his company's creative research.

TOPICS

1. How would you go about selecting the vocations for which you are best fitted?
2. Sidney Edlund lists four basic principles to follow in applying for a job. Which do you think is the most important—and why?
3. In what ways could an applicant "be different and still be sincere"?
4. Let's suppose that you are hiring a salesman to work for you. What qualities would you look for in this man?
5. What are the advantages of submitting a written presentation of your qualifications when you call on a prospective employer? Why should it be graphic?

EXERCISES

1. List six careers for which you think you might be suited. Check the one for which you think you are best fitted. Tell why.
2. Select the career that appeals to you most and list 10 points by way of qualifications which might appeal to a prospective employer.
3. Suggest five "extras" a salesman might work up in order to win favor with a prospective employer.
4. Suggest six ideas to enable your school or college or business to save money.
5. If you were an employer, what three questions would you ask of an applicant in order to evaluate his creative ability?

REFERENCES

BELDEN, CLARK, *Job Hunting and Getting*. Boston. L. C. Page and Company, 1935.

EDLUND, SIDNEY and MARY, *Pick Your Job and Land It*. New York. Prentice-Hall, Inc., 1938.

HURST, EDWARD, *The Technical Man Sells His Services*. New York. McGraw-Hill Book Company, Inc., 1933.

LARISON, RUTH H., *How to Get and Hold the Job You Want*. New York. Longmans, Green and Company, 1950.

LYONS, GEORGE J. and MARTIN, HARMON C., *The Strategy of Job Finding*. New York. Prentice-Hall, Inc., 1939.

MCCLURE, MATTHEW THOMPSON, *How to Think in Business*. New York. McGraw-Hill Book Company, Inc., 1923.

TERZIAN, LAWRENCE, *How to Get the Job You Want*. New York. Grosset and Dunlap, 1950.

THOMPSON, C. B. and WISE, M. L., *We Are Forty and We Did Get Jobs*. Philadelphia. J. B. Lippincott Company, 1938.

WELLS, F. L., WILLIAMS, RUTH and FOWLER, PHILIP, "One Hundred Superior Men." *Journal of Applied Psychology*. August 1938, pp. 367–384.

Chapter XXVII

Creativity in leadership and in professions

IN PUBLIC life or in business, creative thinking is vital to leadership. Although an executive must possess judicial judgment to a marked degree, he cannot be solely a judge—he must also excel in resourcefulness. Then, too, he needs to recognize the value of creativity, and to know how to tap and encourage the creative power of his associates.

A business leader has to combine creative thinking with judicial thinking in arriving at decisions. To get surer answers than his own one-man judgment could arrive at, he thinks up ways to pull in the experience of others; he thinks up ways to get *composite* judgment through conference groups, or through surveys; he thinks up ways to put the problem to actual test.

Imagination is vital to precautionary judgment. One of the ablest executives I know recently said to his board of directors: "We're sailing along fine but we ought to be on the lookout for rocks ahead. I made up a list of 20 things that might wreck us. Here they are." Later, he enlisted the help of five creative men with business experience and worked out a check-list of 179 such hazards.

2. *Successful leaders encourage creativity*

The ideal top executive is both a creative pace-setter and a creative coach. He cultivates the creativity of those around him and makes it bloom. Above all else, he must feel a real regard for the power of ideas. He cannot be like a man I know who made a name for himself in the Army despite his habit of looking down his nose and saying, "Ideas are a dime a dozen." Instead, he must be like John Collyer, head of B. F. Goodrich, who, according to his Research Director, Doctor Fritz, "not only welcomes every possible idea but makes us all feel that what he most wants from us is utmost use of our creative imagination."

In a publication of the Society for the Advancement of Management, Ordway Tead emphasized the "responsibility of management to provide situations in which creativity is consciously released." And in the *Harvard Business Review*, Frederick Randall wrote: "Management must learn to mine creativity within its own ranks . . . The ability of management to adapt to new and changing conditions requires thinking *beyond* the established areas of past experience. Indeed an organization may consider a good capacity for creative thinking as one of its most valuable assets."

Morale is a valuable *by*-product of saturating an organization with creative effort. In the *Chicago Tribune* organization hundreds of the staff participated in an organized program of creativity. Pierre Martineau reported as follows: "By making many of our people aware that they are personally contributing to our operations, our brainstorming sessions are doing a great job of building morale."

One of the needs of big business is to bring up the creative power of second-line executives. They sit in plenty of conferences, but they are too often tempted to use their imaginations merely to anticipate how their associates will react. Such anti-creative tendencies can often be overcome by active encouragement on the part of those at the top.

Older leaders must especially guard against letting their long experience make them cynical toward ideas which might seem unpromising at first blush. So warns Clarence Francis, head of General Foods: "Younger executives come to me with what they think are new ideas," said Mr. Francis. "Out of my experience I could tell them why their ideas will not succeed. Instead of talking them out of their ideas, I have suggested that they be tried out in test areas in order to minimize losses. The joke of it is that half the time these youthful ideas, which I might have nipped in the bud, turn out either to be successful or to lead to other ideas that are successful. The point I overlooked was that while the idea was not new, the conditions under which the idea was to be carried out were materially different."

3. *How businesses harvest ideas*

The premium that business places upon ideas is evidenced by the fact that over 6,000 American companies, comprising over 20,000,000 employees, now operate suggestion systems. The worker is thereby encouraged to submit his ideas for the good of the business; and he or she is well rewarded for each suggestion accepted.

Such a plan was first used in Scotland in 1880 by a shipbuilder named William Denny. The first suggestion system in the United States was installed by the Bausch and Lomb Optical Company in 1899. The U. S. Navy established a full-fledged system in 1918. But the great upsurge in such projects came with World War II. During those hostilities, the Army's suggestion system stimulated civilian employees to think up 20,069 new ideas which saved $43,793,000 in 18 months. The Navy conducted similar programs in each of its 48 largest shore establishments. In one of these, over 900 suggestions were received and processed within one fortnight.

In business organizations, such plans are now growing apace. In one year the Eastman Kodak employees received $28,000 more for their ideas than the year before. A total of 9,711 suggestions were adopted, a gain of 1,100 over the previous year. In one Kodak plant, that year, four individuals submitted more than 50 ideas each.

The General Electric Company has paid to employees for their ideas an average of over $50,000 a month. Many companies have paid $5,000 or more for an idea. One man, Charles Zamiska, received over $28,000 for devising a better way to handle cores in the casting department of the Cleveland Bronze Company. That sum represented 25 per cent of the resultant savings during the first six months.

The Suggestions System of General Motors has been outstandingly productive. In just one year, 256,499 suggestions were received and 68,378 were adopted. The winners were awarded a total of $3,260,000 in that year.

At the A. C. Spark Plug Division, Al Simberg has provided courses in creative problem-solving for over 600 employees. He has also conducted considerable research, some of which measured the effect that creative training can have upon contributions to Suggestions Systems. The employees tested were divided into two groups. According to the Suggestions System records, one group had scored unusually high in accepted ideas while the other group had scored unusually low. Both groups received a ten-session course in creative thinking. During the year following this training, the high achievers increased their number of suggestions by 40 per cent; the others upped theirs by 47 per cent.

Before taking the course, the high producers had averaged a $39 reward for each accepted suggestion. After the course, this average increased to $83—as against an all-plant average increase of only $4.

To sustain a national economy based on more-goods-per-hour-of-labor, a continual flow of new ideas is imperative. That's why John A. Barkmeier of Marshall Field recently told 800 leading executives, "The creative thinking of every worker from the bottom to the top of each organization is needed." That's the basic reason why suggestion systems are now more numerous and more solid than ever before.

4. *Creativity in professional pursuits*

We have already dealt with the fact that imagination is the *sine qua non* of scientific and technological achievement. *All* professions likewise call for creativity.

The practice of medicine is a continual challenge to imagination. In diagnosis, a physician must conceive all possible alternatives. Although he can now lean upon instruments and testing procedures which the creative minds of others have devised, he cannot diagnose well unless he forces himself to think up plenty of hypotheses. And when it comes to treatment, here, again, he cannot go solely by book, but must apply his knowledge imaginatively.

And, all along, a physician or surgeon would do well to realize that the brilliant progress of surgery and medicine in recent years has come largely from the creative effort of innovators like Doctor Cushing and Doctor Fleming.

Then, too, a physician needs continually to use his vicarious imagination—to put himself into his patient's shoes. The therapeutic value of this is dramatized in a story about the son of Lord Halifax. A veteran of World War II and a double amputee, he was asked to buck up a legless veteran who was too despondent to help rehabilitate himself. Some weeks later the head of the hospital told Halifax that the veteran was well on his way to recovery. "How did you do so much to restore his spirits?" the doctor asked. "That's easy to understand," said Halifax. "He saw that I was in his shoes!"

Doctors who serve children have a special need for imagination in their patient relations. As a newspaperman in my early days in Buffalo, I heard a lot about a Doctor Borzilleri, who was the idol of that city's large and highly respected Italian colony. He was the creator of a fictitious dog with its tail in *front.* Whenever he had to treat a sick child he would distract its attention by telling about this strange pet. Too often the child would insist on seeing the animal, and as a result the doctor's wife had to buy scores of toy dogs, cut off their tails, and sew them on their noses.

In nursing, too, creative imagination plays a vital part. For this reason, some schools of nursing now include creative orientation. This trend was pioneered in 1955 in the training program at the Newman Memorial Hospital in Emporia, Kansas.

How about pastors? Can you imagine the creative effort they must put into preparing a new sermon each week? Then, too, a successful minister has to use his ingenuity in raising money, in planning programs, in pleasing his flock in countless other ways.

The outstanding teachers have been those who have taught creatively. Many believe that the model teacher of all time was Jesus Christ. One of His techniques was reported by Saint Matthew in these words: "All this Jesus said to the crowds in parables; indeed he said nothing to them without a parable." In this and in other ways, He empowered His teaching with imagination.

As to lawyers, a legal light has remarked: "Give me a young graduate who has had only fair marks in school but has shown that he can think creatively, and I will make a better lawyer out of him than if he were an unimaginative valedictorian."

Lawyers certainly have to think up strategies, and to foresee what their adversaries will contend. And what a strenuous challenge to creativity a jury can be!

In journalism, creative techniques are gaining more and more recognition. Several universities have included creative training in the curricula of their Schools of Journalism. In 1955, the National Association of Industrial Editors converted its annual convention into a "Creative College."

Professional politicians have long followed conventional patterns in their campaigning; but Thomas Dewey had to think up something new to win the governorship of New York State in 1950. The odds were overwhelmingly against him; and yet overnight he reversed the tide by using a new medium in a brand-new way. All day long and all evening, he appeared before a vast television audience, extemporaneously answering questions that came in from voters all over the state. Many of those who heard and saw him marveled at his grasp of public problems and decided to change their ballots in his favor. And in the Eisenhower campaign for the presidency, what an idea it was to have television bring into the nation's living rooms the Republican governors from all over the country—instead of just having the General stand at a lectern and read another long speech!

In the military profession, strategies and tactics are everything; and they depend upon creative thinking. A military leader must also put himself into his enemies' boots. During the nip and tuck of the African campaign, General Montgomery kept on the wall of his mobile headquarters a photo of General Rommel. When asked why, he replied: "So I can look at his picture and keep pondering, 'What would I do if I were Rommel?'"

Recognizing that creative imagination is a prime factor in military leadership, the Navy engaged Dr. J. P. Guilford of the University of Southern California to conduct a long-term research program to determine how to measure the relative resourcefulness of candidates for commissions. This project was started in 1951. After nine years, the net of the findings was this: *Creativity is indispensable to military leadership.*

The need for creative education has become widely recognized in the Armed Forces. The Air Force inaugurated its course in the ROTC early in 1954 and has offered similar training at the Air University and in other establishments. Creative training has also been inaugurated here and there by the Navy and the Marines. As to the Army, an outstanding example is the Management School at Fort Belvoir. Ever since May 1956, creative principles and procedures have been featured. Over 1,900 officers have taken this training there.

The Armed Forces believe in creative training for high-ranking officers as well as for subordinates. At a Creative Problem-Solving Seminar in the U. S. Army Management School, the participants included 10 Generals.

No soldier can be a great general without driving his imagination to the utmost. "How much in military matters depends on one master mind!" said Abraham Lincoln. What is a master mind? It is one which combines mastery of knowledge *with* mastery of imagination. Together they account for outstanding leadership on the field of battle and in every other field.

TOPICS

1. What creative idea was launched in 1880 by William Denny? To what extent is it flourishing today?
2. How many ways can you think of to stimulate the flow of ideas from an organization?
3. Do you believe it is possible to "put yourself in the other fellow's shoes"? To what extent?
4. Do you consider past experience a help or hindrance to thinking up fresh ideas about a problem? Why or why not?
5. How should an employer handle an enthusiastic young employee who suggests an idea which had already been proved worthless?

EXERCISES

1. List 10 factors which might cause a successful business to fail.
2. Write down six ways in which an active imagination could improve the effectiveness of a doctor.
3. Write six alternative headlines for the leading article in yesterday's newspaper.
4. What six steps could a library take to make it more popular?
5. "A tenor is not a voice, it's a disease," said G. B. Shaw. Write a similar epigram on (a) Sophomore (b) Woman (c) Politician (d) Television.

REFERENCES

ACKERMAN, CARL W., *George Eastman.* Boston. Houghton Mifflin Company, 1930.

BUSCH, NOEL F., *Briton Hadden—A Biography of the Co-Founder of Time.* New York. Farrar, Straus and Young, Inc., 1949.

CREATIVE ENGINEERING. New York. American Society of Mechanical Engineers, 1944.

CROWTHER, SAMUEL, *John H. Patterson, Pioneer in Industrial Welfare.* Garden City. Doubleday and Company, 1923.

GOODE, K. and KAUFMAN, Z., *Showmanship in Business.* New York. Harper & Brothers, 1936.

GUILFORD, J. P., "Some Recent Findings on Thinking Abilities and Their Implications." *Informational Bulletin,* Training Analysis and Development, TA&D Directorate, Deputy Chief of Staff Operations, Hq. ATRC, Scott AFB, Illinois, Vol. 3. Fall 1952, pp. 48–61.

GUTH, L. W., "Discovering and Developing Creative Engineers." *Machine Design.* March 1949, pp. 89–94.

MIRSKY, JEANNETTE and NEVINS, ALLAN, *The World of Eli Whitney.* New York. The Macmillan Company, 1952.

OSBORN, ALEX F., "About Ideas; Which Kind of Boss Are You?" *Factory Management.* March 1950, pp. 88–89.

OSBORN, ALEX F. and WEIS, G. F., "Your Ideas; How to Put Them Across." *Factory Management.* February 1950, pp. 68–72.

PROUT, HENRY G., *A Life of George Westinghouse.* New York. Charles Scribner's Sons, 1922.

SEABROOK, WILLIAM, *Doctor Wood.* New York. Harcourt, Brace and Company, 1941.

VON FANGE, EUGENE K., *Professional Creativity.* Prentice-Hall, Inc., 1959.

YOUNG, J. F., "Developing Creative Engineers." *Mechanical Engineering.* December 1945, pp. 843–846.

Chapter XXVIII

Imagination can improve personal relations

"IMAGINATION GOVERNS the world," said Disraeli. And to a large extent it can govern our personal lives. Without it, even the Golden Rule won't work. For we cannot do unto others as we would be done by, unless we mentally put ourselves into their shoes. Even enlightened selfishness depends on use of imagination.

Tact calls for active imagination. Saint Paul in his speech at Mars Hill quickly won his anti-Christian audience by saying that he, too, worshiped an "unknown" God. Time and time again, Christ used superb imagination in making contact with strangers. For example, on the shores of a lake one day He saw two fishermen whom He sought as disciples. They were busy with their nets and talking their trade. To have broken in on them with a plea that they turn to preaching might have invited their snarls. "Come with Me," said Jesus, "and I will make you fishers of men." That word "fishers" helped to win them.

Contrarily, far too many enmities are caused by failure to imagine how the other fellow will react. For example, in a Chinese city the English colony maintained an ostentatious club house, in the front of which a sign shouted: "No Chinamen or dogs allowed." The newspaperman who told me about that went on to remark: "The white man is through in Asia; it can be largely blamed on that kind of tactlessness."

When we say, "Think twice before you speak," we mean not only to weigh what we are about to say, but also to imagine how our remark will be taken. Most of the discourtesies which cause unhappiness are due to our failure to use our imagination to that end.

Harvard University recently made a study of why people lose their jobs. This showed that only 34 per cent are let out because of inability to do their work, whereas 66 per cent are fired for failure in human relations—for inability to put themselves in the other fellow's shoes—for *dis*use of imagination.

By constantly trying to change shoes we can grow creatively; but for a more active exercise—instead of passively applying the Golden Rule—we might make ourselves "go over to the other side," by implementing the Golden Rule. Then we practice what psychology calls *empathy*—"the imaginative projection of one's own consciousness into another being." This should call for thinking up things to *do* for the other fellow and *doing* them, thus bringing into play not merely vicarious imagination but also creativity. By such means we can almost move mountains—as James Keller proved in his book about the Christophers, *You Can Change the World.*

Empathy is the secret of Alcoholics Anonymous. What a shining example of altruism this organization is—and what a tribute to man's power of imagination! Over the years, all the medicines, religions, and "cures" had succeeded in rehabilitating less than four per cent of the alcoholics; but, by changing places with other victims, AA members are putting back on their feet about 50 per cent of those who seek their help.

2. *Imagination in marital relations*

As Ian Maclaren pointed out, "We sin against our dearest, not because we do not love, but because we do not *imagine*."

America's marital record shows that two out of three matings last a lifetime. On the other hand, Doctor Clifford R. Adams made a 10-year study and found that only 17 per cent of married people are really happy with each other. The contentment of the other 83 per cent could certainly be improved by more creative thinking.

"Kiss-and-make-up" may work fine at first but later often runs up against the law of diminishing returns. A far better rule is to kiss and *think* up—think up ways of *avoiding* the clashes which would otherwise call for making up. That kind of imaginative exercise helps us not only to safeguard our happiness, but also to build up our minds.

Divorce has become so common that, when forms were sent out to Harvard's Class of '32 in order to gather biographical data, lines were left to insert *two* marriages and one *divorce*. There are nearly 400,000 divorces a year in the U.S.A. In how many of these cases has the man or woman or relative or friend consciously applied *imagination* in search of ways to avoid the rocks? Psychiatrists have attempted diagnoses in many cases. Lawyers have given lots of advice, but mainly by way of judicial or critical judgment. In hardly one case out of ten has there been any conscious effort to think up the new ideas which might keep the family together.

Stephens College is famous for preparing women for married careers and Doctor Henry A. Bowman, chairman of its Home and Family Division, is an authority on marital problems. "Successful marriage," said Doctor Bowman to his students, "is a *creative* achievement." Only one out of 20 Stephens graduates is divorced, as against the national record of one out of three.

Any man or woman in marital trouble can think up ways to offset unhappiness and thus give marriage more time to mend itself. For instance, a husband became infatuated with a younger woman, and his wife was about to start divorce proceedings, when a friend of hers suggested that she take on new interests which might sublimate her distress. She listed 23 activities, out of which she chose the writing of poetry. This gave her a creative outlet which kept her going until her husband regained his senses.

Timing is a key to continuing marriage, as Nina Wilcox Putnam pointed out in her personal story: "Many times during the past twenty-three years my husband and I have faced down almost every conceivable ground for divorce. . . . Always one or both of us have taken time out for reflection, with the result that a better, stronger relationship has sprung from the ashes of our anger. I believe that in any marriage *time* is of the essence."

The use of time as a tool is but one of many ideas for solving marital problems. Imagination is not only "of the essence" but can be the *key* to successful marriage.

3. *Home chores challenge imagination*

The domestic duties of most wives call for more imaginative effort than do the cut-and-dried jobs of their husbands. "What can I make out of these left-overs?" . . . "How can I get Johnny to bed on time?" . . . "Whom can we find to sit for us this Saturday evening?" On such questions many a woman can, and does, whet her creative wits—day in and day out, from sunrise to lights-out.

Shopping certainly calls for agile thinking, and the leaner the purse, the more imagination meal-planning takes. A husband may look upon meat buying, for example, as a simple routine; but when he sits down to a goulash as tasty as tenderloin but costing far less, he should thank his lucky stars that his wife has used her imagination instead of his dollars.

Many famous writers, actors, and painters practice the culinary art. They recognize cooking as a truly creative exercise. Almost every dish calls for thinking up some way to make it tempting. And there is no limit to the recipes we can invent. In thinking up what to cook and how to cook it—in thinking up new ingredients and new shapes—in every aspect, cooking can challenge imagination.

Laundry work? Even this offers women an opportunity to exercise imagination. An authoress told me: "I can do my best creative thinking while ironing. Any activity which keeps the eyes occupied in one spot, while leaving the mind relatively free, is a distinct aid to mental concentration. In a way it is like fixing the eyes on a single light, as is done in hypnosis."

And laundering is beset with little problems which challenge imagination. For instance, a New Jersey woman loved loopy hooked rugs but detested the marks which clothespins left on them. So she thought up the new stunt of sewing a four-inch piece of muslin on each side before she put them in the tub.

Accessories for home beautification call for plenty of imagination. One woman, instead of covering her flowerpots, has merely polished them. Even window shades need not be drab, as was proved by a Philadelphia housewife who painted the inside of her shades in the colors which would add to the charm of each room.

We can use imagination in planning the size, character, color and framing of pictures. And in this phase of home beautification, ideas can take the place of dollars. Mrs. Edward Cart needed something to brighten up the plain green walls of her apartment and conceived the scheme of using a scenic fabric based on paintings by Grandma Moses. Out of this cloth she cut single pictures and framed each of them with neat black wood.

4. *Creative attacks on parental problems*

If we parents could only nudge instead of nag! Nagging takes only a tongue; but nudging calls for creative thinking. Oh, how we need ideas for leading children through the wilderness of infancy, through the jungles of adolescence, to the land of maturity!

To stop bickering about practicing the piano, a thoughtful mother bought a little notebook and a box of colored stars. Now each of her children sets the timer on the kitchen stove, and practices for 15 minutes. At the end of that period, the mother pastes a star in the child's practice book. On Sunday, the child with the most stars for the week wins a prize. "Their music improved," she told me, "and each child developed a personal sense of responsibility about her practicing." What a simple little idea! Yet how many parents would rather nag than try to think up new ways of any kind!

If parents cannot spare the rod, they can at least think up better ways to spank. And it is better if they pick the right time and place instead of letting their ire tell them when and where.

Even a bit of drama may pay off. One of Canada's legal lights has three little boys; and ever since they could be expected to know right from wrong their father has taken care of the spanking duties. But for each such session he always puts on a garment which he wears at no other time—a wild and woolly sport coat. That helps make his gentle whacks more memorable.

We also need imagination to make the punishment fit the crime—to deal out penalties which the child will deem fair. The Dale Castos do this by changing places. They sit down with their son and carefully discuss the issue. Then they put it up to him to decide what the punishment should be. At one session, the penalty he chose was such that his father found himself saying: "Son, we think you're being too hard on yourself. Instead of not playing ball for a whole week, we think a two-day layoff will be penalty enough."

In contrast, Doctor W. W. Bauer told about a little boy who was late for lunch. "The mother flew at him in a fury, berated him as a little beast and then forced him to eat his food—all of it." After she went out, the boy vomited. That night the parents could not find him. At midnight the police called to report that they had caught the tot trying to hitchhike out of town.

Here's what his mother should have done, according to Doctor Bauer: "When lunch time came and Joe did not appear, she should have eaten her lunch and cleared it away. Then, when Joe arrived, she should have told him to get his own lunch and to clear up afterward. This would have fitted his offense and would have taught him that it didn't pay to be late for meals."

When parents imaginatively discipline their children they help insure the desired result with less danger to amity than when they bawl them out. And by trying to think up these strategies, parents tend not only to keep their homes happier but also to keep their imaginations wider awake.

Parents also do well to induce their children to try to be creative on their own. For example, whenever a child of Mrs. Jean Rindlaub gets restless and whines, "What is there for me to do?" Mrs. Rindlaub's answer is always something like this:

"Come on, Anne—get a pad of paper, take a pencil and write down all the things you might like to do. I'll bet you could think up at least 25. And you'll find that just by writing down that list you'll have lots of fun."

Department-store executive Julian Trivers likewise believes in making his youngsters think up. One evening at dinner he unwrapped a mysterious wooden box with a slot in it. He then told his five children about suggestion systems such as are used in about 6,000 businesses, and he announced that each child was to think up ideas for the family good and stick their suggestions in that box. He then described the entrancing prizes which would be awarded at the end of each month for the best suggestions. The Trivers system didn't create any earth-rocking ideas, but it did help teach the five Triverettes that they were blessed with minds which were meant for creative *use.*

Robert T. Early, who taught Creative Thinking at Northwestern University, used brainstorming as a source of family fun and harmony. On a 2,000-mile automobile trip, his seven-year-old and eight-year-old daughters repeatedly joined him in brainstorm sessions—thinking up solutions to problems like: "How to get home chores done more quickly." Reported Mr. Early, "This made our vacation trip a lot less tiring as well as more pleasant."

Neighborhoods likewise are using brainstorming as a profitable pastime. This trend started in Asheville, North Carolina in 1955. A class of couples was formed to study this text. They met one evening a week at each other's homes and took turns acting as teachers. Having completed the course, the group has continued to meet once a week to brainstorm their own parental problems, civic problems, and other problems of mutual interest.

5. *On getting along with one's self*

Married or single, active use of imagination can enable everyone to get more out of life. It even makes for a more attractive personality, according to Professor H. A. Overstreet:

"People who are creatively alert are much more interesting than those who are not. They seem almost to belong to a different species, or perhaps to a higher level of evolution. They see not only what is but what might be; and the power to see what might be is one of the chief traits that distinguish human beings from one another."

As for getting along with oneself, our contentment largely depends on whether we are creative or non-creative. According to the findings of the Human Engineering Laboratory, much of our restlessness arises from disuse of our aptitudes. Our talents are constantly craving outlet; more than that, they are constantly craving development. When we dam them up, they torment us. Thus the cause of our discontent can often be traced to failure to exercise our creative aptitudes. To paraphrase Ben Franklin: "To cease to think creatively is but little different from ceasing to live."

"High up in our resources for happiness," said F. Robley Feland, "we can place the proved knowledge that we have, in our thinkery, a well-exercised power to think ourselves out of trials and difficulties. Although it is impossible to lift ourselves over a fence by our bootstraps, it is possible—*it can be easy*—to lift ourselves over life's obstacles by the force of our applied imagination."

Even the strongest spirits are prone to sag. Doctor Karl A. Menninger described President Lincoln's depressions as so deep that, during one period, "it was necessary to watch him every hour of the day and night. At one time it was considered advisable to remove all knives, scissors, and other instruments with which he might have taken his life."

There were real reasons for Lincoln's melancholy. On the other hand, the blues that beset most of us are seldom due to crushing causes. These spells can often be prevented, or relieved by the right use of creative imagination.

Instead of just moping, we might even write up our case. The chances are it won't look so gruesome on paper—it may even look ridiculous enough to make us laugh at ourselves. And the very fact of that writing effort may produce an emotional release—may open the gate for some creative thinking on our own.

Or we might take on some physical exercise and, best of all, some creative exercise—as I proved to myself one morning when an untoward incident sent my spirits into a tail-spin. It was important that I get myself back into the right mood for a conference that afternoon at which I was due to preside. So I hit upon the plan of going to lunch alone and tackling a crazy creative project.

A few weeks before, Grantland Rice and I had been talking about a silly idea of mine for a piece of verse. So at the Hotel Statler that noon, on the back of the menu, I scribbled seven quatrains on that theme. The people at nearby tables probably wondered what asylum I was from. But I had fun; and I returned to the office in good spirit.

Then, too, when we know we are in for something that

can't be avoided, it may help if we steer our imagination into it, head on. For instance, during my third fevered day of flu, I said to my wife: "If this runs true to form, I will be all over it by next Monday and then I'll be depressed for two days." A week later I was back at work but almost as low as a dachshund. I would have been even more dispirited had I not projected my imagination—had I not conditioned myself against that mental slump.

We can push anxiety out of our minds by pushing something creative into them. Winston Churchill was never more worried than during the second half of 1915. As First Lord of the Admiralty he had plenty to keep his mind off the heart-rending things that were happening. But, having gone from that exciting post, he had too much time to brood. "I had long hours of utterly unwonted leisure in which to contemplate the frightful unfolding of the war. At a moment when every fibre of my being was inflamed to action, I was forced to remain a spectator of the tragedy, placed cruelly in a front seat. And then it was that the Muse of Painting came to my rescue."

But even better than painting or any other such hobby is the more strenuous exercise of energetically tackling the causes of our despair, and creatively thinking our way through to serenity.

* * *

Imagination makes man "the paragon of animals," said Shakespeare.

"Imagination governs the world," said Disraeli.

"Imagination is more important than knowledge," said Einstein.

We may discount those statements and yet must agree

with Dr. Guilford that the subject of imagination has been "deplorably neglected."

By and large we have failed to recognize the fact that nearly everybody possesses creative imagination, at least potentially. We have failed to find wide-scale ways to develop this gift of our people. We have even failed to find ways to help offset the forces that tend to atrophy this gift.

Only recently has it been generally realized that imagination can be the key to the solution of almost any kind of problem. Only recently has scientific research convinced educators that creativity is teachable.

It is now a known fact that nearly all of us can become more creative, if we will. And this very fact may well be the hope of the world. By becoming more creative we can lead brighter lives, and can live better with each other. By becoming more creative we can provide better goods and services to each other, to the result of a higher and higher standard of living. By becoming more creative we may even find a way to bring permanent peace to all the world.

TOPICS

1. Do you think more people lose their jobs because they can't handle the work or because they can't handle people? Why?
2. What is "empathy" and how would you apply it in your daily life?
3. Instead of "kiss-and-make-up" what is a better rule for marital harmony? Why?
4. Why do you think Alcoholics Anonymous succeeds in so many cases where medical science has failed?
5. Consciously or unconsciously, most of us have developed favorite ways to lift ourselves out of moods of depression—i.e., "to forget our troubles." In what ways could one use his imagination toward that end?

EXERCISES

1. Suppose you have a child who neglects homework in order to watch TV. What six strategies can you think up to help solve this problem?
2. Think up 10 ways to entertain yourself when alone for an entire evening.
3. Think of the person you like least. Then select the one thing about him or her that you find most admirable. Then think up three ways to magnify that virtue in your own mind.
4. Describe the most annoying habit of the person closest to you. Think up six tactics to get that person to change that habit for the better.
5. Write a 50-word cable to the Soviet Premier giving reasons why he should let his subjects hear the true facts about free nations.

REFERENCES

Bauer, William Waldo, *Stop Annoying Your Children*. Indianapolis. Bobbs-Merrill Company, 1947.

Bossard, James H. S. and Boll, Eleanor S., *Ritual in Family Living*. Philadelphia. University of Pennsylvania Press, 1950.

Carroll, Eleanor G., *Two for the Money*. New York. Doubleday and Company, 1940.

Dunn, David, *Try Giving Yourself Away*. Scarsdale, N. Y. Updegraff Press, Ltd., 1947.

Ellenwood, James L., *Just and Durable Parents*. New York. Charles Scribner's Sons, 1948.

Ellenwood, James L., *There's No Place Like Home*. New York. Charles Scribner's Sons, 1938.

Garrison and Sheehy, *At Home with Children*. Henry Holt, 1943.

Gilbreth, F. B. and Carey, E. G., *Cheaper by the Dozen*. New York. Thomas Y. Crowell Company, 1948.

Grossman, Jean S., *Life with Family*. New York. Appleton-Century-Crofts. Inc., 1948.

LURTON, DOUGLAS, *The Power of Positive Living.* New York. McGraw-Hill Book Co., Inc., 1950.

MAGOUN, F. ALEXANDER, *Love and Marriage.* New York. Harper & Brothers, 1948.

MERRILL, FRANCIS E., *Courtship and Marriage.* New York. Wm. Sloane Associates, 1949.

PARKER, CORNELIA S., *Your Child Can Be Happy in Bed.* New York. Thomas Y. Crowell Company, 1952.

REILLY, WILLIAM J., *Successful Human Relations.* New York. Harper & Brothers, 1952.

INDEX

INDEX